D1527521

CRITICAL APPROACHES TO INFORMATION TECHNOLOGY IN LIBRARIANSHIP

Recent Titles in
Contributions in Librarianship and Information Science

The Decision-Making Process for Library Collections: Case Studies in Four Types of Libraries
Beatrice Kovacs

The Librarian, the Scholar, and the Future of the Research Library
Eldred Smith

Social Science Reference Sources: A Practical Guide
Revised and Enlarged Second Edition
Tze-chung Li

Books and Blueprints: Building America's Public Libraries
Donald E. Oehlerts

Dilemmas in the Study of Information: Exploring the Boundaries of Information Science
S. D. Neill

The Library and Its Users: The Communication Process
John M. Budd

Books Behind Bars: The Role of Books, Reading, and Libraries in British Prison Reform 1701–1911
Janet Fyfe

Technological Innovations in Libraries, 1860–1960: An Anecdotal History
Klaus Musmann

Democracy and the Public Library: Essays on Fundamental Issues
Arthur W. Hafner, editor

Research Libraries—Yesterday, Today, and Tomorrow
William J. Welsh, editor

Critical Approaches to Information Technology in Librarianship

Foundations and Applications

EDITED BY

JOHN BUSCHMAN

CONTRIBUTIONS IN LIBRARIANSHIP AND INFORMATION SCIENCE,
NUMBER 74

GREENWOOD PRESS
Westport, Connecticut • London

Library of Congress Cataloging-in-Publication Data

Critical approaches to information technology in librarianship: foundations
    and applications / edited by John Buschman.
            p.   cm. — (Contributions in librarianship and information
    science, ISSN 0084–9243 ; no. 74)
      Includes bibliographical references and index.
      ISBN 0–313–28415–6 (alk. paper)
      1. Libraries—United States—Automation. 2. Information
    technology—United States. I. Buschman, John. II. Series.
    Z678.9.A4U618 1993
    027.073—dc20   93–17866

British Library Cataloguing in Publication Data is available.

Library of Congress Catalog Card Number: 93–17866
ISBN: 0–313–28415–6
ISSN: 0084–9243

First published in 1993

Greenwood Press, 88 Post Road West, Westport, CT 06881
An imprint of Greenwood Publishing Group, Inc.

Printed in the United States of America

The paper used in this book complies with the
Permanent Paper Standard issued by the National
Information Standards Organization (Z39.48–1984).

10 9 8 7 6 5 4 3 2 1

Copyright Acknowledgments

Chapter 2 substantially updates and revises a previous work by Norman Balabanian, "Presumed
Neutrality of Technology," *Society*, vol. 17 3(1980), with permission of Transaction Publishers.

Chapter 5 is reprinted by permission of *Harvard Business Review*. An excerpt from "New Worlds of
Computer-Mediated Work" by Shoshana Zuboff, vol. 60 5(September/October 1982). Copyright
© 1982 by the President and Fellows of Harvard College; all rights reserved.

Chapter 6 contains an excerpt from the poem "Smog," from *Stolen Apples* by Yevgeny Yevtushenko.
Copyright © 1971 by Doubleday, a division of Bantam Doubleday Dell Publishing Group, Inc.
Used by permission of Doubleday, a division of Bantam Doubleday Dell Publishing Group, Inc.

Contents

Acknowledgments

As editor of this volume and author of three chapters, I have a number of people to thank for their help and support in bringing this project to its conclusion. First, I wish to thank Rider College and the Faculty Research and Patent Committee for the award of a Summer Fellowship in support of writing my own chapters. Second, I would like to thank my colleagues for their interest in and support of this volume. In particular, I would like to acknowledge the fine collection at Rider Library that Henry Halpern has built. It was invaluable to me to have this resource available right outside my office door. Third, I need to thank Lynn Taylor at Greenwood Press for her initial interest, encouragement, and support of my work. Fourth, the staff of Rider's Educational Support has greatly smoothed my way in the preparation of this manuscript—especially Wanda. Finally, this book is dedicated to Michael Carbone, who introduced me to the need for critical scholarship on technology, among other things.

CRITICAL APPROACHES TO INFORMATION TECHNOLOGY IN LIBRARIANSHIP

Introduction: Why Do We Need a Critical Approach to Information Technology in Librarianship?

John Buschman

This book begins with an attempt to answer the question posed by the title of this chapter: why do we need a critical approach to information technology in librarianship? Before answering the question, let me first note a few things that the profession does not need. Librarianship does not need more soul searching about the "real" mission or contribution of the profession; we do not need more introspection or self-flagellation for the purpose of motivating librarians to seize the moment or to reform; we do not need exhortations to work harder/smarter or to know more/do more. Each of these has become a self-conscious refrain in our literature; each has some validity and may even appear in this volume. However, the identity and effort of the profession are not the issues here. Rather, the goal is to turn some of that intellectual and professional effort toward redefining the issues around information technology in libraries.

To be clear from the outset, this project is about looking soberly and critically at the phenomenon of information technology in our profession and in our institutions. Many changes have already been wrought by information technologies, and many more are projected. If the profession as a whole (and not just our administrative, library school, and technical elite) is to make responsible decisions about libraries, if we seek to fill a central role in debate about information policy in our institutions and our nation, if we are to aid and further public and scholarly inquiry, and if we are to control (or regain control of) the agendas of our institutions, then we must account for and join that established body of theoretical and critical scholarship which has seriously questioned the role that technology has come to play in Western society; challenged the role of technology as a historical phenomenon in relation to work, power, education, and media; and critically examined the relationship of technology and science.

SOME INDICATIONS OF THE CHANGES

That information technology is changing libraries and the library profession in fundamental ways is not in question. Beyond the frantic catch-up calls, slogans, grave visions of wide-scale professional failure or success, and outright glib enthusiasm, there is a need to establish just what those changes are. I would suggest that they could be described in three areas: purchasing, collections, and services. While this is not an exhaustive overview, a brief summary in each area will indicate the nature of the changes wrought by information technologies.

The purchasing patterns of libraries have changed:

> schools, public libraries, college and academic institutions spend billions of dollars for hardware, software, and related library automation services. . . . If [these] services and products could be isolated from acquisition and book budgets, current industry expenditure estimates would be shown to be conservative. . . . [As it is] the library automation market is growing at approximately 25 to 30 percent per year.[1]

These figures do not include the money spent on online, cataloging, or vendor services. In two 1991 surveys of libraries belonging to the Association of Research Libraries (ARL), all the respondents of one survey offered electronic resources, but "no single model has [yet] emerged for the provision of scholarly electronic information."[2] Seventy-two percent of the respondents of the other survey indicated that they expect expert systems will become important library technologies by or before the year 2000.[3] Our large academic libraries are clearly set to invest in and develop the next generation of electronic resources.

More specifically, in a survey conducted by Kristine Condic and Frank Lepkowski of 122 academic libraries, all but three offered CD-ROM systems.[4] This trend is generalized as indicated by a recent *Library Journal* survey which noted that public libraries expected to spend an average of $13,533 on CD-ROM software in the 1991-92 fiscal year. Academic libraries expected to spend an average of $10,519 during the same period. Total average expenditures on electronic resources for this period (which also included online services and hardware) averaged $37,958 for public libraries, and $22,112 for academic libraries. These expenditures came out of overall average materials budgets of $157,830. CD-ROMs are indeed the electronic "medium of the moment."[5] Clearly priorities and patterns of purchasing have been altered by the information technologies currently being marketed to libraries.

Information technologies are altering our collections as well. Condic and Lepkowski found that 72 percent of the academic libraries owning CD-ROMs have cancelled print subscriptions to indexes or abstracts as a result.[6] In a notable article published in the *Chronicle of Higher Education* in 1991, Paul Gherman outlined just how collection priorities are shifting at university libraries. For instance, he notes that purchases of monographs at ARL libraries dropped 16 percent while spending on electronic information at his own institution grew to 10 percent of the size of the monographs budget. Due to inflation and lack of new money, Gherman's institution planned to cut $300,000 in journal subscriptions. Savings from those cuts will not be spent on monographs, but rather money will go into a fund for faculty to purchase articles they need:

> I expect this fund to continue to grow until by 2000 a majority of our periodical information will be purchased this way. . . . To sum up, new electronic services are high on our list of priorities, on-demand information comes next, sustaining important periodicals next, and monographs get the remainder of our budget. The bottom line is that we will be spending more of our budgets for access to information and less on ownership of information.[7]

In the meantime, text is becoming digitized in the aggressive development of electronic books and journals,[8] and in another important development, that text itself is becoming a multimedia product.[9]

Services, of course, follow the changes in patterns of purchasing and collections. Most of the changes in services due to information technology are well known since it is a popular subject of our literature, particularly those championing the Information Age. Briefly, it is widely known that electronic resources have shifted service emphasis onto interlibrary loan, teaching "information literacy," accommodating outside access to computer catalogs and indexes, merging with traditional computer-center functions and giving reference service to large tape-loaded data banks, and of course accommodating those CD-ROMs and database services offered by one's own institution.[10]

Needless to say, the librarian doing all of this needs retooling. Briefly, an incomplete list of the changes suggested or advocated for our profession might include: more subject knowledge; more communication skills; more

administrative skills; more technical/technological grounding; an enhanced M.L.S.; subject specialization; and of course, flexibility and an
attitude which welcomes change, or at least faces it bravely.[11] This has
been characterized as a paradigm shift in librarianship in which, eventually, paraprofessionals will service and preserve current print and microform collections, and strong subject-grounded librarians will go out of the
library to assist

> clients in framing information problems, interpreting information
> resources, and . . . understanding what is needed . . . in resources and
> in improved access. [Lastly,] systems designers, artificial intelligence
> experts, indexers, linguists, and the like [will be] responsible for
> providing access to the paper-based collections, on the one hand,
> and to the electronic resources on the other. [This will not be] just a
> responsibility for traditional "library" information, but for informa-
> tion and information systems.[12]

By now, it should be clear that the clean distinctions among purchasing
and the business end of libraries, collection development, and services are
being blurred by information technologies far more than they ever were.
It should be equally clear that information technologies are the primary
reasons for those changes. For instance, without delving into an over-
arching examination of serials inflation, it is even apparent in Gherman's
case of journal cancellations that technologies of document delivery are
shaping the response to that inflation by providing an alternative not
previously possible (or acceptable to the library's community), and affecting monograph purchases as well.

THE FRAMEWORK OF THE RESPONSES TO TECHNOLOGY

I have written elsewhere that our intellectual and professional responses
to these phenomena have been inadequate, and uncritically accepting of
the large amount of hype that information technologies receive. We "have
shared fully in the fulsome praise of computers and the benefits of their
use."[13] Librarians have sought to use the emerging role of information
technology in our work to raise the low status of our profession. "Put at
its simplest, our traditional anxiety about image, combined with the high
status of information technology, has led us into some uncritical approaches to new technologies."[14] For example, this rather startling statement was made in the course of a book review on instruction in use of

technology in libraries: "the authors contend that, while the costs of teaching technologies are high and while there are no provable benefits of training, 'designing pedagogically sound instructional programs for library technology is nonetheless extremely important for both the library and the library user.' "[15]

To be sure, the library profession is not alone in either its faith in technology or bloated rhetoric. Theodore Roszak has written about how information and its technology have been thoroughly and successfully hyped in the culture as a whole:

> The computer . . . has been overdressed in fabulous claims [which] have been deliberately propagated by elements in our society that are making some of the most morally questionable uses of computer power. . . . Information . . . has received ambitious, global definitions that make it all good things to all people. Words that come to mean everything may finally mean nothing; yet their very emptiness may allow them to be filled with a mesmerizing glamor. The loose but exuberant talk we hear on all sides these days about "the information economy," "the information society," is coming to have exactly that function. . . . Unburdened of vainglorious ambition . . . the computer . . . may yet become a reasonably valuable public servant.[16]

I have come to realize that the issue of our professional and intellectual responses to information technologies is not as one-dimensional as hopping on a powerful social/cultural bandwagon. There are other factors. First, there has been a long history of governmental, technical, and corporate elites advancing a technological agenda on national information policies. That agenda has come to redefine our work and our institutions. And in a second and closely related development, I have expanded a point made by Michael Winter in his chapter for this volume. I would suggest that library administrators and library science scholars have knowingly or unknowingly realigned themselves with that elite culture, furthering the technological and information agenda that is transforming libraries.[17] In-the-field librarians are in a position of responding to the overwhelming prestige, hype, and social agenda of information technologies, and the alignment of those who employ and train them with that message.

The third factor which complicates librarianship's response to information technology is what Michael Harris and Wayne Wiegand have both identified as a historical tendency to deliver the kinds of library services demanded by the powerful of American society. For instance, Wiegand has noted that library school training traditionally socializes students "to trust the opinions of authority experts from outside fields as a foundation for the library's decisions about what to include and what not to include."[18] Further, "the library's role in American history has been to perpetuate the canons of the dominant cultures . . . [and] occasionally to argue a principle of intellectual freedom."[19] Harris has noted that the purpose of the American public library has shifted over time from the elitism and authoritarianism of assimilation, to an educative function, to protecting the public's right to know, and through the decline of the democratic dogma of universal public enlightenment.[20] Through the process of shifting and adjusting to dominant cultural ideologies, librarians turned away from examining their social role and instead directed a great deal of attention to "modern management and efficiency . . . locating space for burgeoning collections and providing for their care, [and] attempting to reduce library work to a 'mechanical art.' . . . As a result, librarians thought less and less about theoretical questions . . . and spent more and more time dealing with organizational matters."[21] I contend that these institutional accommodations to power and the consequent narrow professional focus continue to characterize the conditions of librarianship today.

Fourth, Harris has identified a key point about library science research: a "positivist perspective now governs the thinking of most serious researchers in library science (and probably all who refer to themselves as 'information specialists')."[22] He has noted the many critiques of positivism in the social sciences:

> [Positivism has] never been able to generate "scientific paradigms," [it] cannot sustain the essential division between the subject and object of research, [and] value free pretensions . . . have been proven to be mystifications designed to camouflage the extent to which the social scientist is governed by prejudgments and domain assumptions. [The] belated, but thorough conversion [of library science] to positivism has come precisely at the time when social scientists in general have dramatically revised their conception of the value of positivist epistemology for generating knowledge about society.[23]

This orientation has led to research which is "policy oriented, designed for immediate professional consumption [and geared toward] professionally palatable findings [and] reductionist answers of 'relevance.' "[24] The curriculum through which library students pass is not designed to socialize them to question these assumptions, as Wiegand notes, and it is reinforced by the higher professional rewards for concentration on smaller, technical questions or effective use of technology rather than work on ethics or the foundations of librarianship.[25]

This social and historical framework has resulted in a professional and research literature which, at best, asks incomplete questions about how best to implement electronic resources without raising critical questions about them. At worst, our literature is plainly celebratory, often exhortative, and full of vague and dire threats of the results if we do not embrace information technology more thoroughly and enthusiastically. There is a need for a new framework through which to examine information technology's role in the library field.

THE NEED FOR A CRITICAL APPROACH AND FRAMEWORK

The time for stepping back and looking critically at the underside of information technology in librarianship is past due. In a previous article, my coauthor and I applied a critical-theoretical analysis from education to librarianship. What we found in doing so was that many of the issues came to coalesce around the role of information technology. Therefore, this volume sets out to form a critical framework for the study of information technology in librarianship. The value of doing so remains the same as in that previous work: "Its influence [will] derive less from research findings than from the distinctively different research priorities it proposes." There clearly have been other critical and theoretical writings on the subject which have paved the way for this volume in addition to the previous works by the authors in Part II.[26] The point of this book is that these previous efforts have been disconnected pieces of dissent in the old framework of technological celebration. If we are to analyze information technology in a serious way, there must be a new framework for those analyses. It does not need to be created from whole cloth. There is a well-established genre of legitimate scholarship which has explored critiques of technology, and that critique has been extended into some disciplines of special relevance to librarianship. In other words, a critical approach to information technology in librarianship already has an intellectual heritage upon which to draw, and to which it is indebted. Finally, in directly confronting some of the slogans, assumptions, and guiding myths about information technology in the library literature, this volume seeks to more firmly establish those arguments and encourage more critical scholarship so that our profession retains and regains control over technology.

We need what Herbert Schiller has called "critical research in the information age." By this he means a recognition that "communication channels . . . are as much a part of the structures of domination as are the military forces and the structures of the international banking system. [They are] a critical element in the overall system of production [and technologically driven changes in them have] consequences [that] are neither inevitable nor . . . necessarily progressive."[27] Such research would focus on production of information rather than consumption; it would focus on sources of power and how it is exercised in relation to information and communication; and it would rest on a strong sense of continuous social and institutional change and history.[28] The impact of information technology should not be studied *"after the fact* of its introduction. This approach has, in effect, excluded technology from detailed scrutiny. . . . This is in keeping with the view of technology as a social construction."[29] It is time that the library profession contribute to this line of scholarship and forge a contribution to critical research in the Information Age.

STRUCTURE OF THE BOOK

Part I is intended to introduce some of the framework of scholarship for critical research on information technology in librarianship. This section as a whole is by no means an exhaustive scholarly treatment of each field or each major author. Rather, this section, combined with the bibliography at the end of the volume, is intended to introduce a basic mode of scholarship, and provide some resources to further an equivalent scholarship in the library field. As such, contributing authors were chosen for their ability to use and convey the critical analysis of technology in their fields, and the relevance of those analyses to librarianship. Still, the resources of this volume are not meant to limit critical inquiry, but rather to serve as a beginning point for our field. These chapters provide a framework through which to view the analyses in Part II and the previously mentioned fragmentary work critiquing information technology in librarianship.

The first section begins with Norman Balabanian's chapter critiquing the assumed neutrality of technologies. This fundamental argument underlies every critical analysis of technology, and is mentioned elsewhere in this volume. Balabanian covers it thoroughly by analyzing the various arguments for the neutrality of technology. Next, Michael J. Carbone's chapter covers the critical scholarship on the educational uses of computers. This chapter has special relevance to librarianship considering the close relationship of most libraries to schools and higher education, and the educative function that libraries fulfill. Sue Curry Jansen follows with an exploration of the basis of critical scholarship on information technologies in the communications field. Jansen provides valuable background, connecting her arguments to the Frankfurt School, and extending her analyses through feminist critiques of science and technology. The following chapter is an article written by Shoshana Zuboff before the publication of her 1988 work, *In the Age of the Smart Machine*. In one of the best short treatments of the relationship between information technology and work, Zuboff clearly and concisely reports the early findings of her field studies and places them in historical perspective. Steve Slaby follows with his account of being an in-house dissident in a school of engineering at an Ivy League institution. He outlines the experiences which taught him to question the role technology played in society and engineering education and the analyses he used to challenge his students and colleagues.

Part II presents some critical analyses of information technology in librarianship. These contributing authors have not read Part I (with the exception of myself, of course), and they were not responsible for explicitly connecting their work to this background. They were chosen, however, for the quality of their analyses and their connection to that framework. These chapters show the legitimate and fertile questioning of technology in librarianship, and establish the scholarly legitimacy and professional and social responsibility of doing so. Along with these chapters, the scholarly framework suggests much more of the kind of critical scholarship that could follow in the library field. By no means have all of the questions been raised, nor all of the possibilities explored in this volume.

Part II begins with my own chapter on issues of censorship and information technology in libraries. Censorship is identified in both its overt forms—denial of access—and covert forms—what the technologies exclude. As such, it is connected to and relies upon some of the research outlined in the fields of education and communications in Part I. Carolyn Gray follows with her chapter on the civic role of libraries and the relationship of information technology to what has happened to information policy. Her work tracks the social policy commentaries identified by Slaby and is a demonstration of the importance of information policy. Michael Winter's chapter looks at the effects of information technology on librarianship through an analysis of the labor process. Winter provides a very valuable and clear connection to the sociological literature relevant to librarianship, and locates his analysis in historical perspective. His contribution parallels Zuboff's chapter and, among other things, forces us to consider carefully the parallel issue of deskilling in teaching noted in Carbone's chapter. John Haar has provided a valuable contribution by locating the electronic resources libraries purchase in a political and economic perspective. He reminds us that our work does not take place in a vacuum and that social and economic issues are frequently played out in our institutions. Again, this extends Jansen's analysis of the powerful strings connected to technologies and media. Lastly, I conclude the volume with a brief examination of the persistent themes of the chapters and their relationship to the emerging entrepreneurial direction of the profession, and a short section assessing where this critical approach stands, and where it might lead.

NOTES

1. Ernest A. Muro, "The Library Automation Marketplace," *Library Technology Reports* July-August 1990: 455–56.

2. Nancy Allen, Joan Chambers, and Irene Godden, "Scholarly Information Centers in ARL Libraries: Flyer 175 and Summary Table of Selected Responses," *SPEC Kit* (175) June 1991.

3. Charles W. Bailey, Jr., and Judy E. Myers, "Expert Systems in ARL Libraries: Flyer 174 and SPEC Survey—Use of Expert Systems in Research Libraries," *SPEC Kit* (174) May 1991.

4. Kristine Condic and Frank Lepkowski, "Survey on Attitudes Towards CD-ROM Indexes," preliminary summary results distributed to participating institutions, 26 May 1992.

5. John Berry, "CD-ROM: The Medium of the Moment," *Library Journal* 1 February 1992: 45.

6. Condic and Lepkowski.

7. Paul M. Gherman, "Setting Budgets for Libraries in Electronic Era," *Chronicle of Higher Education* 14 August 1991: A36.

8. For example, see Kathryn M. Downing, "An Electronic Publishing Primer," *Publishers Weekly* 19 April 1991: 44–46; Nathaniel Lande, "Toward the Electronic Book," *Publishers Weekly* 20 September 1991: 28–30; Reva Basch, "Books Online," *Online* July 1991: 13–23; Raymond Kurzweil, "The Future of Libraries Part 1: The Technology of the Book," *Library Journal* January 1992: 80–82; Raymond Kurzweil, "The Future of Libraries Part 2: The End of Books," *Library Journal* 15 February 1992: 140–41; David Wilson, "Testing Time for Electronic Journals," *Chronicle of Higher Education* 11 September 1991: A23–24; Martin Wilson, "AAAS Plans Electronic Journal Venture with OCLC," *Information Today* November 1991: 19–20; Nancy Melin Nelson, "Academic Networks: Publishers Consider Opportunities in Library Technology," *Information Today* December 1991: 10–12; Mick O'Leary, "Town Hall Brings National Review Online," *Information Today* November 1991: 7–9.

9. For instance, see Bruce Flanders, "Multimedia Programs to Reach an MTV Generation," *American Libraries* February 1992: 135–37; Beverly T. Watkins, "Videodisks Add 'Dimension of Emotion' to Ethics Education," *Chronicle of Higher Education* 4 March 1992: A22–23; Michael Rogers, "Library of Congress Unveils High-Tech Lab," *Library Journal* 1 May 1992: 26–28.

10. Among numerous examples, see "Implications of CD-ROM Reference," *Library Hotline* 6 March 1989: 9; May M. Moore, "Compact Disk Indexing and its Effects on

Activities in an Academic Library," *Journal of Academic Librarianship* 16 (November 1990): 291–95; Virginia Tiefel, "The Gateway to Information: A System Redefines How Libraries Are Used," *American Libraries* October 1991: 858–60; T. R. Reid, "Computer Access System Brings the Library Home," *Washington Post* 2 September 1989: A3; Lawrence J. McCrank, "Information Literacy: A Bogus Bandwagon?" *Library Journal* 1 May 1991: 38–42; Natalie Hall, "A Match Made Online," *American Libraries* January 1990: 70.

11. For instance, see Virginia Massey-Burzio, Alan Ritch, Steven D. Zink, and Martha L. Hale, "Reference Librarian of the Future: A Symposium," ed. Ilene F. Rockman, *Reference Services Review* Spring 1991: 71–80; Clark N. Hallman, "Technology: Trigger for Change in Reference Librarianship," *Journal of Academic Librarianship* 16 (September 1990): 204–8.

12. Pat Molholt, "The Future of Reference III: A Paradigm Shift for Information Services," *College & Research Libraries News* 11 (December 1990): 1048–49; see also Anne Woodworth, et al., "The Model Research Library: Planning for the Future," *Journal of Academic Librarianship* 15 (July 1989): 132–38.

13. John Buschman, "Asking the Right Questions About Information Technology," *American Libraries* December 1990: 1026.

14. John Buschman, "A Critique of the Information Broker: Contexts of Reference Services," *Reference Librarian* 31 (1990): 146.

15. Greg Byerly, rev. of *Teaching Technologies in Libraries: A Practical Guide*, by Linda Brew MacDonald, et al., *Information Technology and Libraries* 10 (September 1990): 244.

16. Theodore Roszak, *The Cult of Information: The Folklore of Computers and the True Art of Thinking* (New York: Pantheon, 1986) ix–x, xii.

17. John Buschman, "Information Technology, Power Structures, and the Fate of Librarianship," Social Responsibilities Round Table, Progressive Librarians Guild, and Alternatives in Print Task Force cosponsored panel, American Library Association Annual Conference, San Francisco, 28 June 1992 (forthcoming in *Progressive Librarian*).

18. Wayne A. Wiegand, "The Socialization of Library and Information Science Students: Reflections on a Century of Formal Education for Librarianship," *Library Trends* 34 (Winter 1986): 395.

19. Wayne A. Wiegand, "The Role of the Library in American History," *The Bowker Annual*, 33rd ed., ed. Filomena Simora (New York: R. R. Bowker, 1988) 75.

20. Michael Harris, "The Purpose of the American Public Library," *Library Journal* 15 September 1973: 2509–14; Michael H. Harris, "Public Libraries and the Decline of the Democratic Dogma," *Library Journal* 1 November 1976: 2225–30; see also Wiegand, "Role."

21. Harris, "Purpose" 2512.

22. Michael H. Harris, "The Dialectic of Defeat: Antimonies in Research in Library and Information Science," *Library Trends* 34 (Winter 1986): 518.

23. Michael H. Harris, "State, Class, and Cultural Reproduction: Toward a Theory of Library Service in the United States," *Advances in Librarianship* 14 (1986): 220–21.

24. Harris, "Dialectic" 525.

25. Wiegand, "Socialization" 396.

26. Jerome Karabel and A. H. Halsey, quoted in John Buschman and Michael Carbone, "A Critical Inquiry into Librarianship: Applications of the 'New Sociology of Education,' " *Library Quarterly* 61 (January 1991): 15–40. In addition to works already

cited, see Colleen Roach, John Buschman, and Mark Rosenzweig, "Towards a New World Information and Communication Order: A Symposium," *Progressive Librarian* 3 (Summer 1991): 5–23; Carolyn M. Gray, "Information Technocracy: Prologue to a Farce or a Tragedy," *Information Technology and Libraries* 48 (March 1987): 3–9; Carolyn M. Gray, "Technology and the Academic Staff, or the Resurgence of the Luddites," *Professional Competencies: Technology and the Librarian*, ed. Linda C. Smith (Urbana-Champaign, IL: Graduate School of Library and Information Science, University of Illinois, 1983); Michael F. Winter, *The Culture and Control of Expertise* (Westport, CT: Greenwood, 1988); John M. Haar, "The Politics of Information: Libraries & Online Retrieval Systems," *Library Journal* 1 February 1986: 40–43; John M. Haar, "The Reference Collection Development Decision: Will New Information Technologies Influence Libraries' Collecting Patterns?" *Reference Librarian* 22 (1988): 113–25; Marcia J. Nauratil, *The Alienated Librarian* (New York: Greenwood, 1989) 68–73; Herbert I. Schiller and Anita R. Schiller, "Libraries, Public Access to Information, and Commerce," *The Political Economy of Information*, eds. Vincent Mosco and Janet Wasko (Madison, WI: University of Wisconsin Press, 1988) 146–66; Herbert I. Schiller, "Public Information Goes Corporate," *Library Journal* 1 October 1991: 42–45; Herbert I. Schiller, "The Global Commercialization of Culture," *Progressive Librarian* 2 (Winter 1990/91): 15–22; F. William Summers, "The Need to Know," *Effective Access to Information*, ed. Alphonse F. Trezza (Boston: G. K. Hall, 1989) 1–11; James F. Govan, "The Creeping Invisible Hand: Entrepreneurial Librarianship," *Library Journal* January 1988: 35–38; Patricia Glass Schuman, "Reclaiming Our Technological Future," *Library Journal* 1 March 1990: 34–38; Patricia Glass Schuman, "Making the Case for Access," *RQ* 29 (Winter 1989): 166–72; Nancy C. Kranich, "Information Drought: Next Crisis for the American Farmer?" *Library Journal* 15 June 1989: 22–27; Judith A. Adams, "The Computer Catalog: a Democratic or Authoritarian Technology?" *Library Journal* 1 February 1988: 31–36; David Linton, "Pro-Machine Bias: The Fate of the Luddites," *Progressive Librarian* 4 (Winter 1991/92): 7–16; Henry T. Blanke, "Libraries and the Commercialization of Information: Towards a Critical Discourse of Librarianship," *Progressive Librarian* 2 (Winter 1990/91): 9–14; Mark Rosenzweig, "Libraries at the End of History?" *Progressive Librarian* 2 (Winter 1990/91): 2–8.

27. Herbert I. Schiller, "Critical Research in the Information Age," *Journal of Communication* 33 (Summer 1983): 250–52.

28. Schiller, "Critical" 253.

29. Schiller, "Critical" 255.

I

Critical Approaches to Information Technology in Librarianship: Foundations

2

The Neutrality of Technology:
A Critique of Assumptions

Norman Balabanian

Contemporary technological society is experiencing a profound multidimensional crisis. It has not always been so. From at least the time of the Industrial Revolution in England, a general feeling of optimism pervaded Western society. It was commonly believed that the growth of scientific knowledge knew no limits, and that scientific knowledge could always be applied to the problems of society. Since science and technology were so successful in producing marvelous inventions, they could eventually solve any human problem.

This attitude was exemplified at the Chicago *Century of Progress* World's Fair in 1933. The motto of the Fair was: *Science Finds—Industry Applies—Man Conforms.* The Guidebook to the Fair amplified the idea further: "Science discovers, genius invents, industry applies, and man adapts himself, or is molded by, new things. . . . Individuals, groups, entire races of men fall into step with science and technology."

Such sentiments were expressed in obvious satisfaction. The irony that human beings should bend willingly to the dictates of a technological imperative, when for ages they have struggled to be free of human tyrants, seemed to escape the "happy technologists" of that day.

A similar outlook exists among technological optimists of today, typified by Simon Ramo, who writes:

We must now plan on sharing the earth with machines. . . . But much more important is that we share a way of life with them. . . .

This chapter substantially updates and revises a previous work by the author, "Presumed Neutrality of Technology," *Society*, vol. 17 3(1980), with permission of Transaction Publishers.

We become partners. The machines require for their optimum performance, certain patterns of society. We too have preferred arrangements. But we want what the machines can furnish, and so we must compromise. We must alter the rules of society so that we and they can be compatible.[1]

Does Ramo really mean "compromise"? He does not say that if the "patterns of society"—the way we live—are not optimum for the machine, then we might redesign the machine. On the contrary, we must change society, we must change people to make them conform to the machine. There is no "compromise" here. It is not that the machine will be constructed to be compatible with human processes, but that humanity must accept the social patterns needed by machines since we "need" them.

But for some time now, and at an increasingly rapid pace, it has begun to register on the consciousness of many that the benefits to contemporary society flowing from science and technology have been purchased at a very high price. The questioning is not merely a superficial probing of the merits of this or that technology, but a profound questioning of the foundations of science and technology. People are questioning a view-of-the-world that can contemplate with equanimity the shaping of human beings, their society, and their culture in accordance with what its champions say are the dictates of technology.

The social problems associated with science and technology are well known. They point up the nature of the crisis. A non-exhaustive, brief taxonomy of the crisis-level problems would include:

1. *Environment*: Pollution, resource depletion, population explosion, habitat destruction.

2. *Medical/Health*: Dangers to human health from industrial production processes, products, and wastes.

3. *Psychological/Emotional*: A substitution of machine values for human values; transformation of the nature of work from craftsmanship to meaninglessness, leading to worker alienation; a feeling of citizen powerlessness in the face of a complexity said to be understandable only by an expert elite, and so, alienation from politics; social malaise exhibited in symptoms of increasing crime, senseless vandalism, anxiety, disharmony and tension, apathy, loss of agency, and loss of a feeling of community.

4. *Military:* Technology-based militarization and potential annihilation.

5. *Social:* Increasing centralization, bureaucratization, authoritarianism.

CONTEMPORARY TECHNOLOGY

Just what *is* contemporary technology? What do commentators mean when they use this term? Perhaps the first image conjured by the term "technology" is "machine"—a physical object. This was, no doubt, the original embodiment of technology but it is hardly an adequate conception for the contemporary scene. Like the term "society," technology is an abstract concept. A society is not simply a collection of people, but also the interrelationships among them. In the same way, technology means not simply a collection of machines, but the relationships among them, their uses, and the relationship between them and people. A single word cannot adequately represent the rich texture of language, so also a single machine, or a collection of machines, cannot adequately represent contemporary technology. One-dimensional observations—as of the proverbial elephant—are inadequate to describe that multidimensional, abstract concept: technology.

Contemporary technology cannot be understood without considering at least the following dimensions or elements:

1. *Physical Objects*[2]
    a. Hardware: tools, instruments, machines, weapons, appliances.
    b. *Structures:* bridges, buildings, plants, dams, networks (road, rail, telephone, pipeline, electric).
    c. *Materials:* metals, plastics, drugs, chemicals, synthetic fibers.

2. *Know-how:* not abstract, scientific knowledge but procedures, methods, processes, *technique.* Accumulated knowledge is as much a part of technology as a machine. For Harvey Brooks, technology is nothing but certain kinds of know-how; technology "is not hardware but knowledge, including the knowledge of not only how to fabricate hardware to predetermined specifications and functions, but also of how to design administrative processes and organizations to carry out specific functions, and to influence human behavior toward specified ends."[3]

3. *Personnel*: not autonomous human individuals but standardized people, largely interchangeable with one another, having the appropriate know-how to manipulate the physical objects.

4. *Organization and System*: the organized structure, the mechanisms of management and control, the integrated systems within which hardware and physical structures are embodied and technique employed by personnel; the linkages that tie together hardware, technique, and personnel with the social institutions.

5. *Political and Economic Power*: this dimension is implicit in the preceding one but it should be acknowledged explicitly.

Technology is not simply the computer, for example, but large-scale computer networks linked through telecommunications systems; it is command-and-control systems; it is data banks, the know-how and the software to manipulate them, and the power implicit in controlling them. Any analysis of contemporary technological society which fails to account for this multidimensional nature of technology, especially the notion of technological system, will be deeply flawed.

MODELS AND THEIR SUPPORTING PREMISES

In going about their everyday lives people carry in their heads models or paradigms of what the world is like, what society is like. Walter Lippmann noted that individuals create for themselves a *pseudo-environment*, an internal representation of the world, built up over a lifetime. People's perceptions of events are determined by the images, the preconceptions, the premises that underlie this pseudo-environment. Most people tend not to question these preconceptions, even when the consequences of acting in accordance with their images of reality lead to anomalies that the paradigm cannot reconcile.

In science, when such anomalies develop, some creative individuals question the old paradigm and its premises, and develop a whole new image of the world based on an entirely new way of looking at things. For example, Newtonian mechanics gave way to relativistic mechanics. On another level, many people *are* aware of the anomalies between the rhetorically cultivated presuppositions of the social system and the adverse effects of the realities they experience on the receiving end. Such people *do* seriously question the premises on which the social system is founded; and sometimes this questioning leads to a violent "paradigm shift"—

through revolution. But more often than not, their questioning is "contained."

Historically, whenever a paradigm shift has been necessary (in science or social structure), this shift has been resisted by those who have an interest in the old paradigm (an intellectual, emotional, or financial interest). It is difficult for people who have invested a lifetime in the service of a particular world view to switch to a different outlook. Even if they intellectually understand the need for it, their entire previous life leaves them unprepared to carry on comfortably in the new paradigm.

Contemporary technological society is now facing anomalies which baffle the social and economic preconceptions most of us carry around. These preconceptions are built strongly into the social structure and culture, but reality cries out for a paradigm shift. It is essential, then, to identify and critically examine the premises—both explicit and hidden—that underlie the now inadequate contemporary model. The following are five of the major premises.

1. *Self-Seeking:* The preferred behavior mode for human beings is one of self-seeking, of pursuing one's own self-interest—at least what is *perceived* to be such. The foundation of the capitalist ethos is that such self-seeking behavior will lead to social good through the operation of an "invisible hand" in the "market."

2. *Elastic Wants:* Human wants are infinitely elastic; they expand without limit. So it is necessary to have continual economic growth in order to satisfy them.

3. *Dominating Nature:* The physical world (nature) is there for "man" to subdue, conquer, dominate, subjugate, and exploit. Descartes said that by scientific knowledge "we may be able to make ourselves masters and possessors of nature."

4. *Neutrality of Technology:* Technology is morally and politically neutral; it is a mere tool which can be used for good or evil. If it is not used properly, "man" is to blame.

5. *Freedom of Choice:* Individuals in our free market system have free choice. The root cause of such ills as wasteful consumption, urban congestion, pollution, and the specific designs of inappropriate "products" lies in the free choice exercised by autonomous individuals.

Each of these ideas which underlie the dominant paradigm in contemporary technological society fails to withstand critical examination. They must all be rejected if transformation to a humane society is a goal. The first three refer to the presumed nature of human beings. Although I will devote some brief thought to them, the bulk of my analysis in this essay will be reserved for the last two.

HUMAN NATURE: SELF-SEEKING AS A PREFERRED VALUE

The premise or assertion that self-seeking behavior is the preferred mode for humans tends to encourage an aggressive, contentious, noncooperative spirit; it cultivates self-aggrandizement, greed, and envy—a looking out for Number One at the expense of the community. Furthermore, say its proponents, this is human nature anyway, and you can't change it. The type of social structure fostered by this outlook is a hierarchical one, with individuals engaged in a scramble for status on the ladder of success, elbowing their lonely way to the top. The capitalist culture and social system require individuals to act in a self-centered, contentious manner. The proper operation of the system *demands* it. How convenient, then, to ascribe this attitude to basic human nature! Writing in 1930, John Maynard Keynes said: "For at least another hundred years we must pretend to ourselves and to everyone that fair is foul and foul is fair; for foul is useful and fair is not. Avarice and usury and precaution must be our gods."[4]

Why did Keynes think that self-seeking should be encouraged? Because it was useful to the operation of the capitalist system! But he at least recognized that it was not laudable, and that you had to work at it to make avarice and greed appear as gods. Perhaps it is true, says Samuel Florman, "that the common man would be 'happier' if he did not have the urge to scramble upward to a high station in life. But this is irrelevant, because the common man does have the urge . . . human nature is at the root of our problems."[5]

But is the greedy, status-seeking pursuit of self-interest a consequence of unalterable human nature? To demonstrate that it is not requires only to find counterexamples. We would ask: have humans ever acted selflessly? If we could find any such cases (and we need not look only to the lives of saints—Francis of Assisi and Mahatma Gandhi come to mind—but to ordinary people in common situations to find many counterexamples) we would have to conclude that the proposition that self-seeking is unalterable human nature is, at the least, not proved. With a bit of further thought, we would have to say that some humans act selflessly, others selfishly; that *any* human *sometimes* acts one way, sometimes the other; even that individual humans often have conflicts within themselves, when faced with a given situation, as to whether they should respond to the situation in a self-seeking manner or in a cooperative, communitarian manner.

It can just as validly be assumed that human beings—far from being, by nature, selfish—are, by nature, cooperative and fraternal. How they *actually* behave in given situations depends on their socialization, on the reinforcements they receive for their behavior. If the culture, the social order, continually reinforces them for self-seeking, for personal aggrandizement, the chances are they will act this way more often than not. An outside observer would then notice that most people, much of the time, behave in noncooperative, self-seeking, status-enhancing ways. Such an observer who might conclude that such behavior is simply human nature would be a naive observer, indeed. Even the happy technologist will occasionally and unknowingly concede this. Florman says: "Man, for all his angelic qualities, is self-seeking and competitive; conceding to humans noble, as well as ignoble qualities."[6]

INFINITELY EXPANDING HUMAN WANTS

Economists postulate that human wants are infinite and insatiable—no sooner has one want been served, than another is stimulated; that humans are incapable of saying "enough." Says Florman: "Contemporary man is not content because he *wants* more than he can ever have."[7] This being the case, is the argument, it is essential to maintain economic growth and increased levels of consumption. The serious flaw in these assertions is the failure to distinguish between those wants that are basic and absolute *needs*—such as food, clothing, shelter, sex—which humans will experience independent of the condition of other human beings around them—and those which are socially-induced and relative.

It is clearly untrue that basic human needs cannot be satisfied. The sight of food is not tempting to a person who has just finished dinner; such a person would then prefer to spend his or her time on other pursuits. It is also clear that some basic human needs are not at present satisfied for a substantial fraction of the world's population. To this extent "growth" is still needed; not generalized growth, but increases in those areas of production intended to satisfy the basic needs of those now inadequately served. Perhaps "redistribution" rather than "growth" is the operative concept.

The second category of wants may well be insatiable. But what is their nature? These wants are experienced only in a relative sense, only if a feeling of superiority to others is achieved, only if vanity or status is enhanced. These wants require continual comparison with others and feverish activity in pursuit of inequality. They are not ennobling, but base. In a sane society, pursuing this satisfaction would be discouraged. But in a society dominated by the capitalist ethos, it is encouraged and cultivated through high-powered persuasion and promotion. Herbert Marcuse[8] refers to such wants as "false needs," not to deny that they exist but as a judgment of their worthiness. The flourishing of false needs is a reflection not on human nature but on the values consciously cultivated by the social system. It makes no sense to actively promote ego trips, feelings of vanity and prestige, desires for superiority and status—and then to demand economic growth in order to satisfy these desires—at the expense of ignoring the crises we now face.

Furthermore, the effort of satisfying these wants is doomed to failure. "For it is obvious that, over time, everybody cannot become *relatively* better off."[9] If people's satisfactions depend almost entirely on status, ego-gratification, and feelings of superiority, then increasing levels of consumption cannot yield increasing satisfaction to society as a whole. The superiority and enhanced status of some imply the inferiority and reduced status of others.

HUMAN SUBJUGATION OF NATURE

The idea that human beings should have dominion over the earth and all that it contains (now extended to the entire universe) was an early tenet of Western civilization; it even carried Biblical sanction. And mankind has not been reticent in carrying out this injunction. But there are at least two fallacies in this outlook.

The first relates to depletion. Clearly, intrusive human activities carried out over a period of time can have, and have had, devastating effects on nature and on human society. In the past, the wholesale destruction of forests and improper cultivation procedures led to soil erosion. Similar activities have had major detrimental effects on the present conditions of many parts of the earth. But the scale, intensity, and quality of current human interventions in nature dwarf those of the past. The final vanishing of a great deal of the wealth of the earth seems to be imminent.

Whatever utility the concept of domination and control of nature by humans may have had in the past, it is now counterproductive. Rather than subjugating nature, human beings must learn to live in harmony with it, to cooperate with its processes. That does not mean that human beings must lie down supinely before nature, but that their activities should take nature's processes into account. Humans should avoid building their structures over faults in the earth's plates, for example. Or they should avoid building their towns in the flood plains. Cooperating with nature also means understanding its limits and its carrying capacity, and thus minimizing those activities that put pressure on those limits and exceed the carrying capacity of the earth.

The second fallacy is the mistaken assumption that nature is one thing and human beings are something else, outside of nature. That is false, of course; human beings are as much a part of nature as mountains and birds. If the earth were destroyed, human beings would cease to exist also. Human domination and exploitation of nature implies the proposition of human domination and exploitation of other humans. Although this proposition was accepted practice in the past, slavery, imperialism, and other institutions of exploitation should no longer be tolerated. Their rejection implies the rejection of the parent concept: the subjugation and domination of nature by humans.

It is clear that the preceding analysis of the three premises of the dominant contemporary paradigm lumped under the heading of "human nature" requires further expansion. Nevertheless, the remainder of this essay will focus on the other two premises.

NEUTRALITY OF TECHNOLOGY

Although champions of "advanced technology," or "high-tech" (i.e., the happy technologists) may approach their subjects from different perspectives, there seems to be a common refrain to their individual verses that amounts to a litany of technology:

- that technology is just a passive tool whose consequences depend on the uses to which it is put;
- that if technology is used harmfully, "man" is to blame;
- that there are no values embodied in technology;
- that technology plays an entirely passive role with respect to issues of power and control;
- that the prime reasons for introducing innovations in production processes are increased efficiency and productivity;
- that the prime reasons for introducing innovations in products is to satisfy a human need, "to satisfy it more safely, reliably, and at lower cost to the user."[10]

Here is what some of the happy technologists say:

Simon Ramo:

> [I]t was not really technology but rather the selector and user of
> it—man—who should be faulted. Surely everyone understands that
> science and technology are mere tools for civilized man.[11]

Melvin Kranzberg:

> Technology *per se* can be regarded as either good or bad, depending
> on the use man makes of it.... Nuclear power provides a good
> example, for the power within the atom can be used for constructive
> or destructive purpose, as man chooses.[12]

Peter Drucker:

> The only positive alternative to destruction by technology is to make
> technology work as our servant. In the final analysis this surely means
> mastery of man over himself, for if anyone is to blame, it is not the
> tool but the human maker and user.[13]

Samuel Florman:

> A basic human impulse precedes and underlies each technological
> development. Very often, this impulse, or desire, is directly respon-
> sible for the new invention. But even when this is not the case, even
> when the invention is not a response to any particular consumer
> demand, the impulse is alive and at the ready.[14]

This litany of the happy technologist constitutes an ideology.[15] The
ideology of technology has purposes quite remote from explaining reality
to members of society. It fails to take political power and economic
interests into account and masks their predominant role. It promotes a
model which ascribes to technology an objectivity, a value-neutrality,
which technology does not in fact possess. A useful clue to the ideological
nature of a statement purporting to be explanatory is the ascribing of
action to vague collective nouns and pronouns, as in:

> "*Man*" is to blame (collectively).

> "*Mind* determines the shape and direction of technology."[16]

"If technology is sometimes used for bad ends, *all* bear responsibility."[17]

"[M]ake technology work as *our* servant."[18]

"Thus *we* manufacture millions of product to enhance our physical comfort and convenience. . . . But in doing this, *we* overlook the need to plan ahead."[19]

Are we all equal in responsibility, or aren't there some who are more equal than others? Who are the "we" who do the manufacturing? Is that the same "we" who forgot to plan? Doesn't somebody's profit enter the picture at all? Surely it is some specific minds that shape technology, not an abstract "mind." The preceding manner of speaking conceals the existence of very specific, powerful groups and individuals whose activities in pursuit of their interests are major factors in the problems of contemporary technological society.

Some insight into the role played by technological ideology can be obtained by analogy, through an examination of the role of economics in our society. Like any other science, says John Kenneth Galbraith, economics has the purpose of understanding, in this case, the economic system and how it works, what is the nature of money, labor, capital, taxation, the market, and so on. But economics also has an instrumental function: to serve the goals of those who have power. It creates images in the minds of people, thus contributing to their model of society. Those images are not at all consonant with the reality of the economic system, at least with the 50 percent of the economy represented by what Galbraith calls the "planning system": the large corporations and their activities. The instrumental function is to induce people to behave as if the image were the reality. It is to conceal from people the true nature of most of the economy as a *planned* system—not free enterprise—with the planning being done by a handful of large corporations in their own interest.[20]

Like economics—which has both a scientific purpose and an instrumental function as an ideology—technology also has two goals. Quite apart from the purpose of enhancing our physical comfort and convenience, technology and technical expertise serve an ideological instrumental function. This function is again image making and concealment, that is, the covering of political and economic power in a cloak of technical objectivity. The image is created that decisions and actions serving the interests of those in power are simply the consequences of objective facts, carried out for objective reasons such as efficiency.

Innovations in Production Processes

Let us first examine the issue of technological innovations and their introduction. The ideological assertion is that these serve the objective goals of efficiency, increasing production, and satisfaction of human needs. Those holding the images that make up the dominant paradigm see this as reasonable but it does not stand up under closer scrutiny.

In his study of the development of the textile industry during the Industrial Revolution in Britain, David Dickson[21] shows that the rise of the factory system and the organization of work in factories was largely a managerial necessity, rather than a technological one. It was done for the purpose of "curbing the insolence and dishonesty of men." The rising capitalist class made no bones about it, that the specific machines introduced had as their major purposes the subduing and disciplining of workers. Speaking of one invention in the textile industry, Andrew Ure, an early champion of the factory system, says: "This invention confirms the great doctrine already propounded that when capital enlists science in her service, the refractory hand of labour will always be taught docility."[22]

Further confirmation is provided by Samuel Smiles, the biographer of several industrialists of the period:

> In the case of many of our most potent self-acting tools and machines, manufacturers could not be induced to adopt them until compelled to do so by strikes. This was the case of the self-acting mule, the woolcombing machine, the planing machine, the slotting machine, Nasmyth's steam arm and many others.[23]

Technological innovation was not so much determined by a concern for production efficiency as it was a management tactic to maintain a fragmentation of workers, authoritarian forms of discipline, hierarchical structure, and regimentation.

Similar lessons can be learned from other events in the history of industrial development. Cyrus McCormick was a manufacturer of agricultural equipment in Chicago. In 1880, unhappy with working conditions in the McCormick plant, the skilled workers were attempting to organize into a union, something McCormick violently opposed. He installed a $50,000 machine—a truly tremendous amount for the time. The machine required only unskilled workers to operate it. It was very inefficient and produced goods that were greatly inferior to what had previously been produced. Further, after two years, it was abandoned once it had served its purpose of getting rid of the "troublemakers," destroying the union, and cowing the workers. The same story is evident down to the present. After analyzing the demands that the contemporary corporation imposes on employees, Richard C. Edwards concludes that the complex hierarchy of the modern corporation grew not from the demands of technology but from the desire of greater control over workers.[24]

Innovations in Products

Next consider the introduction of technological innovation in "consumer products." To a significant extent, such innovations arise as a consequence of research and development (R&D) activities. Although small entrepreneurs also contribute to product innovation, a great deal of R&D activity directed toward product development is carried out in the laboratories of large, technology-intensive corporations. What are the goals of these corporations? Simply stated, they are: survival; growth in sales; growth in profits.[25] All the activities of corporations—production, sales, marketing, and R&D—are carried out to reach these goals. Product innovation, no less than production or marketing, serves corporate purposes and so would be carried out, independent of social need.

Would a lack of need suffice to thwart the corporations' desire to increase sales and profit? Of course not; if a market does not exist, "it must be developed."[26] That is, it must be created, cultivated, and nourished. The entire arsenal of persuasion is unleashed to convince potential consumers that the new innovation will not only perform the specific function for which the product is ostensibly designed, but will also enhance status, satisfy vanity, increase personal appeal, and so on. People are thus sold the idea that their self-worth is measured by the goods they possess and consume, in general, and by this specific product, in particular.

The preceding analysis seriously weakens the claims of technological objectivity and value-neutrality. The nature of a society's technology is intimately related to issues of power, control, and economic organization, and reflects the dominant paradigm in terms of which reality is interpreted. A society in which economic growth is a high value necessitates a particular kind of technology: one with a high level of "innovation" quite independent of social need. Policies leading to economic expansion must be reflected in the particular form of technology through which this expansion is achieved. Hierarchical forms of social control become reflected in the technology. The presumed neutrality of technology then lends legitimacy to the resultant social policies.

Like other happy technologists, Simon Ramo repeatedly and explicitly claims the value-neutrality of technology. Without realizing it, however, he makes an amazing concession contradicting this position and acknowledging an instrumental function for technology. In reviewing the space program and justifying the spending of large resources on this program, he concludes:

> The pattern we are developing—to be far-sighted, to be bold, to want to pioneer, to be willing to take some risks, to carry with us as a part of our way of life the exploration of the unknown—it is these habits that we cultivated when we carried out our space program.[27]

This is a remarkable concession that a specific technological development has an agenda quite unrelated to the primary goal; *that the program served the ideological purpose of cultivating certain habits.* Can it be denied that less glorious-sounding attitudes than the ones admitted by Ramo—greed, status seeking, self-aggrandizement, contentiousness—may also be on the agenda? The general truth cannot be escaped: technology serves an instrumental function.

FREEDOM OF CHOICE

Not only is technology passive and neutral, according to the happy technologists, but whatever evil consequences are associated with the deployment of technology result from autonomous individuals exercising their free choice. Not only that, but people perversely choose to use technology even though this fact leads to environmental degradation, depletion of resources, and other unpleasant things they themselves experience. Furthermore, technology itself is liberating and enhances individual freedom. Here is a sampling of their assertions:
John Gardner:

> Everyone lampoons modern technology but no one is prepared to give up his refrigerator.[28]

Samuel Florman:

> However much we deplore our automobile culture, clearly it has been created by people making choices, not by a runaway technology. Experts underestimate the inclination of ordinary people to make choices contrary to what appears to be their best interest.[29]

Melvin Kranzberg:

> Similarly, the American small town of the beginning of this century, to which many of our contemporaries look back longingly, may not have been as idyllic; how are we to account for the fact that so many Americans fled from the small towns? . . . That kind of spatial freedom vanished from the onrush of urbanism; but people apparently want to live together in large agglomerations.[30]

Alvin Weinberg:

> A social problem exists because many people behave, individually, in a socially-unacceptable way. . . . Too many people drive cars in Los Angeles with its curious meteorology, and so Los Angeles suffocates from smog. . . . What right does the water resources expert have to insist that people use water less wastefully? Green lawns and clean cars and swimming pools are part of the good life, American style . . . and what right do we have to deny this luxury?[31]

Emanuel Mesthene:

> The freedom of individual decision-making is a value we have cherished that is built into the institutional fabric of our society. The negative effects of technology . . . are traceable less to some mystical autonomy presumed to lie in technology and much more to the autonomy that our political and economic institutions grant to individual decision making.[32]

Simon Ramo:

> National control is really the only answer, and that can come only if a majority of Americans are willing to accept interference in their freedom to choose automobiles.[33]

Daniel P. Moynihan:

> Freedom is choice and technology greatly enhances choice. [Therefore,] technology has vastly enhanced human freedom.[34]

These assertions constitute a second litany. To be generous, one would ascribe the origins of this litany not to a deliberate agenda, ideologically promoted, but to a fundamental confusion about what technology is. As noted earlier, the *systems* within which the separate components of technology are incorporated are its essential features. Failure to understand that the term "technology" subsumes organized and integrated systems implies a profound misunderstanding of the nature of contemporary technology.

It should be evident that the two major propositions—that technology is passive and neutral, on the one hand, and that it enhances human freedom and autonomy, on the other—are incompatible and mutually exclusive. If technology is value-neutral, how can it be biased toward freedom? And if it plays an active role with respect to one moral issue (namely, freedom), then is it possible to claim that technology is neutral toward other ends? Notwithstanding this fundamental contradiction, the same individuals who make the one claim, more often than not, also make the second one. But this logical fallacy does not rule out the possibility that one claim or the other might be true, even if both cannot be. In the previous section I have argued that the technology-is-passive-and-neutral proposition is not true. This section will do the same for the technology-enhances-freedom claim.

Autonomous Individual Choice?

Let me use the term "life-style" to designate the manner in which individuals in a society go about their daily activities at home, at work, at play, and so on. In American society, the general perception exists that life-style is a matter for individual choice, at least for a vast majority. But is one free to choose to have a refrigerator or not? Is it a simple matter of life-style choice or do other institutional arrangements of society impinge implacably with demands of their own? Is it the kind of choice referred to by Justice Oliver Wendell Holmes when he said: "In its evenhanded majesty, the law forbids rich and poor alike to sleep under a bridge"?

A refrigerator (including freezer) performs several functions. It stores perishable food (a necessity) and cools beer or produces ice for cooling drinks (a comfort or luxury). The latter (luxury) category is not an essential function. The desirability of cold beer, for example, is culturally or socially induced; other cultures (the British) find warm beer more desirable. But even the necessary functions are questionable. Other societies, like France a decade or two ago, made it possible for people to purchase their perishable foods on a daily basis in markets or small shops, easily accessible and within walking distance of their homes, even in the largest cities. *This option is not now available to most contemporary Americans.*

The supermarket as a social institution has its own imperatives. One buys for a week of eating, not for a day, so storage in a refrigerator becomes essential to living. It is a life-style necessity induced by an economic system of food distribution over which individuals have little control. To chide individuals for recalcitrance or perversity for their unwillingness to "give up" a refrigerator is to profoundly misjudge the nature of contemporary technology and its induced social change.

No value judgment about the merits of different life-styles is implied in the preceding scenario. It is irrelevant to the argument whether or not a supermarket/refrigerator society has advantages over the other. The only question is: do individuals have the autonomy to freely choose not to utilize a certain technology?

The Automobile Culture

A similar and even stronger case can be made about the automobile. "The love affair of Americans with their cars" is an image commonly used to explain our automobile culture. The question, again, is one of choice. During the period of gasoline shortages in the early 1970s it was customary for American leaders to exhort the people to conserve gasoline by driving less. The implication was clear: driving by Americans is mainly discretionary and it is only the perverse exercise of individual free choice that causes our current ills. The arguers for the existence of free choice gaze out at society as it exists at a given period of time, with the social structure and state of technology as they exist. Within this framework, they claim, individuals can choose. They can choose to buy this model car or that, this color or that, this upholstery material or that, this option or that. The one fact that belies all of this apparent freedom is that the majority of individuals cannot choose *not to* buy a car—if they also want to participate in the normal life of the society, such as going to work, buying food or clothing, attending a concert, and so on. The design of cities, the location of services, places of employment, shopping centers, and so on, are all predicated on the motor car as the dominant mode of transportation.

Many communities in the United States had electric railway systems that served admirably in the first third of this century. It was not the autonomous choice of individuals that killed these existing urban and interurban mass public transportation systems, and prevented their improvement and expansion. In more than one case, they were purchased by automotive corporations (the major culprit being General Motors, abetted by Gulf Oil) and converted to motor buses, and then allowed to die in order to promote the use of the private automobile.[35]

A case in point is Los Angeles. It had an extensive electric streetcar and interurban rail system in the early part of this century. During the 1920s the Pacific Electric Railway operated 1,200 miles of interurban rail service. When the population of the area was only 1 million in 1924, the system carried a volume of 109 million passengers. (By comparison, 45 years later when the population was 8 to 9 times greater, public transit using buses carried only 75 percent more passengers annually.) The reason we have smog in Los Angeles, says Alvin Weinberg, is because too many people drive cars! A much more accurate reason is that General Motors bought the Pacific Electric Railway system and destroyed it. Not individual autonomy, but the technological order, capped by the power of large corporations, is the major cause, not only for smog but for the fact that over half the land area of Los Angeles—including freeways, streets, driveways, parking lots, gas stations, automobile showrooms, and so on—is dedicated to the automobile.

It can also be observed, parenthetically, that the same results to be achieved by driving fewer miles can be achieved by driving more efficient cars. But U.S. auto producers long resisted designing and producing automobiles with better fuel efficiency. The conventional argument that manufacturers "give the public what they want" doesn't wash. Chrysler is a case in point. From 1976, after Chrysler management was informed by its own market analysts that there was increasing public resistance to large cars, they made no plans for introducing more fuel-efficient models because profits on large cars were greater. In 1979, when it had to seek federal assistance in order to avert bankruptcy, Chrysler had to entice people to buy its backlog of fuel-inefficient cars by offering large price reductions, but it had few fuel-efficient cars to sell in order to obviate the need for public welfare.

Ramo decries federal "interference" in setting safety regulations, emission standards, and so on, because it would control people's "freedom to choose automobiles." But many, many government actions have had and continue to have, a major impact in instituting, cultivating, and maintaining the American automobile culture. Among these are the investment tax credit that encouraged auto manufacturers to produce cars, and the oil depletion allowance that encouraged oil companies to produce fuel for them. But of far greater significance were the establishment and the method of funding of the federal interstate highway system in the late 1950s. This was one of the most far-reaching acts of "interference" by government.

People were not asked to debate the merits of different transportation systems and then choose what they favored. Specific corporate interests, in order to promote their own welfare, brought about the current state of the U.S. transportation system. It is not descriptive of reality to say now that people have free choice in their mode of transportation. To set up the transportation system so that individuals are compelled to buy cars just to be able to participate as members of society, and then to sneer at them because they are unwilling to give them up, is to add insult to injury. It is like blaming the victim for the crime. For most contemporary people in the United States, most of the time, driving a car is not discretionary—it is mandatory.

THE EFFECTS OF EXTERNAL COSTS

Even within the context of a market and the regulation of technological developments by the market, is it possible to describe accurately the current status of specific technologies (e.g., the transportation system) as the collective consequence of untrammeled individual choice guiding the invisible hand? Market prices can be kept artificially low by transferring some of the costs associated with production or use from the manufacturer and/or user to third parties—that is, to the rest of us. This can be, and has been, done in at least three ways: (1) by subsidies from the government; (2) by failure to account for "external costs" or negative "externalities" in setting prices; and (3) by accounting procedures that treat nonrenewable resources as flow rather than capital.

All of these processes have operated widely to distort price structures. Vast sums have been transferred to corporations in subsidies by the federal government, either directly (through grants and low-interest loans) or indirectly (through the taxing mechanism or by having the government assume responsibility for certain components of technological systems, such as highways and airports). "External" costs are both tangible—just to clean up the effects of corporate activity on the environment will take decades and hundreds of billions of dollars—and intangible, yet real. Inestimably huge external costs, both privately borne and socially borne, have been transferred from manufacturers and users to others. Purchasing decisions are obviously influenced by prices that are artificially depressed in such ways. If this circumstance permits a large-scale technological development to take place, which then induces major changes in the way people live, would it be meaningful to assert that the detailed forms of the resulting society are consequences of individual "free choice"?

It might be argued that, in a democracy, citizens are the ultimate determiners of government actions, so if government subsidies result in the development of certain technologies, it must be the result of individual choice among candidates. Political scientist James Carroll has provided a cogent and compelling analysis of such issues.

> [T]echnology often embodies and expresses political value-choices that, in their operations and effects, are binding on individuals and groups, whether such choices have been made in political forums or elsewhere. . . . Technological processes in contemporary society have become the equivalent of a form of law—that is, an authoritative or binding expression of social norms and values from which the individual or group may have no immediate recourse.[36]

Furthermore, says Carroll, there are often no appropriate political processes for "identifying and debating the value choices implicit in what appear to be technical alternatives." Technological processes are technically complex and occur in administrative organizations (either government agencies or corporations) to which citizens have no access. So, ordinary people on the outside have neither the opportunity nor the means to identify the value questions, far less to resolve them in the public forum. Consequently, *de facto*, the locus of the political value choices becomes the technological processes themselves; there is no public debate and issues are posed and resolved in technical terms. Individuals have no autonomous choice in the matter.

But even if, in some historical period, the development of some specific technology had been a political issue, had been fully debated in political forums, and had subsequently become the subject of a referendum or legislation, would that settle the issue? Not for later generations, it wouldn't. The resulting configuration of technology would become a given for subsequent generations and, to the extent that other options have been foreclosed by the adoption of the technology in question, individuals in those generations would have no choice. And we, now, are the "later generation" of earlier times. One might respond in rejoinder that that's life; people in one era must accept what those in another era left behind—not just in technology, but in laws, mores, and so on. At least two arguments can be advanced in rebuttal: (1) Precisely! the rejoinder grants the premise that individuals have no choice; and (2) laws can be repealed and mores can be violated by future generations, but the dependence on technology cannot be easily transcended.

The design of cities, and the location of services, places of employment, shopping centers, and so on, are all based on the private motor car as the dominant mode of transportation. Mass transportation is not an alternative. People cannot decide to buy either at the supermarket or at the corner grocery—they must buy at the supermarket because there are no longer many corner groceries. They cannot choose to buy unpackaged, unwrapped, unboxed products because such products don't exist in most places. Only now in the 1990s can some choose to recycle much of the "waste" materials (paper, glass, plastics, metals) which they are compelled to bring into their homes as a result of supermarket packaging. Until recently few recycling facilities were available in most places.

EMPLOYEES AS AUTONOMOUS CHOOSERS OF TECHNOLOGY

In contemporary technological society, vast numbers of human beings are employed as personnel and embedded in an organized employment structure in which they perform specific, well-defined functions. For its proper functioning, the technological order requires that the totality of these functions be carefully coordinated and articulated. In this context, how can the concept of technology as a neutral tool for autonomous individuals to use as they choose be reconciled with the plan and control needed to make systems work? It is ludicrous to imagine human beings—in the capacity of employee and personnel, from the user of the most sophisticated equipment on the assembly line, to the airline pilot, to the supermarket checkout person, to the hamburger slinger at the fast-food outlet—to be autonomous wielders of neutral tools to achieve their individually chosen goals. Since the "job" of employees is "usually their sole livelihood, there is strong pressure for strict discipline and obedience. One appears at a pre-established time, for precisely- determined work, for an exactly-designated reward."[37] As employees, individuals have little discretion or autonomy in the manner in which they will utilize the technology appropriate to performing their function.

THE FREE MARKET

And what about the invisible hand that operates through the mechanism of the "free market" to optimize the conditions of life? Perhaps an example will shed some light on the subject. It has long been known that lead and the human body are incompatible. When the body absorbs lead (by breathing the fumes from leaded gasoline, by drinking water delivered through lead pipes, by exposure to lead-based paint, etc.), the body is damaged. Most susceptible are children. For many years it has been known that lead is dangerous and various actions have been taken to get lead out of the environment. By the 1980s cars that use leaded gasoline were no longer being built. Water pipes in new buildings can no longer be made of lead; lead paint is no longer being sold. But there are millions of homes and apartments that still carry lead-based paint—peeling and chipping though they may be. Children ingesting chips and the dust of such paint are at great risk. The harmful health effects of exposing children to lead-based paint were well known through many studies. But a new dimension was added when the results of a long-term study were released in 1990 showing that children exposed to lead-based paint had lower grades throughout their schooling, tended to drop out of high school at greater rates, tended to take drugs more, and so on. And it wasn't just a few percent more but *seven times* more than their contemporaries.

How was a reduction of lead use brought about? Was it through free market forces? Was lead removed from gasoline because people were lured into unleaded gasoline by the market—through lower prices? Did auto makers design engines to use unleaded gas because market forces drove them to do it; that is, because such engines were cheaper so people surged to buy the cheaper car, thus forcing other manufacturers to go no-lead?

None of this was the case. The design of engines and the lead content of gasoline were *regulated*. Regulations forced manufacturers to design engines to use unleaded gas. Regulations forced gasoline refiners to remove lead from gasoline. (Actually, they were forced not to add lead to gasoline, which was the previous practice.) If we had relied on the market, we would still be inhaling gas fumes laced with lead, with the resulting damage to the health and welfare of millions of people. The same is true for lead-based paint and lead water pipes. Without regulation, the health of millions of people would still be at risk from these sources. The assertion that guidance and control of technology can be achieved through the mechanism of the market is an ideologically based article of faith, far removed from reality.

CONCLUSION: HARMONIOUS TECHNOLOGY

In this essay I have presented a critique of what appears to me to be ideologically based views about technology. I will now conclude by summarizing my analysis and adding a final thought.

- Technology is not a neutral, passive tool devoid of values; it takes the shape of and, in turn, helps to shape, its embedding social system.

- The ideologically promoted, neutral-tool, use-abuse model of technology conceals the issues of economic and political power relationships among different groups in society. It, thus, serves the instrumental function of legitimating the dominant ideology.

- Far from increasing freedom, contemporary technology limits individual autonomy and imposes a style of living concerning which individuals have little choice.

- The needs to which technology is said to respond are social system-induced. In a social order with different values and goals, the needs would be different and so the nature of technology would be correspondingly different. Resource conservation, cars with high fuel efficiency, and electrically efficient appliances, for example, are antithetical to the values of the present social system— growth, consumption, profit. Hence, they are neglected.

- The crisis of contemporary society cannot be resolved if the contemporary form of technology remains dominant; it must be replaced by a technology of a different nature. But since technology is intimately tied to matters of political power and social control, changing the technology implies a profound change in the social order.

- The crisis is not one *within* technological society which can be overcome by patching up the system, but a crisis of the contemporary technological system *itself*. The major question is not *who* is to control the means of production, but *what* the means of production shall be and *what* shall be produced. It is not *where* to locate the nuclear power plants, but *whether* to have nuclear power at all. It is not merely a question possibly of limiting growth but of radically altering the very nature of technology.[38]

- Contemporary technology is based on a narrowly conceived economic efficiency, on social control, and on profit. I would like to characterize a needed alternate technology as *harmonious*. It would be based on different criteria:

  Harmonious technology would respect ecological values and be in symbiosis with nature. This does not mean there would be no human intervention in nature, just that such intervention would not be destructive and exploitative, but in harmony with ecological values; consequently, harmonious technology would rely mainly on renewable energy and would be minimally consumptive of nonrenewable resources.

Harmonious technology would be responsive to direct social needs and would not require a hierarchical, exploitative, and alienating relationship among human beings. It would not oppress people nor treat them as mere appendages to machines, but would be emotionally and intellectually satisfying to work with.

Harmonious technology would value the durability and quality of products, the decentralization of production, agricultural diversity over monoculture, and pluralism in life-style and culture.[39]

What is needed to bring about the transformation is a new consciousness that sees the interrelationships among the physical, biological, and social spheres; collectively they constitute a system of which humanity is a part. What is needed also is a new style of living which is in harmony with the natural world—a harmonious technology in a harmonious society. An appropriate motto might be:

SCIENCE DISCOVERS—HUMANITY DECIDES—
TECHNOLOGY CONFORMS

NOTES

1. Simon Ramo, *Century of Mismatch* (New York: David McKay, 1970) 2.

2. I am indebted to David P. Billington of Princeton University for the distinction between structures and machines. By their nature, structures are stationary and have a degree of durability. This renders them relatively inflexible and not subject to rapid change. Structures are often of unique design, reflecting the requirement of a particular physical or social setting. Machines, on the other hand, are dynamic, have a relatively short life, and are compatible with rapid change. It might be fruitful to study whether this distinction contributes differentially to contemporary images of technological reality. There will be no further considerations of the distinctions in this essay.

3. Harvey Brooks, "The Technology of Zero Growth," *Daedalus* 102 (Fall 1973): 139.

4. John Maynard Keynes, *Essays in Persuasion* (London: Rupert Hart-Davis, 1952) 372.

5. Samuel C. Florman, *The Existential Pleasure of Engineering* (New York: St. Martin's Press, 1976) 77.

6. Florman 84.

7. Florman 75.

8. Herbert Marcuse, *One Dimensional Man* (Boston: Beacon Press, 1964) 5.

9. Ezra J. Mishan, "Ills, Bads, and Disamenities: The Wages of Growth," *Daedalus* 102 (Fall 1973): 84.

10. R. M. Glorioso and F. S. Hill, Jr., *Introduction to Engineering* (Englewood Cliffs, NJ: Prentice Hall, 1975) 4.

11. Ramo, *Century* vi.

12. Melvin Kranzberg and Carroll Pursell, eds., *Technology in Western Civilization*, vol. II (New York: Oxford University Press, 1967) 705.

13. Peter F. Drucker, "Technological Trends in the Twentieth Century," *Technology in Western Civilization*, vol. II, eds. Melvin Kranzberg and Carroll Pursell (New York: Oxford University Press, 1967) 32.

14. Florman 61.

15. The dictionary definition of an ideology is: (1) a collection of errors, illusions, and mystification which present an inverted, truncated, distorted reflection of reality; (2) a manner of thinking or a set of values which is characteristic of a group; it is the integrated assertions, theories, and aims that constitute a socio-political program.

16. Bruce O. Watking and Roy Meador, *Technology and Human Values* (Ann Arbor, MI: Ann Arbor Science, 1978) 55.

17. Watking and Meador 157.

18. Drucker 32.

19. Simon Ramo, *Cure for Chaos* (New York: David McKay, 1969) 1.

20. John Kenneth Galbraith, *Economics and the Public Purpose* (Boston: Houghton Mifflin, 1976).

21. David Dickson, *The Politics of Alternative Technology* (New York: Universe, 1974) 71-83.

22. Quoted in Dickson 80.

23. Quoted in Dickson 81.

24. Richard C. Edwards, *Contested Terrain: The Transformation of the Workplace in the 20th Century* (New York: Basic Books, 1979).

25. Galbraith.

26. Glorioso and Hill 24.

27. Ramo, *Century* 51.

28. John Gardner, Godkin Lecture at Harvard University, *New York Times* 30 March 1969: E9.

29. Florman 60, 24.

30. Kranzberg and Pursell 700.

31. Alvin Weinberg, "Can Technology Replace Social Engineering?" *Technology and Man's Future*, ed. Albert H. Teich (New York: St. Martin's Press, 1977) 22-30.

32. Emanuel G. Mesthene, *Technological Change: Its Impact on Man and Society* (Cambridge: Harvard University Press, 1970) 40.

33. Ramo, *Century* 117.

34. Daniel P. Moynihan, Honors Convocation Lecture, *Syracuse University Record* 1 February 1979: 3.

35. Bradford C. Snell, *American Ground Transport*, sent to the Subcommittee on Antitrust and Monopoly of the Committee on the Judiciary, U.S. Senate (Washington: G.P.O., 1974).

36. James D. Carroll, "Participatory Technology," *Technology and Man's Future*, ed. Albert H. Teich (New York: St. Martin's Press, 1977) 336.

37. Langdon Winner, *Autonomous Technology* (Cambridge, MA: MIT Press, 1977) 201.

38. Ivan Illich, *Tools for Conviviality* (New York: Harper and Row 1973).

39. Clearly, this is an inadequate characterization of harmonious technology. A more detailed exploration of its shape and dimensions to convey the rich possibilities it has for human society is deferred for later development.

3

Critical Scholarship on Computers in Education: A Summary Review

Michael J. Carbone

INTRODUCTION

Since the early 1980s, computers have become an important issue in the debate about American education. The widespread introduction of these machines prompted such headlines from "Here Come the Micro Kids" and "Schools Are in the Grip of a Computer Mania" to *Time* celebrating the computer as "Man of the Year" in 1982.[1] As Michael Apple has pointed out, in the early 1980s, the growth of the new technology was definitely not a slow movement. He wrote that in 1985 alone, there was a 56 percent reported increase in the use of computers in U.S. schools, and of 25,642 schools surveyed, over 15,000 reported some computer usage. He went on to suggest that it is estimated that over 350,000-plus microcomputers have been introduced into the public schools since 1980.[2] With the growth of computer technology and its introduction in schools came critical analyses of this trend. This chapter will serve to review that literature.

The promise of the computer to revolutionize American education came through high-tech decrees about academic excellence, readiness for an information society, and a future demarcated by the need for "computer-literate workers" in preparation for the world competitive high-tech job market. So deeply convincing were these mantras that in 1983 the National Commission on Excellence in Education recommended computer training as one of the five New Basics, along with English and science.[3] After all, the publication of *A Nation At Risk* in 1983 had forcefully warned Americans of a "rising tide of mediocrity" in our schools, and boldly claimed that if a foreign nation had done to us what our schools were doing, or in this case not doing, it would be considered an act of war against the United States. Thus, in a broad constellation of widely publicized accounts from educational, governmental, and private sectors, the computer was heralded as the newest and, to date, the most promising tool for the salvation of an economy held captive by Japanese and German competition. All in all, it was a fairly auspicious inauguration. As Douglas Sloan has suggested, the computer seems to have come on the scene as a veritable *deus ex machina* to put all things right.[4]

It is no secret that educational policy in the United States is often characterized as being driven by a "bandwagon" mentality and highly subject to faddish thinking. It seems that most educators are always searching for a "magic bullet" which will solve the complex problems facing our schools and country—problems which are deeply complex, structurally embedded, and often organic to larger economic, social, and political currents. To wit, the slippage of the middle class during the Reagan years made a perfect target for early Apple computer advertising suggesting to anxious middle-class parents that school performance was contingent upon the acquisition of a home computer. No child should be without one. While most of the early literature about computers and education and the teaching of "computer literacy" was quite celebratory, a small but dissenting voice began to appear in the midst of this newest educational fashion. The minority status of this critical voice is the consequence of many complex factors, notably among them the technical, faddish mentality of educational thinking, our blind faith in technology, and educators' often stubborn refusal to question issues of power and control behind forces of educational policy making. Yet, despite its marginal status, the body of critical literature has steadily continued to probe the deeper recesses of the meaning of technology, and its widespread introduction into our classrooms and the cognitive and emotional lives of our children.

The character and scope of the critical literature concerning technology and education is diverse. In fact, Michael Young argued in 1984 for the need to conceptualize technology not just as information technology if sociologists of education were to make critical contributions to issues of educational policy and practice.[5] He went on to speak of the necessity of what he called "a sociology or politics of technology." Young warned critical educational sociologists against "ending up with, at least implicitly, an anti-technology argument, which would offer nothing to teachers or anyone else. [What we need is] to develop a view (or more ambitiously, a theory) of people's relation to technology as the products of other people's work embodied in artifacts or commodities."[6] Douglas Sloan has also suggested that professional responsibility demands much more than the mindless sloganeering of educators "urging to outdo one another in thinking of new ways to use the computer in all manners and at every level of education possible."[7]

In questioning the belief in the inexorability of the computer-communications revolution, Sloan reminds educators, as does Young, that human beings have choices in shaping, restraining, and directing this "revolution." These critiques have come to represent, for the most part, an unpacking, a probing and thoughtful look into what C. A. Bowers calls the "cultural dimensions of educational computing." The parameters of inquiry have been broadly drawn from a body of literature which has been asking questions about the relationship of the socio-political nature of technology to: work, culture, social environments, cognitive processes, hidden biases, school/corporate relationships, "frames" of thinking, literacy, public spaces, and democratic educational practices. These domains of inquiry have taken scholars deeper and deeper not only into the processes of technology, but also into the deep cultural and structural foundations of schooling and the institutional nature and relations of classrooms, machines, learners, teachers, and curricula.

In order to gain a full appreciation of the critical response to computers and technological forces in education we will now turn to a more specific look at the arguments and questions these inquiries raise. It is to the idea of "computers as social artifact" that we now turn. Recalling Michael Young's preliminary thoughts on the need for a theory about people's relations to technology, I intend to explore the critical literature in terms of social and cultural relations and reproduction. The following areas constitute some of the important social and cultural critical responses to education and technology: the deskilling of teachers' work and erosion of professional autonomy and control; the influence of computers on the cultural reproduction of and constructions/meanings of literacy; the fostering of a particular form of rationality and the seeming "neutrality" of technology, the economic pressures behind the drumbeat for computers in schools and their consequences for the democratic ends of education; and lastly, the transformation of schools into marketplaces for technological innovations and the ideology of computer literacy.

THE DESKILLING OF TEACHERS' WORK AND
ISSUES OF PROFESSIONAL AUTONOMY

As technology enters the workplace, work is altered. There is no reason to assume that teaching will be exempt. In fact, as Michael Apple has argued, because teaching has developed as a feminized world of work, or "women's paid work," it is particularly vulnerable to issues of hierarchy, authority, and control of work. Apple writes,

> because of these conditions [of gender bias] it has been exceptionally difficult for women to establish recognition of the skills required in their paid and unpaid work. They must fight not only against the ideological construction of women's work, but against the tendencies for the job to become something different and for its patterns of autonomy and control to change as well.[8]

In other words, because of the gendered nature of the teaching profession, it tends to respond differently to issues surrounding the important questions of autonomy and control. Computers are having an effect on the psychology of teachers' work. Their influences are felt in the domains of teachers' use of professional knowledge, communications among themselves regarding the aims and purposes of education, student-teacher relationships, and professional autonomy.[9]

It must also be noted that schools as a world of work have, at least since the turn of the century, always been interpreted as economies of scale. The drive for greater productivity in education and, in fact, the modernization of education require the transformation from a labor-intensive to a capital-intensive operation. It is certainly the promise of greater efficiency and control that has been the prime objective to justify expenditures in new instructional technologies.[10]

It would be unfair and one-dimensional to say that the deskilling of teachers' work is solely the product of technological forces alone. Certainly state-mandated curricula, outcomes-based educational assessment, teacher-proof material, and all other sorts of efforts to rationalize and standardize the school's curriculum play a significant part. Educational policy shows a long history of the attempts of "educational managers" to control the shop floor, so to speak. To the extent that control is now facilitated, enhanced, and aided by technological means—primarily computers—teachers' work may be transformed.[11] It is now possible for an entire curriculum to be embedded within a computer system, either in an individual classroom or within an entire school, for example, GEMS—or Goal-based Educational Management Systems.[12] As a result, work processes are altered as well as one's relationship to one's work. The ability of authority to be built into the machine, so as to seem invisible to the implementor/user, comes to characterize a very sophisticated form of control. Maxine Greene has characterized this as a "world where people will be expected to tap into vast storehouses of data that will often be authorless and therefore will seem to have an objective existence in the world."[13] The GEMS system, as studied by Robert Bullough, Stanley Goldstein, and Ladd Holt, offers some particular insight.

The GEMS program as developed for the Jordan School District represents the ability of educational computer technology to easily exploit the ever-increasing concern created by technocratic systems, which seem to require an increasingly higher degree of order to function efficiently. Public notions of accountability in education in pursuit of cost-effectiveness are easily satisfied by more rational and efficient forms of educational delivery. Bullough and his coauthors, in studying teachers' interactions with what they called the "rational curriculum," found deskilling as well as an uneasy acquiescence on the part of teachers as they responded to such technological curricular systems. Teachers seemed to vacillate somewhere between sensing the control of the system and liking the fact that it took the guesswork out of teaching and thus provided an odd sense of potency derived from a clear statement of educational purposes and outcomes. The authors write:

Since the curriculum is presented in the form of an organized, complete, and obviously powerful system, it is as though it was created by nonhumans or superhumans rather than by humans who might have their own particular and peculiar axes to grind. Teachers have reified the system and its objectives into something that transcends human beings and their abilities to make good judgments.[14]

The intended or unintended reduction of teachers to clerks is one possible outcome of the computerized school, and of the rationalized curriculum. Technology, insofar as it represents a form of rationalized control, may well contribute to significant changes in the structure and nature of teachers' work. Michael Apple and Susan Jungck write:

[W]hen individuals cease to plan and control a large portion of their own work, the skills essential to doing these tasks which have built up over decades of hard work—setting relevant curricular goals, establishing content, designing lessons and instructional strategies, "community-building" in the classroom, individualizing instruction based on an intimate knowledge of students' desires and needs, and so on—are lost.[15]

This in fact is what Bullough et al. found in their studies. Teachers who worked with the "technological curriculum" tended not to raise questions about the values or the goals/aims toward which they were working, in short, the normative questions of educational policy.

There is little evidence in the literature that suggests teachers have harnessed technology for their own instructional purposes. Most teachers simply do not have the time, facilities, or knowledge to create their own software, and as a result tend to rely on commercially produced material. This lack of time and the consequent pressure in teachers' work are not likely to recede in the near future. Again Apple and Jungck observe that intensification of the work day is one of the most concrete ways in which the working conditions for teachers have eroded. Intensification can be caused by greater accountability forces, cutbacks, and other sorts of efficiency-minded reforms. The upshot is that intensification increasingly forces people to rely on "experts" (read: technological solutions) to tell them what to do, leading people to cut corners.[16] The irony might just be that in relieving one problem—work intensification—teachers end up with another, greater one: deskilling and increased work alienation.

It is clear that technology and working conditions have a complex relationship. Computers now provide ways for authorities to represent themselves within the work lives of teachers in a relatively benign fashion. Whether embedded within a particular software program, or more complexly within entire curricular packages, teacher work can be monitored, structured, and rendered more routine.

Of course the question presents itself: does technology in the school inevitably lead to work degradation? There are those who believe that such does not have to be the case. Critics such as Tom Snyder argue that the technological revolution will only be educationally meaningful when programs are created that put computers in teachers' hands, and serve as a tool for teachers' own purposes. He envisions computers as storehouses of information that teachers can draw on to inform their opinion and give substance to their views—in other words, his vision is one of teacher empowerment.[17] However, given the realities of the current structure of our schools, the climate of accountability, our emphasis on standardization, and the intensification of teachers' work in a hierarchical work environment, I think Mr. Snyder's vision of technology highly unlikely. However, even if it were likely, there are other issues which critics have raised. These questions serve largely to reopen inquiry into the normative purposes of education and the nature of learning. It is to this constellation of interrelated and interdependent issues that I would like to turn.

INSTRUMENTAL RATIONALITY, LITERACY, AND CULTURAL REPRODUCTION

Similar to the critiques of educational technology and teachers' work, critical responses within the broad areas of literacy, technology, and social reproduction contextualize technology within social and political frameworks. As a consequence, when computers are viewed within these larger human issues, different questions about technology and education begin to surface. In fact, technology itself becomes something more, something other than just an assemblage of parts, circuits, and plugs. Its essence, its human associative meanings begin to be revealed in powerful ways which challenge the basic cultural myth of the "neutrality of technology." Thus, this broader, more socially contextualized response to educational technology and schooling has been characterized by a more fundamental reexamination of the aims and processes of education, requiring, as Maxine Greene notes, interpretations and ways of seeing from vantage points educators too seldom consult.[18] The relationship of schools as sites which reproduce instrumental and technical forms of literacy, thinking, and political dispositions to issues of the environment, democracy and equity, human subjectivity, and quality of life become vital and apparent. Key to these critiques, and a pivot upon which they rotate, is an unpacking of what John Broughton, et al. calls the "invisible pedagogy" of computers, systems, and technology, or what Douglas Noble has called the "imperatives of high technology."

Several very important conceptual domains seem to constitute the core of this literature. These include but certainly are not limited to critiques of: computers and their relationship to instrumental forms of rationality, as well as a critique of instrumental reason itself; the ideology of computer literacy and its reproduction in the schooling process; and an exploration into computers as "framers" of thinking.

I want to begin with computers and instrumental rationality. This argument revolves around a critical inquiry into the values of technology. The computer embodies a certain kind of rationality, as John Broughton argues, which is "the condition of the possibility of computer technology, its fundamental presupposition."[19] Its technical rationality represents a closed system of thought, dealing solely in the realms of what can be quantified, measured, and observed. This instrumental rationality only recognizes explicit forms of knowledge and values the production of measurable data that determines both efficiency and effectiveness. Bowers notes that technology's underlying metaphor involves viewing the world as a machine, and the task of the rational-calculatory mind is simply to reengineer the various systems in order to improve prediction, control, and efficiency.[20] Implicit forms of knowing, which enable us to be effective cultural beings, are discounted or devalued and the contextual is often ignored. As Bowers puts it:

> [T]he technicist mind-set (as formed by instrumental reason) privileges experimental innovation over substantive tradition, abstract and theoretical ways of thinking over implicit forms of understanding, the autonomous individual over the collective memory and interdependence of the cultural group, and a reductionist, materialistic view of reality that denigrates the forms of spiritual discipline necessary for living harmoniously.[21]

The machine both informs the way computers represent, symbolize, and reproduce a particular form of rationality and the way knowledge is treated and limited by the form of the computer as a medium. Together, these represent the ideology of the invisible pedagogical dimensions of the electronic learning environment. It should be noted that implicit within this critique is the rejection of computers as just tools. Their value in teaching and learning is not simply a matter of adequately supporting the needs of the user to acquire the necessary skills, attitudes, objectives, and behaviors to apply new instructional technology or methods effectively. Technology is not a neutral tool which can be used for either beneficial or detrimental ends.

Another important aspect of the critique of the hidden curriculum of computer learning is its particular contribution to notions of thinking and the socialization of students into a particular understanding of literacy. Sloan has argued persuasively for the role of image in thinking. He suggests that new insights present themselves in new images. Images form and underlie thought, even though these images must then be developed through more formal logical and calculatory forms of thinking. A rich vital imagery and imagery-making capacity of the mind are essential for new insight. Images, he argues, will shape the kind of world we come to know, the kind of world we give ourselves. "It is particularly in relation to the centrality of the image in all thinking that much serious thought must be given to the appropriate educational use of the computer with its powerful but highly specific, and exceedingly limited, form of imagery."[22] The computer and its function, both symbolically and actually, represent and reproduce a mechanistic imagery, an imagery basically reproductive of the instrumental reason which has come to dominate our age. Questions of educational meaning naturally flow from this analysis. What should be the role of education in a machine-dominated age? What role should computers play in the life of children, considering their affective life and need for sensory experience and image making?

In the same sense, in privileging instrumental forms of thinking—forms which are highly organized around information—Theodore Roszak warns of the danger of confusing information with ideas. He argues that information does not create ideas. Ideas are generated, revised, or unseated by other ideas. He concludes that the principal task of education should be to teach young minds how to deal with ideas, evaluatively and adaptively.[23] This is closely linked with Sloan's idea of images. Images and ideas imply a domain of knowledge which is outside of but not exclusive of the technical, measurable, and observable. John Davy writes, "Computers, by their very nature, and whether operated with LOGO or otherwise, are potent training grounds for thinking about thinking in purely functional, operational, and instrumental terms." Using the metaphor of light for the computer, he too warns us that the "light is flat, and there is little room to move around. Compared to the mysteries of hide-and-seek among moving shadows, it is a limited world [and] is sited on the slopes of the mountain of instrumental reason."[24]

Critics have raised powerful questions about the nature of the machine, its power to structure, suggest, represent, or reproduce forms of knowing which they assert must be assessed in the rich and complex context of schools and educational aims, in a society characterized as dominated by Newtonian rationalistic thinking, bureaucracy, and complex human and environmental questions. The very essence of their critique forces one to dig into what Larry Cuban calls the DNA of the school and the classroom, forcing an investigation of those features of technology and computers that are hidden—recessed into inner logics and the subtle dimensions of interaction. In *Experience and Education*, John Dewey wrote about collateral learning, a phenomenon which he referred to as what is learned in addition to the obvious lesson at hand. To ignore this domain is, he thought, a great pedagogical fallacy, an educational blind spot. The sum of these arguments gives us plenty of reason to pause and take seriously the question Harriet Cuffaro asks: what does a youngster learn when she presses the keyboard to call up cars and garages on a screen to figure out how to park a car? She argues that the unanticipated lessons that children acquire informally when working with microcomputers should indeed give educators some sense of caution before plunging ahead with all sorts of new technologies. She writes:

It is the presence of these collateral learnings—the distance and narrowing of the physical reality, the magical quality of pressing keys, the "invisible" sharing of control, the oversimplification of process, the need for precision and timing—that merit great attention when thinking about young children's learning and the use of microcomputers.[25]

ECONOMIC AGENDAS, TECHNOLOGY, AND CORPORATE CONTROL

Computers and computer literacy have come to symbolize and act as the metaphor for the conservative American educational reform movement which began seriously in 1983. As such, computers have generated a good deal of critical inquiry into the relationship between schools and economic agendas. Areas of major concern are: schools as marketplaces for technology; empowerment of a technological imperative and elite; a critique of the mantra of the social and economic need for "computer literacy"; educational equity and opportunity issues; and lastly, the potential demise of schools as public spaces devoted to critical forms of literacy for democratic ends.

Historical studies of the development of schools in the United States are increasingly pointing out the close relationship between educational and economic issues. Revisionist scholars have written at length about schooling as an integral part of the establishment of social stability for a growing industrial capitalist economy. The role of the common school in easing class conflict and the triumph of the social efficiency ideology in the early curriculum are well documented as examples of the school's relationship to economic issues.[26] The bureaucratic, hierarchical, and differentiated character of the modern school is no accident. Clearly the rise of the "industrial school" has served the hierarchical and class-based needs of American corporate capitalism well.

When in 1983, economic imperatives were offered as compelling reasons for educational reform, schools quickly, and almost reflexively, responded. The conservative educational reform argument suggested that the recovery of American economic strength lies in a more rigorous school system, an undoing of the excessive "progressive" reforms of the 1960s. There has basically been a concerted effort to reintroduce authority into the curriculum[27] and to tie the ends of education to corporate economic needs and the promise of high technology. Greene again has characterized the essential questioning of this movement: "Nowhere is it written that American schools are required to track, test, control, and sort in response to the demands of the Pentagon or to those obsessed with exploiting markets overseas."[28] Thus, the call for computer literacy as a curricular basic and the wide-scale introduction of computers into schools have been viewed by critics as binding schools ever tighter to the needs of capital and its required social constructs of class stability, gender differentiation, and racism.

The very core of this critique is, as Apple notes, the ideological and ethical issue concerning what schools should be about and, most importantly, whose interests they should serve. He writes:

> The language of efficiency, production, standard cost-effectiveness, job skills, work, discipline, and so on—all defined by powerful groups and always threatening to become the dominant way we think about schooling—has begun to push aside concerns for a democratic curriculum, teacher autonomy, and class, gender, and race equality.[29]

Will a high-tech revolution in our schools usher in a new era of productivity and economic power for the United States? Critics say no. In fact, when examined closely, the two actually have little relation to one another. The occupations that will contribute the greatest number of jobs not just in high-tech industries but throughout the society by 1995 will include mostly service jobs—building custodians, cashiers, secretaries, office workers, waiters, truck drivers, and health-care workers. This is certainly not a prescription for high-tech literacy. In fact, it is estimated by economic forecasters that only about 25 percent of those jobs will require people with a college degree.[30] Ernest Kahane and Andrew Oram note that "most of the created jobs have as little connection to programming as putting a bank card into a cash machine."[31] It is estimated that the widespread computerization of the business world will actually create a net loss in jobs, especially among women.[32] What then might be the reason for the technological push in education? As I have noted, some suggest that it represents another triumph for corporate capitalistic hegemony. Is it to produce more critical thinkers? Even if computers did foster critical thought, which I have suggested many believe they don't, there are little objective data confirming the contention that computer programming enhances intellectual functioning or problem solving. What students do learn by programming computers has little carryover into non-computer situations.[33] In his conclusion, Apple notes that these are not inconsequential points, and along with Douglas Noble, believes that computer literacy does not prepare people for potent, intellectual work. Even if it did, such work will be a rare commodity in tomorrow's labor market. There is instead every indication that computers will be used to preserve existing relations of knowledge and power on the job rather than to disturb them, and that there will be little room at the top.[34] Before we give our schools over to the requirements of the new technology and the powerful corporation, we must seriously think of who will win and who will lose, and how this all will reinforce those who already possess great economic and cultural power.

There is also the possibility that the school itself has been transformed into a lucrative market for technological innovation. Paul Hurly and Denis Hlynka have noted how this will serve to benefit and empower a technological elite. The modernized school system could become dependent upon the providers of innovation, and thus highly subject to outside control (I have already written about how this could serve to further deskill teachers). An example of such a scenario might well be found in the current push for the electronic classroom characterized by interactive video systems. Apple states bluntly that "teachers' jobs themselves are on the line here."[35]

"What has apparently convinced an entire population that something as vague and worthless as computer literacy is essential to their lives?" Douglas Noble asks.[36] It all seems to play on our hopes for a better future and our fears about an economy in decline. But the manipulation of these basic human issues is cynical and, as many have tried to warn us, perhaps even downright dangerous. The wholesale appropriation of educational aims and normative language may well deliver the final blow to notions of education that have to do with participatory citizenship, human development, and the nurturing and development of those domains of knowing that lie outside of the empirical, technical, and instrumental. The ideology of computer literacy itself, as fueled by visions of economic recovery, serves as a form of educational practice which does not seem to include a critical social or political analysis of technology, computers, or visions of a high-tech future. It exploits the notion that the Information Age is already here and that if we don't hurry we'll be left behind. All of this rhetoric about computer literacy implies the idea that technological imperatives exist outside of the realm of human intervention and thus ties us and our lives closer to its own logic. In the process, the debate about technology and computer literacy in our schools becomes seriously depoliticized and irrational. We are left to believe that all other forms of education are valueless in that they have no economic clout and are not translatable into spendable and powerful social currency. Critics have noted that creating spaces for critique and possibilities for alternative technological scenarios should become a priority among educators.

SCHOOLS AS PUBLIC SPACES, AND THE
TECHNOLOGICAL/ECONOMIC AGENDA

Perhaps Henry Giroux has raised the best argument against the economic/technological imperative in education. Bearing in mind the argument that a large part of the blame for U.S. economic problems is our lack of high-technology industries, and a large part of the solution is sought in making our schools and their curricula more responsive to industrial and technological needs, Giroux sketches out critical changes in public policy. The hegemony of the corporate sector rests upon the attempted reproduction of particular forms of consciousness conducive to consumerism and ideas of inexhaustible natural resources. Notions of progress that he characterizes as "new and improved," and what Noble has called a gee-whiz glance at the marvels of the future, explain at least part of the uncritical rush of schools to embrace the dictates of the corporate agenda.

In a short, but I think very important article entitled "Public Philosophy and the Crisis in Education," Giroux argues forcefully against such an uncritical acceptance of a *de facto* change in public policy: "First, does this new public philosophy, which has defined the parameters of the existing crisis and the varied recommendations to resolve it, adequately name the nature of the crisis? And second, does this philosophy itself represent as much of a threat to our nation as the problems it has identified?"[37] The danger, according to Giroux, is that as an ideal, a model of economic rationality is becoming the basis for new relationships between schools as public institutions and the private economic sector. This model represents an ideology that undermines the importance of critical public spheres, where the capacity for learning is not defined by economic or technical considerations. This of course poses a direct threat to the public good, because such a view of public policy provides the philosophical basis for launching an assault on the relevance of any public sphere dedicated to goals other than those which can directly benefit the economic needs of corporate America or its inherent technical logic.[38]

Giroux gives us pause to think seriously about the costs of allowing the narrow agendas of technical and economic expansion to become the underlying basis for educational policy. We must ask what is being lost educationally in terms of democratic issues, human development for all of our citizens, and spaces for critical inquiry which are not beholden to such economically reductive ideologies and pressures. Once again, Maxine Greene perhaps summarized the issue best when she wrote: "In a time when so much time is spent watching . . . and manipulating, a time when linear forms work in strange dialectic with the swirling images of video, we need to provide spaces for speech, for dialogue, for giving voice to what remains silent amid the sounds of machines."[39] These are not issues to be taken lightly. Giroux ends by stressing the need to construct a public philosophy that is committed to "developing forms of knowledge, pedagogy, evaluation, and research that promote critical literacy, and civic courage."[40]

CONCLUSION

When reviewing the more recent literature regarding the issue of computers and technology in education,[41] it is evident that the flurry of activity in critical scholarship was indeed in the early period of the debate. There are perhaps several reasons for this. One is that the computer revolution in education never really materialized beyond the initial acquisition of machinery and software. Another may be attributed to the nature of much of the educational software available—little of it goes beyond what can be done in a good workbook. Too, the promise of student motivation has not met the heights originally touted, and there has not been anything close to adequate programming or incorporating computers into the teacher's or the school's curricular goals. Many now are looking to these reasons for the computer failure and to these same areas as sites for its rejuvenation. In fact, parts of the school restructuring movement are working on ways of rethinking and talking about restructuring in a technological/computer framework. The direction of all of this remains to be seen. However, I want to note, and I want to do this rather forcefully, that the early inquiries into what I have called elsewhere the "underside" of computers in education are still very much relevant, potent, and essential. We ignore this scholarship only at our own peril. I think Michael Apple says it best:

> The new technology is not just an assemblage of machines and their accompanying software. It embodies a form of thinking that orients a person to approach the world in a particular way. Computers involve ways of thinking that are primarily technical. The more the new technology transforms the classroom in its own image, the more a technical logic will replace critical, political, and ethical understanding. . . . Where are computers used? What are they used to do? What do people actually need to know in order to use them? Does the computer enhance anyone's life? Whose? Who decides when and where computers will be used?[42]

These are extremely important questions. They are not peripheral, they are not anti-technology, they are not anti-progress, they are not technophobic, they are not the musings of Luddites or radical leftists; they are human questions—questions which delve into the human domain and the intersection between our inventions and our lives. They are normative questions about ourselves and the reproduction of our society. As Apple writes: "They are fundamentally choices about the kind of society we shall have and about the social and ethical responsiveness of our institutions to the majority of our future citizens."[43] If these issues don't matter then I can't imagine any that do. The future must be of our own making, and we need to begin the kind of debate which will truly sustain such a notion.

NOTES

1. Larry Cuban, *Teachers and Machines: The Classroom Use of Technology Since 1920* (New York: Teachers College Press, 1986) 72.

2. Michael Apple, *Teachers and Texts: A Political Economy of Class and Gender Relations in Education* (New York: Routledge and Kegan Paul, 1986) 151.

3. Ernest Kahane and Andrew D. Oram, "Where Computers Are Taking Us in the Education Field," *The New Servants of Power: A Critique of the 1980s School Reform Movement*, eds. Christine M. Shea, Ernest Kahane, and Peter Sola (New York: Greenwood Press, 1989) 67–74.

4. Douglas Sloan, ed., *The Computer in Education: A Critical Perspective* (New York: Teachers College Press, 1984) 3.

5. Michael Young, "Information Technology and the Sociology of Education: Some Preliminary Thoughts," *British Journal of Sociology of Education* 5 (1984): 206.

6. Young 207.

7. Sloan 1.

8. Apple 57–58.

9. The impetus for the idea to study computers as "social artifact" was taken from Harry Braverman's book *Labor and Monopoly Capital* (New York: Monthly Review Press, 1974) and formed the thesis for an earlier article I published in which I called for a more thoughtful and critical examination of computers in education primarily as social and political phenomena (see note 12 in this chapter). In this piece I suggested that the notion of teacher work become a primary focus of study as it relates to the introduction and implementation of educational technology.

10. Paul Hurly and Denis Hlynka, *Prisoners of the Cave: Can Instructional Technology Improve Education?* Paper presented at the National Conference on Instructional Technology, National Research Council of Canada, 1982, ERIC ED 244 608, 3.

11. Hurly and Hlynka 3.

12. Michael J. Carbone, "Computers in Education: A Cautious View, Technology as Social Artifact," *Contemporary Education* 56 (1985): 209.

13. Maxine Greene, "Microcomputers: A View from Philosophy and the Arts," *Computers in the Schools* 1 (1985): 11.

14. Robert Bullough, Stanley Goldstein, and Ladd Holt, *Human Interests in the Curriculum: Teaching and Learning in a Technological Society* (New York: Teachers College Press, 1984) 32.

15. Michael Apple and Susan Jungck, "You Don't Have to Be a Teacher to Teach this Unit: Teaching, Technology, and Gender in the Classroom," *American Educational Research Journal* 27 (1990): 232.

16. Apple and Jungck 234.

17. Quoted in Peter West, "Developing Educational Software to Empower Teachers," *Education Week* 8 January 1992: 21.

18. Maxine Greene, foreword, *The New Servants of Power: A Critique of the 1980s School Reform Movement*, eds. Christine M. Shea, Ernest Kahane, and Peter Sola (New York: Greenwood Press, 1989) x.

19. John M. Broughton, "The Surrender of Control: Computer Literacy as Political Socialization of the Child," *The Computer in Education: A Critical Perspective*, ed. Douglas Sloan (New York: Teachers College Press, 1984) 103.

20. C. A. Bowers, *The Cultural Dimensions of Educational Computing: Understanding the Non-Neutrality of Technology* (New York: Teachers College Press, 1988) 9.

21. Bowers 9.

22. Sloan 6.

23. Theodore Roszak, *The Cult of Information* (New York: Pantheon, 1986).

24. John Davy, "Mindstorms in the Lamplight," *The Computer in Education: A Critical Perspective*, ed. Douglas Sloan (New York: Teachers College Press, 1984) 19–20.

25. Harriet K. Cuffaro, "Microcomputers in Education: Why Is Earlier Better?" *The Computer in Education: A Critical Perspective*, ed. Douglas Sloan (New York: Teachers College Press, 1984) 23.

26. For an insightful and complete history of the triumph of the "social efficiency" mentality in American education, see Raymond Callahan's *Education and the Cult of Efficiency* (Chicago: University of Chicago Press, 1962) and Herbert Kleibard's *The Struggle for the American Curriculum 1893–1958* (Boston: Routledge and Kegan Paul, 1986).

27. Ira Shor argues this point persuasively in his text *Culture Wars* (Boston: Routledge and Kegan Paul, 1986). He credits the Nixon administration, and primarily his Secretary of Education, Sidney P. Marland, as instrumental in reshaping American educational goals to a more career-minded track in order to quell what they both thought the excesses of liberal education to be—the campus radicalism of the late 1960s and early 1970s.

28. Greene, foreword, ix–x.

29. Apple 153.

30. Apple 157.

31. Kahane and Oram 73.

32. Apple 337.

33. Douglas Noble, "Computer Literacy and Ideology," *The Computer in Education: A Critical Perspective*, ed. Douglas Sloan (New York: Teachers College Press, 1984) 66; and Cuban 94.

34. Noble 68; and Apple 160.

35. Apple 165.

36. Noble 69.

37. Henry A. Giroux, "Public Philosophy and the Crisis in Education," *Harvard Educational Review* 54 (1984): 187.

38. Giroux 190–91.

39. Greene, "Microcomputers" 17.

40. Giroux 194.

41. Surveys of the recent commentary on computers in education either deal with why they failed to become as pervasive as was originally touted, or deal with the idea of a revival of technology in education as an integral part of the current school restructuring debate. For example, see Sharon Shrock, "School Reform and Restructuring: Does Performance Technology have a Role?" *Performance Improvement Quarterly* 3.4 (1990): 12–33; Doris Ray, "Technology and Restructuring," *The Computing Teacher* (March 1991): 9–20; Karen Sheingold, "Restructuring for Learning with Technology: The Potential for Synergy," *Phi Delta Kappan* (September 1991): 17–27; Allan Collins, "The Role of Computer Technology in Restructuring Schools," *Phi Delta Kappan* (September 1991): 28–36; Robert S. Daniels, *What We Have Learned From Instructional Technology*, ERIC ED 266 080; Michael R. Simonson, ". . . Mere Vehicles . . ." *A Symposium on the Status of Research in Instructional Technology*, ERIC ED 785 519; Walter Hathaway, *High Tech: High Touch—The Agony and Ecstasy of School District-Based Educational Improvement Effects*, ERIC ED 254 904.

42. Apple 171–73.

43. Apple 174.

4

Censorship, Critical Theory, and New Information Technologies: Foundations of Critical Scholarship in Communications

Sue Curry Jansen

INTRODUCTION

This chapter will introduce some of the main sources of scholarly critique of information technology from the field of communications research. The grounding work of Marxist scholarship and its revision and extension in the work of the Frankfurt School of Critical Theory will be examined first. Second, the analysis of the culture industry and information capitalism will be explored. Current research and arguments in several areas of scholarship on gender, information, and technology will follow. I will finally turn to research which seeks to expose the hidden curricula of information technologies before offering some conclusions.

The "Dreams of Reason"[1] that secure the scientific outlook also vaunt the claim of technological neutrality: the idea that technology is value-free. These Cartesian dreams purport to scrub away all of the fingerprints of *homo faber*—the living, breathing, calculating, crafting, mortal technician—leaving in his or her stead pristine objects that may be used for good or evil. This move transfers virtually all of the responsibility for creating and inscribing meaning and value to technology from designers or producers to consumers.

The Siamese twins of technological autonomy and technological necessity are also children of this dream. They impute an inherent order to things: an immanent logic that has, for example, purportedly led to simultaneous inventions in vastly different cultural contexts. These tech-

Parts of this chapter are more fully developed in Sue Curry Jansen, *Censorship: The Knot that Binds Power and Knowledge* (New York: Oxford University Press, 1988).

nological imperatives, in turn, provide the auspices for theories and ideologies of technological determinism, evolution, and progress.

Karl Marx challenged the efficacy of the Cartesian dream by identifying a ghost, "a spectre," in the machine: that spectre was, of course, capitalism, the social and commodity relations that have underwritten technological development in the West.[2] Informed in large part by the technological determinism of the anthropologist Lewis Henry Morgan, Marx's own theoretical positioning in relationship to technology and technological evolution is also problematic. His analysis is more cogent than his diagnosis because he never entirely surrendered the Cartesian dream of a clean machine. He favored retooling the engine of history—the organization of the relations of production—to redirect its trajectory toward a more egalitarian future. In developing his blueprint for this future, however, he largely reproduced Morgan's assumptions of technological necessity and evolutionary progress.

A generation later his epigones, Max Weber and the young Georg Lukacs, were far less sanguine. Weber described the social relations of production and administration that accompanied the development of modern capitalism as "an iron cage" that deprived workers of both authenticity and emancipatory possibilities.[3] Lukacs saw this cage and the material and conceptual tools used to manufacture it as possessing a "phantom objectivity."[4]

THE FRANKFURT SCHOOL OF CRITICAL THEORY

By the time Lukacs reached middle age, the Enlightenment's dreams of reason had been transformed into a totalitarian nightmare for much of Europe. Within the rather esoteric realm of academic social theory, the possibility of effecting a synthesis of the ideas of Marx and Freud appeared to hold some promise for making sense of the nightmare.

Friedrich Pollock, Max Horkheimer, Theodor Adorno, Walter Benjamin, Karl Mannheim, Erich Fromm, Franz Neumann, Herbert Marcuse, and others entered into a sustained collaborative effort to bring that synthesis to fruition.[5] In doing so, they gave birth to the Frankfurt School of Critical Theory. Their work provided the auspices for a radical rethinking of the dialectic of power and knowledge. Horkheimer, Adorno, and others persuasively demonstrated that the Cartesian dream, as embodied in the Western Enlightenment, had transformed and deformed reason into a purely instrumental process: a process that became naturalized and reified in what Benjamin called "the age of mechanical reproduction."[6]

The Frankfurt School is now frequently criticized or dismissed because its diagnosis of the modern condition is profoundly pessimistic.[7] Benjamin, himself, committed suicide. The iron cage of modern culture, described by critical theory, had sturdy bars but no doors. As a result, it supported emancipatory visions of social reality, but it could not locate any passages to their realization. In short, it offered no reliable recipes for resistance.

While such assessments are both plausible and persuasive, they nevertheless underestimate the achievements of this extraordinary and extraordinarily diverse group of thinkers. These assessments blame the messenger for the message: a message articulated during the darkest period of the twentieth century. The Nazi was literally at the door when some of the most significant works of the Frankfurt School were conceived.

Mannheim claimed that schools of thought ought to be judged by the significance of the questions they raise, not merely by the answers they provide.[8] The Frankfurt School identified and articulated fundamental questions about the philosophies of the Enlightenment, the constituents of rational thought, the limits of instrumental thinking, the relationship of power and knowledge, the nature of objectivity, and the ghost in the machines of modernity—questions that all serious social analysts continue to struggle with regardless of whether they call themselves critical theorists, deconstructionists, postmodernists, standpoint theorists, or, in some cases, even feminist theorists. To be sure, during the post-World War II period, Existentialism, especially the works of Heidegger and Sartre, sketched a new landscape of critical thought that later thinkers such as Foucault, Lacan, and Derrida would color. Nevertheless, the Frankfurt School framed the questions of our time in ways that remain compelling to those who seek a critical lens for analyses both of structures of knowledge and of knowledge industries.

Jurgen Habermas's inaugural address at the University of Frankfurt in 1965 is usually cited as marking the formal end of the Frankfurt School.[9] The heir-apparent of critical theory renounced the skepticism of his teachers, Horkheimer and Adorno, and with it, apparently, their legacy as well. Committed to "an unabridged and critique-enabling concept of reason,"[10] Habermas, like his mentors, has nevertheless also distinguished himself by persistently raising fundamental questions about the constituents of rational thought, ethics, democratic communication, and the positionings of technology and technological expertise in contemporary authority structures. In the quarter century that has passed since his installation at Frankfurt, he has also repeatedly displayed a strong penchant for engaging hyperbolic rhetoric to mark his distance and autonomy from other thinkers who occupy adjacent territories (e.g., Foucault, Gada-mer, etc.);[11] so much so that his inaugural disclaimer has lost some of its weight. In my judgment, it has become increasingly apparent that Haber-mas sees so far and so well because he is standing on the shoulders of giants.

In the next section, I survey some of the territory that can be seen from the shoulders of these giants, and identify some of the ways the ideas of the Frankfurt School can be used to assess new information technologies for creating, organizing, and distributing knowledge. I will then show that even giants see by not seeing. I locate and mark some of the blindspots in contemporary critical discourses about knowledge and power, and show how these blindspots can be explained and illuminated by analyzing their gendered constituents. I also suggest some of the ways feminist epistemolo-gies can amplify the explanatory powers of critical theory and expand our conceptual resources for technology assessment. After that, I identify some of the ways new information technologies and structures of knowl-edge support what I call "constitutive censorship."[12] In the conclusion, I propose an alternative to Cartesian dreams of reason that restores the human fingerprints to technological ingenuity. This reflexive alternative encourages us to recognize fully that our classificatory systems and tech-nologies are, in Donna Haraway's words, "clackety structures": artifacts of human craftsmanship, interests, perceptual limits, and priorities.[13]

ON THE SHOULDERS OF GIANTS: THE CULTURE INDUSTRY AND INFORMATION-CAPITALISM

In *The German Ideology* (original 1846), Marx and Engels broke with the French philosophes' theory of knowledge by asserting that the ab-stract, formal language of philosophers that creates the impression that thought is free of practical interests is only "the distorted language of the actual world": a language that secures and is secured by the prevailing form of the social division of labor. Marx and Engels maintained that, under capitalism, even the categories that lie behind our semantic conventions and classificatory systems are homologous with property relations, so that "in language [as in life] the relations of buying and selling have been the basis of all others."[14]

This insight lent itself to two interpretations. The first supports a crude, mechanical form of economic reductionism. The second provides the grounds for development of sociologies of knowledge. Marx the revolutionary and coauthor of *The Communist Manifesto* forcefully as-serted the first position. Marx the scholar carefully developed the second position.

The Frankfurt School took its inspiration from the scholarly Marx. As a result, the sociology of knowledge that its members articulated owes almost as much to Marx's sources, especially Hegel, as it does to Marx. Their radical rethinking of the structures of consciousness and the problem of alienation was influenced by Goethe, Schiller, Heine, von Humboldt, Grimm, Nietzsche, Dilthey, Weber, and others, as well as Marx and Freud.

In short, the Frankfurt School translated Marx's definition of critique as "the self-clarification of the struggles and wishes of the age" into practice.[15] In the twentieth century, this practice requires revision and extension of Marx's analyses of the commodity relations of bourgeois cultures, but it also mandates critique of Marx and of formations of power that carry his signature.

Technological Designs as Social Designs: The Culture Industry

Current fashions in critical scholarship favor attributions to Gramsci, Foucault, Althusser, Williams, Hall, and others; however, the works of Horkheimer, Adorno, and Marcuse remain exemplars for responsible critical studies of knowledge industries. They systematically attend to the dialectical relationship that links forms of consciousness and the institutional arrangements that manufacture, package, and distribute commodified forms of consciousness. Adorno's and Horkheimer's concept of "the culture industry" effectively captures and foregrounds this dynamic focus.[16]

If the formulations of critical theory are over-determined (and they often are), they nevertheless manifest more responsible commitments to critique—to the pursuit of self-clarification—than most currently ascendent forms of critical theory such as Americanized versions of "cultural studies." Cultural studies approaches are frequently so eager to find "resistance" in popular forms, including tabloids, MTV, and Madonna, and their fans, that they increasingly ignore the institutional interests and arrangements of power that sponsor these forms.[17] We live in an age of unprecedented conglomeration, concentration, expansion, and globalization of media, entertainment, and information industries and technologies. Adorno's configuration may therefore be a better template for describing emerging formations of the culture industry than it was for mapping the system of domination that operated in his own time.

To be sure, the formulation is only suggestive: it provides a provocative metaphor for organizing theoretical dialogues that can produce informed and "enabling" critiques of knowledge industries. Indeed, its primary heuristic value may actually be its temptation to hyperbole. This hyperbole serves as an insistent reminder of the constant importance of attending to the material and institutional arrangements of what is currently being ideologized as "the information society."

The sociology of knowledge supported by critical theory conceives of technological designs as social designs. It affirms the conclusion that cultural values, economic interests, and political decisions are as integral to the composition of these designs as mathematical calculations, motors, cams, circuits, and silicon chips. Technologies are, in the words of Dallas Smythe, "teaching machines": they invite us to do some things, and make it difficult, although not impossible, to do others.[18]

The ambitious historical inquiries of Horkheimer and Adorno trace the development of instrumental thinking in the dualisms of Western thought from antiquity to the twentieth century.[19] They show how instrumentalism promotes forms of information and information technologies that are based on design principles that incorporate values such as efficiency, hierarchy, standardization, profitability, expansibility, redundancy, and control.

Information-Capitalism

Horkheimer and Adorno's analysis foreshadows and continues to illuminate current developments within contemporary culture industries. Thus, for example, it anticipates the current global movement toward privatization of information: the transfer of the production, control, and distribution of knowledge from public to private organizations and interests. Under the privatization of "information-capitalism," what was once regarded as a public good and cornerstone of democracy—Western culture's accumulated social knowledge or "wisdom of the ages"—is increasingly absorbed into the commodity system.[20] As a result, public libraries, education, broadcasting, museums, galleries, performances, and so on are increasingly brought under the discipline of the logic of profit. Under information-capitalism, then, the marketplace of ideas is no longer conceived as a public utility which serves all who seek its goods. Increasingly it becomes a private enterprise which serves only those who can afford to pay a price for the commodities it markets to consumers.[21]

Information-capitalism not only changes conditions of access to knowledge, it also changes the social role and structure of knowledge as well as the forms of knowledge that are produced. Under this "new world order," the production of knowledge becomes a basic industry like the production of oil, steel, and transportation.[22] The transfer in economic activity from production of material goods to the production of information has, to date, occurred in three ways. The first is through automation, especially robotics and other computer-assisted forms of manufacturing which result in reorganization of the efforts of the human workforce toward research, planning, design, and development of knowledge that is applied in manufacturing material goods. This step also eliminates high-paid blue collar jobs and contributes to the so-called "feminization of labor" in electronics industries. The second is through the emergence of high-tech enterprises which specialize in the production and sale of "commodified 'producer information'" (i.e., design, software, databases, expert systems, etc.)—information resources which are used by other firms in the productive process. The third is through acceleration of the production, promotion, and marketing of consumer information goods such as computers, VCRs, videos, fax machines, and other up-scale technological commodities.[23]

Privatization changes the relationship of the citizen/shopper to knowledge because unlike oil, cornflakes, or automobiles, knowledge is not used up when it is consumed. It may be lost, forgotten, destroyed, or censored, but it does not deplete itself, rust, or wear out. Moreover, once it has been produced, as every college freshman knows, knowledge can be copied, pirated, or plagiarized. This, of course, creates problems for both the producers and the gatekeepers of commodified knowledge. Under the "free-market of ideas" ideology that was valorized by industrial capitalism, knowledge was, at least in theory, communal property and not private property. Hence, it could not turn a profit.

Knowledge can only become a profitable commodity if democratic access is restricted by removing it from the public sphere and limiting the channels available for its distribution. For this reason, librarians and educators now find themselves policing access to photocopies, computer software, and video equipment. And, more ominously, they find themselves and their institutions increasingly held accountable by the legal system for violations that occur within their venues.

The New Enclosure Movement

Ironically, the denial of democratic access to knowledge is effected under the ideological cover of democracy, albeit a cover that makes corporations, rather than individuals, the "citizens" of a new form of "democracy" based upon free enterprise in a global marketplace. To effect the transformation of production of knowledge from a public trust to a private enterprise, a close alignment of the knowledge-producing capacities of business and government is required. The new information brokers have a vested interest in keeping information secret. For this reason, Ivan Illich has characterized the information revolution as a "new enclosure movement."[24]

To effect this enclosure, information industries put pressure on governments to stop giving away the goods: to stop producing and distributing information free (or at cost) through government publications, statistical services, census reports, health and educational services, and so on. U.S. government information policy has been very responsive to these pressures during the Reagan and Bush administrations. This policy has reduced government's information-related responsibilities and services in several ways: (1) through "deregulation," which has eliminated much of private industry's responsibility to report its activities to government agencies; (2) by narrowing the federal government's production and distribution of knowledge so that information that was previously gathered and analyzed by the federal government for local governments is no longer provided; (3) by restricting access to previously available information by expanding the range of information protected by government classification; (4) through sharply increasing the price of information available through the Freedom of Information Act; (5) by significantly reducing the number and volume of publications available through the Government Printing Office, and by making future government publication decisions contingent on profitability; (6) by subjecting the writings and speeches of current or former officials to prior censorship; (7) by restricting access to non-strategic scientific and technological information produced in universities under government contracts and grants; (8) by reducing the operating budget of the Library of Congress and thereby the services it can provide users; and (9) by cutting federal government aid to state and local communities, which, in turn, reduces the discretionary funds available for allocation to universities, public radio and television, libraries, and other cultural institutions.[25]

These pressures are exacerbated by three related developments within information-capitalism. First, the high costs of computerizing and automating library and other information resources as well as the costs of training personnel and clientele to use these resources reduces funds available for supporting traditional forms of information collection and acquisition. Second, concentrations of ownership and control in publishing and distribution networks are responsible for increases in the consumer costs and corporate profits of books and serial publications. Third, concentration has also greatly increased the redundancy factor in the content of mass-marketed information commodities by repackaging essentially the same material for different target markets or "windows."

Privatization of information means that information that was formerly available as a part of a citizen's right to know within a democratic system is now only available if that citizen can afford to pay for it. Under information-capitalism, as Herbert Schiller has frequently pointed out, information that cannot be counted upon to bring in a profit will not be produced.[26] Thus, for example, privatization in Britain, and the self-interest of a conservative government, have been responsive to market forces in ways that have gradually resulted in the elimination of the collection and publication of poverty statistics.[27] It has also led to a kind of reverse colonization whereby the advertising logos of American corporate sponsors are now prominently displayed on the programs and promotions for special exhibits at the British Museum and The National Gallery.

Market Censorship

Under the rule of information-capitalism, the concept and practice of censorship are also transformed. The chancery and state house are no longer the exclusive or even the primary sites of censorship. To the contrary, as Smythe points out, the act of modern censorship is essentially a decision as to what is to be mass-produced in the cultural area.[28] So long as current cultural production is in the hands of privately owned giant corporations, they must also make decisions as to what is to be mass-produced in the cultural area and what will not be produced. Because in monopoly capitalism, privately owned giant corporations are regarded as legal persons, we are accustomed to yield them the same privileges to which natural persons are entitled. It is as accurate therefore to refer to corporate decision making in the cultural area as being censorship as it is to refer to government decision making by that pejorative term. In their attempts to rationalize their production decisions and marketing strategies, corporate decision makers, like the censors of Rome, assume the mantle of mediators of public morals. These market censors determine what ideas will gain entry into "the marketplace of ideas" and what ideas will not. They "inspect" books, magazines, dramatic pieces, films, television programming, computer software, and so on, prior to production, to ensure that they contain nothing that will seriously challenge the tenets or the existence of the corporate system. That is, they decide what products of the culture industry are likely to

ensure a healthy profit margin. Because sensation—sex and violence—
sells, market censorship is far more libertine than church or state
censorship, but its discipline is, if anything, more thorough. Although
the system is not totally determined, most of the time the products that
survive the prior censorship of marketing research—the books, news,
scripts, games, coupons, programmed learning modules, syllabi, styles,
visuals, advertisements, party platforms, and so on—incorporate ideology and values that celebrate the corporate system and question the
loyalty, integrity, and sometimes even the sanity of its critics.[29]

Market censorship also exercises its discipline at the cash register.
Some would-be consumers of information and users of information
technologies are barred from access by the very presence of price tags.
Others have differential access based upon how much they are able or
willing to pay either for the information commodities themselves or for
acquisition of the skills necessary to use and appreciate them. Market
segmentation exercises a particularly interesting form of discipline. On
the one hand, it has a leveling effect by making some information
commodities available at very low prices. On the other hand, however,
it provides the more affluent and better educated both greater quality
and quantities of information resources. The effect of this discipline is
to create the impression of greater choice; when, in fact, for most market
segments, there are simply more choices as the same relatively narrow
range of material is re-packaged for delivery through different media
windows. For example, one sometimes hears the cable subscriber who
pays thirty dollars a month for access to thirty-plus channels complain
that "there is nothing on television."

Under information-capitalism, then, information becomes a form of
capital; and restriction and control of access to information becomes a
fundamental structural principle of the market system as well as a
significant constituent of the social reproduction of the class structure.
Socially structured gaps in the distribution of information increase the
number of potential target markets for information products. Conversely, new information technologies such as desktop publishing,
videotext, and computer information services like CompuServe and
Prodigy dramatically reduce dependence upon economies of scale when
producing information commodities for affluent market segments. With
information-capitalism as with industrial capitalism, "the rich get richer
and the poor get poorer." The difference is that the "phantom" democracy of the new system makes it far more resistant to criticism than the
visible structures of social inequality that were produced by industrial
capitalism.

SEEING BY NOT SEEING: GENDER, INFORMATION, AND TECHNOLOGY

Market segmentation and target marketing of information commodities reflect and contribute to the social reproduction of inequalities and differences based upon gender, race, class, education, age, and other social traits. In this section, I examine some of the gendered constituents of information and information technologies. I focus on gender because it is the most elementary and therefore the most pervasive marker of difference. As Stuart Hall puts it, all social practices and forms of domination— including the politics of the Left—are always inscribed in and to some extent secured by sexual identity and positioning.[30] If we don't attend to how gendered identities are formed and transformed and how they are deployed politically, we simply do not have a language of sufficient explanatory power at our command with which to understand the institutionalization of power in our society and the secret sources of our resistances to change. To assert that information is gendered is to posit both a profound and mundane claim. To assert that certain commodities, media genres, and message systems are marketed to and sought by female consumers is to say the obvious. To assert, however, that the deep structure of information is gendered is a very provocative move.

Blindspots in Critical Theory

I have developed this argument more fully elsewhere.[31] In the space available here, however, I can only offer a brief summary of my argument. Positioning my claim within the context of critical theory is a rather unfashionable move. The social theory of the Frankfurt School from Pollock to Habermas is silent about, indeed blind to, the gendered constituents of structures of knowledge.[32] Yet, the discourse of the Frankfurt School is itself a gendered discourse. It is what Mikhail Bakhtin calls "the word of the fathers,"[33] or what the new feminist epistemologies characterize as androcentric or "malestream" theory.[34] This is why its staying power resides primarily in the cogency it brings to the analysis of (1) instrumentalism, a Western masculinist construction and practice of rationality, and (2) culture industries, historically and still male-dominated institutions.

Critical feminism, a perspective that is both critical of and aligned with critical theory,[35] amplifies the conceptual powers of both feminism and critical theory. Feminist theory illuminates and partially repairs the gendered blindspots of critical theory. Conversely, critical theory provides feminist theory with some rudimentary tools for annexing study of public sphere issues. Those issues have, until very recently, remained less analyzed and under-theorized within its critical frameworks.[36]

Information: A Gendered Concept?

The most ambitious and successful demonstrations of the gendered character of information have, in my judgment, been articulated within five fairly discrete disciplinary constellations: (1) developmental psychology; (2) language, communication, and literary studies; (3) science and technology studies; (4) studies of pornography; and (5) explorations of what might be called the "collective unconscious" of Western art and knowledge structures.

Developmental Psychology. Carol Gilligan's contributions to developmental psychology are by now widely known and therefore require relatively little explication here. Suffice to say she has persuasively demonstrated that females and males in our culture typically attend to different aspects of moral dilemmas, make sense and reach decisions differently, and follow different developmental paths in reaching moral maturity. Her recent work attributes these differences to differential and unequal treatment of girls in the socialization process. To be sure, Gilligan's generalizations are based upon limited and biased samples. Most of her subjects are middle- and upper-class whites. Nevertheless, within this affluent population, she decisively documents the presence of gendered ways of knowing.[37] Others have documented gender-based differences in cognitive styles and learning patterns within less privileged groups.[38]

Language, Communication, and Literary Studies. Available studies of gendered differences in conversational styles, in writing and interpretive practices, and in reader reception are now so voluminous that it would require a fairly sizeable library to house them.[39] These studies demonstrate that language practices are marked by significant gender-based differences. This is so much so that some researchers claim women and men speak different languages,[40] while others contend women are without language and will only gain voice by constructing new languages based upon female embodiment.[41] For our purposes, it is sufficient to note that the differential cognitive styles identified by Gilligan and others produce and/or are produced by different ways of speaking, writing, and reading.

Science and Technology Studies. Studies of science and technology, informed by feminist perspectives, have brought powerful new insights to the history and sociology of science. Among the founding mothers of feminist studies of science are Ruth Hubbard, Ruth Bleier, Carolyn Merchant,

Evelyn Fox Keller, Sandra Harding, Donna Haraway, and Dorothy Smith.[42] Early feminist technology studies focused primarily on reproductive technologies,[43] but they now encompass the entire range of technologies including information technologies.[44] Feminist science and technology studies do not merely claim that science and technology are man-made. They maintain that the epistemologies and theories of knowledge that produced these discourses are systematically skewed by both Euro- and andro-centric interpretive and textual practices. According to these studies, then, the substantive claims of science are neither "neutral" nor "neutered."[45] Feminists conceive of the forms of reason valorized by scientific "objectivity" as contingent cultural artifacts: artifacts that were crafted by formalizing and codifying the "subjective" views of the men who participated in the founding conversations of modern science. Feminist studies in science and technology have identified some of the gendered practices that shaped these artifacts: they are rooted in the misogyny of Western culture;[46] the vision of science is secured in highly sexualized and sexist metaphors;[47] and the categories of science emphasize discrete boundaries, hierarchies, binary logics, and abstractions.[48] Feminist analyses of science and technology do not claim that the discoveries or the laws of the Sciences of Man are invalid or obsolete. Feminists do claim, however, that these sciences are not only partial, but also incomplete. Moreover, they reject all strategies for redressing this partiality that do anything less than undertake a comprehensive revision of existing categories and structures of knowledge. In contrast to the "God's-eye" perspective, feminist epistemologies maintain that all forms of knowledge are "situated knowledges": historically, culturally, and linguistically mediated, finite, and secured within, but not necessarily homologous with, a field of power relations.[49] This does not require embracing relativism or the "apartheid" approach to knowledge. To the contrary, it is the first move toward a "no-nonsense commitment" to the hard work necessary to provide a science that is "friendly to earthwide projects of finite freedom, adequate material abundance, modest meaning in suffering, and limited happiness."[50] Some feminist epistemological studies have documented differences in the ways women frame and secure arguments,[51] do science,[52] and use technology.[53] For purposes of advancing my argument, it will suffice to point out that existing categories, classificatory systems, and structures of knowledge bear the inscriptions of the conceptual practices of "the fathers."[54] The deep structure of these inscriptions appears to be located in the primitive "totemic" of gender.[55] Gender does not simply classify body types or prescribe norms for their representation; it "inflects an entire universe of objects and behaviors with masculine or feminine attributes, most of which remain unstated."[56]

Studies of Pornography. Pornography occupies a crucial position in a gendered sign system because it is the site where the implicit, the "unstated," becomes explicit.[57] For the purposes of my argument, this excursion into the underworld of pornography is intended to alert readers to how much our culture has been sacrificed in its pursuit of clean machines, efficient instruments, and discrete categorical structures and logics. The language, formulas, and narrative structures—the "poetics"—of pornography represent the underside of the Cartesian dreams. It is where reason goes, when, in Heinz Pagels's eroticized Cartesian dreams, it goes out the window.[58] It is the graveyard and refuge heap of the subject/object, mind/body split that Baconian and Cartesian dualisms valorize. Susan Griffin proclaims that "the pornographer is a censor."[59] Pornography censors men's memories of childhood feelings, attachment, wholeness, and vulnerability. It censors the "weakness" of men who long to be more than "instruments," more than machines, Terminators, or Robocops. Repressed and denied by the official discourses of male culture, religion, science, and civic culture, Robert Romanyshyn contends that passion and desire could only reappear in the underground world of male sexual fantasies and pornography.[60] The critical theory of the Frankfurt School identified, catalogued, and traced the historical genesis of these sacrifices, but its authors failed to apprehend the gendered constituents of what they called anti-humanism.[61]

The "Collective Unconscious" of Western Art and Knowledge. Technology is, of course, a product and enactment of the human imagination. In its primitive forms—club, hammer, pot, rope, and so on—its relationship to the human body is readily apparent. Technology is a prosthesis that extends and magnifies the power of human muscles, appendages, and senses. Modern scientific and technological knowledge, the form of knowledge that had its genesis in the Renaissance, relies heavily on visual prosthesis: lens, numbers, print. The etymology of the word "paradigm" betrays this visual bias; from the Greek, it means "to show," to "lay side-by-side." Romanyshyn shows how the geometrization of Western culture during the Renaissance allowed the technological imagination to take flight in both the figurative and literal sense. He locates the genesis of this move in the discovery and codification of linear perspective in Florence in the fifteenth century. Linear perspective achieves "a kind of geometrization of the world, and within that space we become observers of a world which has become an object of observation." It transforms "the eye into a technology" and creates "a world of maps and charts, blueprints and diagrams . . . in which we are . . . silent readers of the printed word and users of the camera . . . [and] in which we have all become astronauts."[62] It creates "bourgeois perception," a kind of tunnel-vision which privileges the visual over other senses.[63] However, Romanyshyn's "we" is not a fully inclusive we. It is the collective we of elite, Western, male discourse: the "astronaut," scientist, technologist, capitalist, "the fathers," who distance and objectify the world and its inhabitants and then re-present this view as the "objective" and omniscient view. In short, it is the "we" of male-gendered information.

Information Theory

Information theory represents one of the purest articulations of the Cartesian dream of a clean machine.[64] The Cartesian recipe maps the coordinates upon which Claude Shannon positioned his mathematical theory of information and Alan Turing devised his theory of computational numbers and conceived his "logic machine."[65] Their work, in turn, provided partial blueprints for development of modern digital computers.

In relocating the sites of numbers and arithmetic operations from mind to electronic circuits, Shannon and Turing's clean machines reduce information to the kinds of messages these circuits can accommodate [see discussion of C. A. Bowers in Carbone chapter and my chapter on censorship—Ed.]. Magoroh Maruyama labels the truncated form of information valorized by information theory as "classificatory information." He points out that this mode of reasoning is only one of the kinds of information routinely used by human beings in the Western world to organize and analyze data. Maruyama maintains that human "information processors," unlike their electronic surrogates, also regularly rely upon "relational," "relevance," and "contextual" informations in making sense, reaching decisions, constructing arguments, and communicating with one another.[66]

"Classificatory information" is the language of Romanyshyn's astronaut, of Griffin's pornographers, of the discourses of science and technology deconstructed by feminist epistemologies, and of the "morality of rules" described by Gilligan in *A Different Voice*. In short, the language or espiteme[67] of the new information technologies that are currently revolutionizing our tools for knowing, classifying, organizing, storing, and retrieving knowledge naturalizes and reifies both instrumental and gendered structures of knowledge. Not only knowledge industries but also the deep structure of what now qualifies as knowledge bears the fingerprints of "the fathers."

IN PRAISE OF NOISY MACHINES

The new information technologies, the prostheses, that are becoming increasingly prominent in our homes, schools, libraries, hospitals, and offices are extraordinary tools and teaching machines. Exposing the hidden curriculum of these machines does not undermine or negate their utility. To the contrary, it re-situates them within human history, culture, priorities, and interests. It restores their human fingerprints, and opens up possibilities of approaching technological assessment and implementation reflexively. It also makes it possible to write alternative programs and to envision alternative design aesthetics for information machines.

Democratic Technics

Luddite forms of resistance may still have some strategic uses on the shop floor and in the office;[68] however, critical feminism can no longer afford to leave the boys alone with their toys. "Astronauts" preparing to exit the planet with "golden parachutes" are not to be trusted to mend the hole in the ozone layer or to keep the Star Wars in the movie theaters.

Prevailing forms of "info-tech" privilege binary data structures: structures that are enhanced by the parallel processing units supported by what Pagels describes as "the new sciences of complexity."[69] A critical feminist aesthetic would presumably try to subvert, invert, and divert capital-intensive information systems which currently advance information-capitalism's instrumental agendas. It would challenge present commitments to what Lewis Mumford calls "authoritarian technics," system-centered, immensely powerful, but inherently unstable technologies.[70]

A critical feminist approach would embrace "democratic technics": social designs that incorporate human-centered, diverse, resourceful, and durable technologies. It would support development of decentralized, egalitarian, accessible, process-oriented alternatives that advance expressive as well as instrumental values.[71]

Democratic technics do not surrender the controls to masters: artisans, designers, producers, or technoscientific experts. They do not bury the wires or scrub away the evidence of human agency. To the contrary, they display the signatures of their makers and demand accountability. Rendering the gendered constituents of the design aesthetics of information technology visible is a first step toward accountability.

"Clackety Structures"

Those who would advance democratic technics need to build alliances with artisans and theorists who are exploring alternative ways of constructing and using information technology: ways that will unlock what John Wyver refers to as "the enabling potentials of the technology."[72] Some examples of enabling alternatives using existing technologies follow: (1) creation of feminist computer networks and bulletin boards[73]—in the immediate aftermath of the 1991 Clarence Thomas–Anita Hill television hearings, these networks operated overtime organizing support for Hill and sharing data on sexual harassment; (2) the "electronic salon" facilitating an interactive conference format for feminist analyses of technoscience organized by Deborah Heath at Lewis and Clark College;[74] (3) using CD-I digital interactive systems, developed by SONY, to explore and advance democratic communications; (4) experiments in digital imaging and virtual reality technologies by conceptual artists advancing counter-hegemonic agendas such as David Hockney, Nancy Burson, Jill Scott, Simon Biggs, Jeffery Shaw, and Tjebbe van Tijln.[75] Jill Scott's installation *Machine Dreams*, for instance, presents a dystrophic vision of women's relations with the sewing machine, typewriter, and telephone switchboard.[76]

The counter-hegemonic efforts use existing digital technologies. They do not abandon binary logics, base-2 number systems, digital circuits, polarities, or rhetorics of antithesis; they do, however, engage these devices self-consciously, deliberately, with awareness that the "tunnel" is not the horizon. In effect, they treat them as what Haraway calls "clackety" structures.[77] They remind us that these sleek new technologies and conceptual practices, like the clubs, picks, steam-pumps, and oil-burners that came before them, are just prostheses; and that, in their own ways, they also whirr, chug, smoke, sputter, and spit. That is, these counter-hegemonic efforts mark the limits and display the biases as well as exploit the potentials of binary data structures. They read or, more accurately, program against as well as within the design aesthetics of information-capitalism.

To be sure, these resistant exercises and entertainments are the efforts of a very privileged, "information-rich" minority: academics, artists, and artisans who have routine access to advanced information technologies. To date, they have had little to say about or to the vast majority of workers employed in the new "electronic sweatshops."[78] Moreover, such efforts can provide no solace to segments of the population rendered unemployable by the new enclosure movement: the poor who are getting poorer. They need to be supplemented and surpassed by practices which, in Smythe's words, put "needs before tools."[79]

CONCLUSION

We are creatures of print who have already crossed over the threshold into cyberspace. The design aesthetics of information-capitalism would make astronauts or cyborgs of women as well as men, and pornographers of us all.

What is required to resist the new enclosure movement is nothing less than a second renaissance in the ways we conceive, create, code, theorize, and use space, technologies, gender, information, epistemology, and communications. Some potential building blocks or data structures for giving birth to embodied, planet- and species-friendly forms of life may already be emerging. Valorizations of local cultures, bio-regionalism, standpoint epistemologies, and situated knowledge can all be seen as, in part, forms of resistance to the reified fictions of the naturalized, essentialized human of humanism that has historically denied the subjectivities of women, sexual minorities, people of color, and the poor.

The astronaut is still in flight, but the damage he is doing to himself and to the planet is becoming increasingly transparent. Those who would bring him down to earth now appear to have more to contribute than he does toward "self-clarification of the struggles and wishes of the age."[80] The new enclosure movement is, however, rapidly shutting down the hearing spaces available for democratic communications.

NOTES

1. Heinz Pagels, *The Dreams of Reason* (New York: Simon and Schuster, 1988).

2. Karl Marx and Frederick Engels, *Basic Writings on Politics and Philosophy*, ed. Lewis S. Feuer (Garden City, NY: Anchor Books, 1959); and Karl Marx and Frederick Engels, *The German Ideology* (New York: International Publishers, 1970).

3. Max Weber, *The Protestant Ethic and the Spirit of Capitalism* (London: Unwin, 1985).

4. Georg Lukacs, *History and Class Consciousness* (Cambridge, MA: MIT Press, 1971).

5. All of these people were not formally associated with the School. Benjamin, for instance, was part of the Frankfurt intellectual and social circles, but not part of the School itself. Moreover, not all were affiliated at the same time or shared the same intellectual visions. Although all were influenced to a greater or lesser degree by Marx, the interest in Freud's work was not universal.

6. Walter Benjamin, *Illuminations* (New York: Schocken, 1969) 217–52.

7. Jurgen Habermas, *Knowledge and Human Interests* (Boston: Beacon, 1971); Martin Jay, *Adorno* (Cambridge, MA: Harvard University Press, 1984); and Martin Jay, *The Dialectical Imagination: A History of the Frankfurt School and the Institute of Social Research, 1923–1950* (Boston: Little, Brown and Company, 1973).

8. Karl Mannheim, *From Karl Mannheim*, ed. Kurt A. Wolff (New York: Oxford University Press, 1971).

9. Habermas; Jay *Adorno*; and Jay *Dialectical*.

10. Gerhard Wagner, "Review of *The Structural Transformation of the Public Sphere* by Jurgen Habermas," *Theory, Culture, and Society* 8.4 (1991): 119.

11. David Held and John B. Thompson, eds., *Habermas: Critical Debates* (Cambridge, MA: MIT Press, 1982).

12. Sue Curry Jansen, *Censorship: The Knot that Binds Power and Knowledge* (New York: Oxford University Press, 1988).

13. Donna Haraway, Presentations and Discussions, National Endowment in the Humanities Summer Institute, "Science as Cultural Practice," Wesleyan University, Middletown, CT, June 2–Aug. 3, 1991.

14. Marx and Engels, *German* 119, 102.

15. Karl Marx, *Karl Marx: Early Writings*, ed. L. Colletti (New York: International Publishers, 1975) 209.

16. Max Horkheimer and Theodor W. Adorno, *Dialectic of Enlightenment* (New York: The Seabury Press, 1972).

17. Alan O'Connor, "The Problem of American Cultural Studies," *Critical Studies in Mass Communication* 6 (1984): 405–27; and Joel Pfister, "The Americanization of Cultural Studies," *The Yale Journal of Criticism* 4.2 (1991): 199–228.

18. Dallas Smythe, *Dependency Road: Communications, Capitalism, Consciousness, and Canada* (Norwood, NJ: Ablex, 1981).

19. Horkheimer and Adorno; and Max Horkheimer, *Critique of Instrumental Reason* (New York: Continuum Publishing, 1974).

20. Tessa Morris-Suzuki, "Capitalism in the Computer Age," *New Left Review* (November/December 1986): 81.

21. Anita R. Schiller and Herbert I. Schiller, "Who Can Own What America Knows?" *The Nation* 17 April 1982: 461–64.

22. Smythe *Dependency*.

23. Morris-Suzuki; and Jansen *Censorship*.

24. Ivan Illich, *Tools for Conviviality* (Berkeley: Heyday Books, 1973).

25. Donna Demac, *Keeping America Uninformed: Government Secrecy in the 1980s* (New York: Pilgrim Press, 1984); and Jansen *Censorship*.

26. Herbert I. Schiller, *Who Knows: Information in the Age of The Fortune 500* (Norwood, NJ: Ablex, 1981); Herbert I. Schiller, *Culture, Inc: The Corporate Takeover of Public Expression* (New York: Oxford University Press, 1989); and Schiller and Schiller.

27. Philip Elliot, "Intellectuals, the 'Information Society' and the Disappearance of the Public Sphere," *Mass Communication Review Yearbook*, vol. 4, eds. Ellen Wartella, D. Charles Whitney, and Swen Windahl (Beverly Hills: Sage, 1983).

28. Smythe, *Dependency* 235.

29. Jansen *Censorship*.

30. Stuart Hall, "Brave New World," *Marxism Today* October 1988: 29.

31. See Jansen *Censorship*; Sue Curry Jansen, "Gender and the Information Society: A Socially Structured Silence," *Journal of Communication* 39.3 (Summer 1989): 196–211; Sue Curry Jansen, *Gendered Knowledges: Information, Technology, and Public Policy* (New York: Oxford University Press, forthcoming, 1993); Sue Curry Jansen, "The Ghost in the Machine: Artificial Intelligence and Gendered Thought Patterns," *Resources in Feminist Research, RFR/DRF* (1988): 17, 4–7; Sue Curry Jansen, "Information and Gender," *Inquiry: Critical Thinking Across the Disciplines* 8.4 (December 1991): 1, 21–24; and Sue Curry Jansen, *Mind Machines: Myth, Metaphor, and Scientific Imagination*, ERIC 1990 ED 311 522.

32. Nancy Fraser, *Unruly Practices: Power, Discourse and Gender in Contemporary Social Theory* (Minneapolis: University of Minnesota Press, 1989); and Jansen "Gender."

33. Mikhail Bakhtin, *The Dialogic Imagination* (Austin: University of Texas Press, 1981) 242.

34. Sandra Harding, *The Science Question in Feminism* (Ithaca, NY: Cornell University Press, 1986); and Cheris Kramarae, ed., *Technology and Women's Voices: Keeping in Touch* (New York: Routledge and Kegan Paul, 1988).

35. Donald S. Sabo and Sue Curry Jansen, "Men, Sports, and the Media," *Men, Masculinity, and the Media*, ed. Steve Craig (Newbury Park, CA: Sage, 1992).

36. Kathy E. Ferguson, *The Feminist Case Against Bureaucracy* (Philadelphia: Temple University Press, 1984); Nancy Hartsock, *Money, Sex, and Power* (Boston: Northeastern University Press, 1985); Dorothy E. Smith, *The Conceptual Practices of Power: A Feminist Sociology of Knowledge* (Boston: Northeastern University Press, 1990); and Dorothy E. Smith, *The Everyday World as Problematic: A Feminist Sociology* (London: Open University/Milton Keynes, 1988).

37. Carol Gilligan, *In a Different Voice* (Cambridge, MA: Harvard University Press, 1982); Carol Gilligan, Nora P. Lyons, and Trudy J. Hanmer, eds., *Making Connections* (Cambridge, MA.: Harvard University Press, 1990); Carol Gilligan, Janie Victoria Ward, and Jill McLean Taylor with Betty Bardige, eds., *Mapping the Moral Domain* (Cambridge, MA: Center for the Study of Gender, Education, and Human Development and Harvard University Press, 1988).

38. Mary Field Belenky, Blythe McVicker Clinchy, Nancy Rule Goldberger, and Jill Mattuck Tarule, *Women's Ways of Knowing: The Development of Self, Voice, and Mind* (New York: Basic Books, Inc., 1986); see also Combahee River Collective, "A Black Feminist Statement," *All the Women are White, All the Blacks are Men, But Some of Us are Brave: Black Women's Studies*, eds. Gloria T. Hull, Patricia Bell Scott, and Barbara Smith (New York: The Feminist Press, 1982) 13–22.

39. Robin Lakoff, *Language and Woman's Place* (New York: Colophon Books, 1975); Dale Spender, *Man Made Language* (London: Routledge and Kegan Paul, 1980); and Barrie Thorne and Nancy Henley, eds., *Language and Sex* (Rowley, MA: Newbury House, 1975).

40. Deborah Tannen, *You Just Don't Understand* (New York: Morrow, 1990); and Lakoff.

41. Helene Cixous, "The Laugh of the Medusa," *New French Feminisms*, eds. Elaine Marks and Isabelle de Courtivron (New York: Schocken, 1981) 134–264; and Helene Cixous and Catherine Clement, *The Newly Born Woman* (Minneapolis: University of Minnesota Press, 1986).

42. Ruth Hubbard, *The Politics of Woman's Biology* (New Brunswick, NJ: Rutgers University Press, 1990); Ruth Hubbard, M. S. Henefin, and B. Fried, eds., *Biological Woman: The Convenient Myth* (Cambridge, MA: Schenkman, 1982); Ruth Bleier, ed., *Feminist Approaches to Science* (New York: Pergamon Press, 1986); Carolyn Merchant, *The Death of Nature: Women, Ecology and the Scientific Revolution* (New York: Harper and Row, 1980); Evelyn Fox Keller, *A Feeling for the Organism: The Life and Work of Barbara McClintock* (New York: Freeman, 1983); Evelyn Fox Keller, *Reflections on Gender and Science* (New Haven, CT: Yale University Press, 1985); Harding *Question*; Sandra Harding, *Whose Science? Whose Knowledge? Thinking from Women's Lives* (Ithaca, NY: Cornell University Press, 1991); Sandra Harding and Merrill Hintikka, eds., *Discovering*

Reality: Feminist Perspectives on Epistemology, Metaphysics, Methodology and Philosophy of Science (Dordrecht, Germany: Reidel, 1983); Donna Haraway, "A Manifesto for Cyborgs: Science, Technology, and Socialist Feminism in the 1980s," *Socialist Review* 15.2 (1985): 65–108; Donna Haraway, "Situated Knowledge: The Science Question in Feminism and the Privilege of Partial Perspective," *Feminist Studies* 14.3 (1988): 575–99; Smith *Conceptual*; and Smith *Everyday*.

43. Gena Corea, *The Mother Machine* (New York: Harper and Row, 1985); Mary Daly, *Gyn/Ecology* (Boston: Beacon, 1978); Barbara Ehrenreich and Deidre English, *Complaints and Disorders: The Sexual Politics of Sickness* (Old Westbury, NY: The Feminist Press, 1973); and Barbara Ehrenreich and Deidre English, *Witches, Midwives and Nurses: A History of Women Healers* (Old Westbury, NY: The Feminist Press, 1973).

44. Cynthia Cockburn, *Machinery of Dominance: Women, Men, and Technological Know-How* (Boston: Northeastern University Press, 1988); Ruth Schwartz Cowan, *More Work for Mother* (New York: Basic Books, 1983); Cynthia Enloe, *Bananas, Beaches, and Bases* (Berkeley: University of California Press, 1990); Barbara Garson, *The Electronic Sweatshop* (New York: Simon and Schuster, 1988); Sally Hacker, "Doing it the Hard Way": Investigations of Gender and Technology (Boston: Unwin Hyman, 1990); Sally Hacker, *Pleasure, Power and Technology: Some Tales of Gender Engineering and the Cooperative Workplace* (Winchester, MA: Unwin Hyman, 1989); Jansen *Censorship*; Jansen "Gender"; Kramarae; Maureen McNeil, *Gender and Expertise* (London: Free Association Books, 1987); Lana Rakow, "Women and the Telephone: The Gendering of Communications Technology," *Technology and Women's Voices: Keeping in Touch*, ed. Cheris Kramarae (New York: Routledge and Kegan Paul, 1988) 207–88; Joan Rothschild, ed., *Machina Ex Dea: Feminist Perspectives on Technology* (New York: Pergamon Press, 1983); Judy Smith and Ellen Balka, "Chatting on a Feminist Computer Network," *Technology and Women's Voices: Keeping in Touch*, ed. Cheris Kramarae (New York: Routledge and Kegan Paul, 1988) 82–97; Judy Wajcman, *Feminism Confronts Technology* (University Park, PA: The Pennsylvania State University Press, 1991); and Jan Zimmerman, *The Technological Woman: Interfacing with Tomorrow* (New York: Praeger, 1983).

45. Catherine MacKinnon, "Feminism, Marxism, Method and the State: An Agenda for Theory," *Signs* 7.3 (Spring 1982): 515–44.

46. H. R. Trevor-Roper, *The European Witch-Craze of the Sixteenth and Seventeenth Centuries* (New York: Harper and Row, 1969); Merchant; Brian Easlea, *Fathering the Unthinkable: Masculinity, Science and the Nuclear Arms Race* (London: Pluto Press, 1983); and Heinrich Kramer and Jacob Sprenger, "Malleus Maleficarum," *Witchcraft in Europe 1100–1700: A Documentary History*, eds. Alan C. Kors and Edward Peters (Philadelphia: University of Pennsylvania Press, 1972).

47. Merchant; and Keller *Reflections*.

48. Hilary Rose, "Hand, Brain and Heart: A Feminist Epistemology for the Natural Sciences," *Signs* 9.1 (1983): 73–90; Keller *Reflections*; and Susan Bordo, *The Flight to Objectivity: Essays on Cartesianism and Culture* (Albany, NY: State University of New York Press, 1987).

49. Haraway "Situated."

50. Haraway, "Situated" 584; T. Minh-ha Trinh, *The Native Other* (Bloomington, IN: Indiana University Press, 1989).

51. Alison Jagger, *Feminist Politics and Human Nature* (Totowa, NJ: Rowman and Allanheld, 1983); Karlyn Kohrs Campbell, *Man Cannot Speak for Her: A Critical Study*

of Early Feminist Rhetoric (New York: Praeger, 1989); and Phyllis Rooney, "Gendered Reason: Sex Metaphor and Conceptions of Reason," *Hypatia* 6.2 (Summer 1991): 77–103.

52. Keller *Feeling*; Keller *Reflections*; and Bleier.

53. Rakow; Smith and Balka.

54. Smith *Conceptual*; Smith *Everyday*.

55. Harding, *Question* 104.

56. Nancy Armstrong, "The Gender Bind: Women and the Disciplines," *Genders* 3 (Fall 1988): 2.

57. Susan G. Cole, *Pornography and the Sex Crisis* (Toronto: Amanita Enterprises, 1989) 9.

58. Pagels uses the following quotation as a header to the first chapter (p. 19) of his widely praised book, *The Dreams of Reason*: "When the penis goes up, reason goes out the window" (from Robert M. Hutchins's film, *Zuckerkandel*).

59. Susan Griffin, *Pornography and Silence: Culture's Revenge Against Nature* (New York: Harper and Row, 1981).

60. Robert D. Romanyshyn, *Technology as Symptom and Dream* (London: Routledge, 1989) 209.

61. Indeed Horkheimer seems to know this without knowing that he knows it. In *The Eclipse or Reason* (New York: Seabury, 1974) 176, he maintains, "The disease of reason is that reason was born from man's urge to dominate nature, and the 'recovery' depends on insights into the nature of the original disease, not a cure of the latest symptom." Also cited, in a similar conjunction, by Easlea.

62. Romanyshyn 33.

63. Donald M. Lowe, *History of Bourgeois Perception* (Chicago: University of Chicago Press, 1983).

64. Jansen "Gender."

65. Claude Shannon, "The Mathematical Theory of Communication," *The Mathematical Theory of Communication*, eds. Claude Shannon and Warren Weaver (Urbana: University of Illinois Press, 1964); Jansen "Gender"; and David Bolton, *Turing's Man: Western Culture in the Computer Age* (Chapel Hill: University of North Carolina Press, 1984).

66. Magorah Maruyama, "Information and Communication in Poly-Epistemological Systems," *The Myths of Information*, ed. Kathleen Woodward (Milwaukee: University of Wisconsin Press, 1990) 28–40.

67. Michel Foucault, *The Order of Things: An Archaeology of the Human Sciences* (New York: Vintage, 1970).

68. Barbara Ehrenreich and Annette Fuentes, "Life on the Global Assembly Line," *Crisis in American Institutions*, 5th edition, eds. Jerome H. Skolnick and Elliott Currie (Boston: Little, Brown, 1976).

69. Pagels.

70. Lewis A. Mumford, "Authoritarian and Democratic Technics," *Technology and Culture* 5.1 (Winter 1964): 1–8.

71. Cockburn; Ferguson; Jansen "Gender"; McNeil; Merchant; and Rose.

72. John Wyver, "Altered Sight," *Marxism Today* April 1991: 42.

73. Smith and Balka.

74. Deborah Heath, "Technoscience I," Eleventh Annual Gender Symposium, Lewis and Clark College, Portland, OR, April 12–15, 1990.

75. Wyver.

76. Wyver 43.

77. Haraway 1991.

78. Garson.

79. Dallas Smythe, "Needs Before Tools? The Illusions of Electronic Democracy," paper presented to the International Communication Association, Honolulu, May 1985. Most of these thinkers are sensitive to this problem and seeing ways of democratizing their efforts; indeed, Smith and Balka explore it in some detail.

80. Marx 209.

5

New Worlds of Computer-Mediated Work

Shoshana Zuboff

One day, in the 1860s, the owner of a textile mill in Lowell, Massachusetts posted a new set of work rules in the morning, all weavers were to enter the plant at the same time, after which the factory gates would be locked until the close of the work day. By today's standards this demand that they arrive at the same time seems benign. Today's workers take for granted both the division of the day into hours of work and nonwork and the notion that everyone should abide by a similar schedule. But in the 1860s, the weavers were outraged by the idea that an employer had the right to dictate the hours of labor. They said it was a "system of slavery," and went on strike.

Eventually, the owner left the factory gates open and withdrew his demands. Several years later, the mill owner again insisted on collective work hours. As the older form of work organization was disappearing from other plants as well, the weavers could no longer protest.

In general, industrialization presented people with a fundamental challenge to the way they had thought about behavior at work. The employer's desire to exploit the steam engine as a centralized source of power, coupled with the drive to closely supervise workers and increase the pace of production resulted in a greater degree of collectivization and synchronization in the workplace. Employers imposed an exact discipline on workers that required them to use their bodies in specified ways in relation to increasingly complex forms of equipment. By the early 1900s, "scientific management" had given supervisors a systematic way to measure and control the worker's body.

Although most workers have accepted the work behavior that industrialization fashioned, the issues behind the New England weavers' resistance lie at the heart of modern labor-management relations. Using collective bargaining, later generations of workers have developed elaborate grievance procedures and work rules that carefully limit an employer's right to control a worker's body.

New forms of technology inevitably change the ways people are mobilized to work as well as the kinds of skills and behavior that are critical for productivity. These changes are rarely born without pain and conflict—nor do they emerge exactly as planners envision them. Instead new conceptions of work organization and behavior emerge from an interaction between the demands of a new technology, its social organization and the responses of the men and women who must work with the new technological systems.

In this regard, the weavers' example is doubly instructive. First it illustrates that during a period of technological transition people are most likely to be aware of and articulate about the quality of the change they are facing. When people feel that the demands a new technology makes on them conflict with their expectations about the workplace, they are likely during the initial stage of adaptation, to resist. Many managers maintain that employees are simply denying change when they cling to familiar patterns and complain as these forms of sustenance are threatened. But resistance can also reveal an eloquent appraisal of the quality of change—a subtle commentary that goes beyond a stubborn attachment to custom.

Second, the weavers' example shows that as a major technological transition recedes into the past and with it the sense of psychological crisis, older sensibilities tend to become subsumed or repressed. However, original sources of resistance, if they are not properly resolved, can continue to influence the management-labor agenda for many years, even though employees may accommodate the demands of a new technology.

Increased use of information technology is altering the technological infrastructure of the workplace. And just as with industrial technology, people who are required to use information systems often resist their introduction. In this article, I outline the principal themes that emerged repeatedly from my interviews and observations, both as they pertain to employees' experiences of information systems and as observable, often unintended, consequences for the organization. Finally, I identify some of the implications of these findings for human resource management policies.

MANAGEMENT POLICIES TOWARD AUTOMATION

In many ways, management policies can determine the effectiveness of automation and the quality of the workplace culture that emerges. In this regard, my discussions with employees and managers reveal two primary concerns.

Substitution and Deskilling of Labor

The purpose of the intelligent technology at the core of a computer system is to substitute algorithms or decision rules for individual judgments. This substitution makes it possible to formalize the skills and know-how intrinsic to a job and integrate them into a computer program. As decision rules become more explicit, the more they are subject to planning, and the less they require a person to make a decision at each stage of execution. For some jobs the word "decision" no longer implies an act of human judgment, but an information processing activity that occurs according to rules embedded in a computer program.

At present, most programmed decision making has been limited to the most routine jobs in an organization such as high-volume operations where tasks can be simplified and rationalized to maximize outputs and minimize skill requirements. For example, partly by limiting a collector's discretion regarding how or in what order he or she should work on an account, an automated collection system makes it possible to increase production goals and reduce the time spent on each account.

Thus for that activity the key to revenue generation becomes volume instead of collection skills. Collection managers I interviewed believe that the system enables them to recoup more funds while reducing their dependence on skilled collectors. One collection manager described the value of the system:

> It gives us a tighter lock on the collector, and we can hire less skilled people. But there's a real loss to the job of skills and know-how. You are being told what to do by the machine.

But job deskilling is not exclusive to the most routine jobs in the organization. A decision-support system installed for a bank's 20 credit analysts was supposed to free them from the most mechanical and boring aspects of the job. Six months after the system was in place, not a single analyst had used it. As one analyst explained it, "I think, then I write down my calculations directly. I know the company and the problem. With this system, I am supposed to type into the machine and let it think. Why should I let it do my thinking for me?"

Automation of Managerial Assumptions

Information systems can embody management's assumptions and values about its employees, especially about their commitment and motivation. The automated collection system provides an example of how this happens.

Bill Smith had managed collection activities for 30 years, and management considered his perspective invaluable. In creating the system, designers spent long hours debriefing Smith, and he helped them make many important design decisions. Senior managers explain key design decisions by saying: "We tried to build Bill Smith's brain into the computer. If we did not build it into the system, we might lose to the competition."

When I talked to Bill Smith, some of the reasons the system eliminated most discretion from the job became clear. As Smith put it: "I like to see people work. I'm a good worker. I don't like to see people take time off. I don't do it."

The depth of memory and extent of communications that computer systems are capable of mean that managerial biases can surround the employee as never before. The cost of Smith's managerial assumptions in the collections operations system was high. A year after the system was in place, turnover had reached almost 100%, and the corporate personnel and employee counseling offices were swamped with complaints from replacements. The new and less-educated collectors presented a different set of problems for management and training. Even with the new staff, turnover remained about three times higher than in the rest of the back-office organization.

COMPUTER MEDIATION OF WORK

As the Bill Smith example illustrates, managerial assumptions can easily get embedded in information systems. But what impact do the new systems have on the organization of work and what actually happens to the people who interact with them?

Work Becomes Abstract

When information technology reorganizes a job, it fundamentally alters the individual's relation to the task. I call the new relationship "computer mediated." Usually, this means that a person accomplishes a task through the medium of the information system, rather than through direct physical contact with the object of the task.

Computer-mediation can be contrasted to other forms of task relationships in terms of the way in which one knows about the object of the task. The potter who turns a pot with his or her own hands has direct experience of the task's object through continual series of sights and tactile sensations. These sensations form the basis for moment-by-moment judgments regarding the success of the process and any alterations that the potter should make. Machines, such as a press or a welding torch, usually remove the worker as the direct source of energy for the labor process, but leave the task's object within sensuous range. Those who work with paper and pencil usually feel "in touch" with the objects of their tasks through the activity of writing and because they are the sources of what they write.

With computer-mediated work, employees get feedback about the task object only as symbols through the medium of the information system. Very often, from the point of view of the worker, the object of the task seems to have disappeared "behind the screen" and into the information system.

The distinction in feedback is what separates the linotype machine operator from the clerical worker who inputs cold type, the engineer who works with computer-aided design from one who directly handles materials, the continuous process operator who reads information from a visual display unit from one who actually checks vat levels, and even the bill collector who works with an on-line, real-time system from a predecessor who handled account cards. The distinctiveness of computer-mediated work becomes more clear when one contrasts it against the classic image of work from the nineteenth century in which labor was considered to be the transformation of nature by human muscle. Computer-mediated work is the electronic manipulation of symbols. Instead of a sensual activity, it is an abstract one.

Many employees I spoke to reported feeling frustrated because in losing a direct experience of their task it becomes more difficult to exercise judgments over it. In routine jobs, judgment often becomes lodged in the system itself. As one bill collector said:

> In our old system, come the end of the month, you knew what you were faced with. With the automated system, you don't know how to get in there to get certain accounts out. You have to work the way the system wants you to.

People in even more complex jobs can also lose direct experience of their tasks. The comptroller of a bank that was introducing information systems to a variety of functions commented:

> People become more technical and sophisticated, but they have an inferior understanding of the banking business. New people become like systems people and can program instructions that don't necessarily reflect the spirit of the operation.

The auditor at one bank is working with a new information system that frees him from traveling to regional branches. The branches feed financial data directly into the information system that he can access in real time. He described his job this way:

> The job of auditing is very different now. More imagination is required. I am receiving data on-line. I don't go to the branches if I don't want to. I don't see any books. What do I audit in this situation? I always have to be thinking about what is in the system. I may be auditing, but it doesn't feel like it.

The auditor now has access to a new level of complexity in his data. He has the possibility of comparing branches according to criteria of his choice and searching out new relationships in the data. But in order to do this, he must now develop a theory of the auditing process. He needs to have a conceptual framework that can guide him through the mass of available information. Theoretical insight and imagination will be the keys to his effectiveness on the job.

By creating a medium of work where imagination instead of experience-based judgment is important, information technology challenges old procedures. Judging a given task in the light of experience thus becomes less important than imagining how the task can be reorganized based on new technical capabilities. In the banking industry, for example, planners are not automating the old, but inventing the new.

While working through information systems seems to require a more challenging form of mental effort, it can also induce feelings of frustration and loss of control.

A collections supervisor described the difference between the manual and computer systems:

> If you work with a manual system and you want to see an account on a given day, you have a paper file and you simply go to that particular

section and pull out the file. When you're on the computer system, in a sense all your accounts are kind of floating around in space. You can't get your hands on them.

Some people cope with this frustration by creating physical analogues for their tasks. In one bank branch, an on-line system had been installed to update information on current accounts. Instead of making out tickets that would be sent to a data center for overnight keypunching, operators enter data directly into terminals; the system continuously maintains account information. Despite senior management's efforts to persuade them to change, the branch manager and his staff continued to fill out the tickets. When asked why, they first mentioned the need for a backup system. The real reason came out when the branch manager made the following comment: "You need something you can put your hands on. How else can we be sure of what we are doing."

People are accustomed to thinking of jobs that require employees to use their brains as the most challenging and rewarding. But instead, the computer mediation of simple jobs can create tasks that are routine and unchallenging while demanding focused attention and abstract comprehension. Nevertheless, the human brain is organized for action. Abstract work on a mass scale seems likely to create conditions that are peculiar if not stressful to many people. While it does seem that those who shift from conventional procedures to computer-mediated work feel this stress most acutely, it's impossible to forecast what adaptation to the abstraction of work will do to people over the long term.

Social Interaction is Affected

Doubtless, once information technology reorganizes a set of jobs, new patterns of communication and interaction become possible. In time, these patterns are likely to alter the social structure of an organization.

When resources are centered in the information system, the terminal itself can become employees' primary focus of interaction. This focus can lead people to feel isolated in an impersonal situation. For example, because functional operations in the back office of one bank have been reorganized, a clerical worker can complete an entire operation at his or her "professional" work station, rather than repeat a single procedure of it before passing the item on to someone else. Although employees I talked to were split in their attitudes toward the new back-office system, most of them agreed that it created an uncomfortable isolation. Because they had few remaining reasons to interact with co-workers, the local social network was fragmented.

Decades of research have established the importance of social communities in the workplace and the lengths to which people will go to establish and maintain them. Since people will not easily give up the pleasures of the workplace community, they tend to see themselves at odds with the new technology that transforms the quality of work life. The comments of one employer illustrate this point:

> I never thought I would feel this way, but I really do not like the computer. If a person makes a mistake, dealing with the computer to try and get that mistake corrected is so much red tape. And it's just taken a lot of feeling out of it. You should have people working with people because they are going to give you what you want, and you're going to get a better job all around.

In a very different kind of application, professionals and managers in the R&D organization of a large consumer goods company find the range of their interaction greatly extended with computer conferencing. While there is some evidence of reduced face-to-face interaction, the technology makes it relatively easy to initiate dialogues and form coalitions with people in other parts of the corporation. Clearly, information technology can offset social life in a variety of ways. It is important to realize, however, that this technology has powerful consequences for the structure and function of communication and social behavior in an organization.

New Possibilities for Supervision and Control

The dream of the industrial engineer to create a perfectly timed and rationalized set of activities has never been perfectly realized. Because face-to-face supervision can be carried on only on a partial basis, employees usually find ways to pace their own activities to meet standards at a reasonable rate. Thus, traditionally, supervision depended on the quality of the relationship between supervisor and worker. If the relationship is a positive one, employees are likely to produce quality work without constant monitoring. If the relationship is adversarial, the monitoring will be continual.

But because work accomplished through the medium of video terminals or other intelligent equipment can be recorded on a second-by-second basis, the industrial engineer's presence can be built into all real-time activities. With immediate access to how much employees are producing through printouts or other visual displays, supervisors and managers can increase surveillance without depending on face-to-face supervision. Thus the interpersonal relationship can become less important to supervision than access to information about the quality and quantity of employee output. One bank supervisor described this new capability:

> Instead of going to someone's desk and physically pulling out files, you have the ability to review people's work without their knowledge. So I think it keeps them on their toes.

Another variant of remote supervision involves controls that are automatically built into systems operations, as in the collections system described earlier. These rules are substitutes for a certain amount of supervisory effort. Because the system determines what accounts the collector should work on and in what order, a supervisor does not have to monitor collectors' judgments on these issues. Managers also see automatic control as the organization's defense against the potentially massive pollution of data that can occur through access by many people to an on-line real-time system.

Remote supervision, automatic control, and greater access to subordinates' information all become possible with computer-mediated work. In some cases, these capabilities are an explicit objective, but too often management employs them without sufficiently considering the potential human and organizational consequences.

With remote supervision, many employees limit their own risk-taking behavior, such as spotting an error in the data and correcting it, developing a more effective approach to the work than the procedures established by the information system, or trying to achieve quality at the expense of keeping up with new production standards.

One reason the initiative to design a custom-made approach to a particular task has become too risky is that many people have difficulty articulating why their approach might be superior to other alternatives. Usually, management has developed a clearly articulated model of the particular task in order to automate it, and if employees cannot identify their own models with equal clarity, they have little hope of having their views legitimated.

Another reason for decreased employee initiative is that the more an information system can control the details of the job, the less even relatively trivial risk-taking opportunities are available. Finally, the monitoring capabilities increase the likelihood that a supervisor will notice a deviation from standard practice. As one bank employee noted:

Sometimes I have a gut feeling I would rather do something another way. But, because it is all going to be in the computer, it changes your mind. If somebody wouldn't listen to the reason why you did it that way, well, it could cause you quite a problem.

Another frequent response to the new relationship of supervision and control involves perceptions of authority in the workplace. Employees can tend to see technology less as an instrument of authority than as a source of it. For instance, one group of bank employees with an especially easygoing manager described the work pace on their computer-mediated jobs as hard-driving, intense, and at times unfair, but thought the manager was friendly, relaxed, and fair-minded.

One collector told about the difference in her attitudes toward her work under the manual system and under the automated system:

When I worked with the account cards, I knew how to handle my responsibilities. I felt, "Hey! I can handle this!" Now I come in every day with a defeatist attitude, because I'm dealing with the tube every day, I can't beat it. People like to feel not that they are necessarily ahead of the game, but that they have a chance. With the tube I don't have a chance.

While this employee knows that her manager is the actual authority in the office, and that he is in turn accountable to other managers, she has an undeniable feeling that the system, too, is a kind of authority. It is the system she must fight, and if she wins, it is the system she vanquishes.

In the Volvo plant in Kalmar, Sweden, a computer system was installed to monitor assembly operations.[1] A feedback device was programmed to flash a red light signalling a quality control problem. The workers protested against the device, insisting that the supervisory function be returned to a foreman. They preferred to answer to a human being with whom they could negotiate, argue, and explain rather than to a computer whose only means of "communication" was unilateral. In effect, they refused to allow the computer to become, at least in this limited situation, an authority. Yet clearly, the issue would never have arisen in the first place were the technology not capable of absorbing the characteristics of authority.

Finally, these capacities of information systems can do much to alter the relationships among managers themselves. A division or plant manager can often leverage a certain amount of independence by maintaining control of key information. Though a manager might have to present the data in monthly or quarterly reports, he or she has some control over the amount and format. With information technology, however, senior managers in corporate headquarters increasingly have access to real-time systems that display the day-to-day figures of distinct parts of the company's business. For instance, a division vice president can be linked to the information system that transmits raw production data from a processing plant in another state. Such data can provide the vice president with a view of the plant that only the plant manager or mid-level managers in the operation previously had.

The new access raises several questions for a corporation. First, some policy decisions must be confronted that address the kind of information appropriate to each level of management. Top managers can quickly find themselves inundated with raw data that they do not have the time to understand. It also creates a tendency for top managers to focus on the past and present when they should be planning the future.

It would seem that this new access capability would expand top management's opportunities to monitor and direct and, therefore, improve the performance of subordinate managers. But as the on-line availability of such information reaches across management hierarchies (in some companies all the way to board chairpersons), reduced risk taking and its effects begin to take hold. Managers are reluctant to make decisions on the basis of information that their superiors receive simultaneously. As one plant manager said to his boss in division headquarters: "I'm telling you, Bob, if you're going to be hooked up to the data from the pumps, I'm not going to manage them anymore. You'll have to do it."

BIRTH OF THE INFORMATION ENVIRONMENT

Another consequence of information technology is more difficult to label, but its effects are undeniable. I call it the "information environment." It refers to a quality of organizational life that emerges when the computer mediates jobs and begins to influence both horizontal and vertical relationships. In the information environment, people generally have greater access to data and, in particular, data relevant to their own decision making. The capacity for follow-up and reorganizing increases as information retrieval and communication can occur with greater ease and convenience than ever before.

One effect of this immediate access to information is a rise in the volume of transactions or operations. This increase, in turn, compresses time and alters the rhythm of work. While people were once satisfied if a computer system responded in 24 hours, those who work with computers now are impatient if information takes more than five seconds to appear. Timely and reliable functioning of the system determines workers' output, and these effects extend up the managerial ladder. Once managers become accustomed to receiving in two hours a report that once took two weeks to compile, they will consider any delay a burden. This speed of access, retrieval, and information processing is allegedly the key to improving the productivity of the organization, but few organizations have seriously considered the appropriate definition of productivity in their own operations. In the meantime, more transactions, reports, and information are generated in an ever-shorter amount of time.

Responses to the information environment usually are accompanied by feelings about power and orderliness. To some people, the increased access to information enhances their power over the contingencies of their work. An account officer for one bank states:

> I never had such a complete picture of a particular customer before. I can switch around the format of the base for my reporting purposes and get a full picture of where the bank is making money. This gives me a new power and effectiveness in my work.

While most people agree that the information environment makes the workplace more orderly, responses to this orderliness tend to be bipolar. Some see the order as "neat and nice," while others perceive it as increasing the regimentation of the workplace. Responses of two collections managers illustrate these differences. The first described the system this way:

> The computer simply alleviates a lot of paperwork. Everything is lined up for you instead of you having to do it yourself. If you are sloppy, the system organizes you.

Another manager in the same organization regards the collections system in a different way:

> Things were a lot more relaxed before the tubes. Before, you scheduled your day yourself, now the machine lines it up for you. This means a more rigid environment because we can track things better.

Greater regimentation can also affect the environment of the professional. A vice president in one organization where professionals have come to rely heavily on electronic mail and computer conferencing puts it this way:

I used to make notes to myself on things I had to follow up. Now those notes go into my electronic mail system. The system automatically tracks these things and they are there in front of me on the screen if I haven't followed up yet. Nothing slips through the cracks, but certainly for the way professionals usually operate, it's more regimented.

Many of the managers and professionals I talked to are wary of systems that seem to encroach on their judgment, their freedom, or the "artistry" of their professional assessments. Instead of feeling that increased information augments their power, these people resist information systems that they see limiting their freedom or increasing the measurability of their work.

At present, most professionals and managers function in fairly ambiguous environments. Information is imperfectly exchanged (often in corridors, washrooms, or over lunch), and considerable lag time usually occurs before the quality of decisions can be assessed. A continual flow of complete information, however, reduces ambiguity. For example, in the marketing area of one bank, an information system provides complete profiles of all accounts while it assesses their profitability according to corporate criteria. Top management and systems developers believed the system could serve as a constant source of feedback to account officers and senior managers, allowing them to better manage their account activities and maximize fee-based revenue. But some bankers saw the flow of "perfect" information as not only reducing ambiguity but also limiting their opportunities for creative decisions and resisted using it.

Limited information may create uncertainty in which people make errors of judgment, but it also provides a "free space" for inspiration. This free space is fundamental to the psychology of professional work. The account officers in the bank had traditionally been motivated by the opportunity to display their artistry as bankers, but as increased information organizes the context of their work, the art in their jobs is reduced.

Employees in back-office clerical jobs also tend to perceive the increased time and volume demands and the measurability of operations as limits on their opportunities to experience a sense of mastery over the work. To overcome these effects, many of the collectors keyed fictitious data into the system of account files. Their managers were confronted with high productivity figures that did not match the size of monthly revenues.

Many managers first respond to such a situation by searching out ways to exert more control over the work process. I am convinced that the more managers attempt to control the process, the more employees will find ways to subvert that control. This response is particularly likely when outsmarting the system becomes the new ground on which to develop and test one's mastery. Managers may dismiss these subversive activities as "resistance to change," but in many cases this resistance is the only way employees can respond to the changes they face. Such resistance can also be understood as a positive phenomenon—it is evidence of an employee's identification with the job.

LISTENING TO THE RESISTANCE

Critics of technology tend to fall into one of three camps. Some bemoan new developments and see them as a particular form of human debasement and depersonalization. Others are ready to applaud any form of technology as progress toward some eventual conquest of dumb nature. Finally, others argue that technology is neutral and its meaning depends on the uses to which human beings press its application. I have found none of these views sufficient.

It is true that information technology provides a particularly flexible set of technical possibilities, and thus can powerfully embody the assumptions and goals of those whom it is designed to serve. Yet, while the value and meaning of a given application must be read, in part, from management's intentions, beliefs, and commitments, this does not imply the ultimate neutrality of the technology itself. To say that information technology is neutral is like saying an airplane is neutral because it can fly to either Washington or Moscow. We know that airplanes are not neutral because we all live in a world that has been radically altered by the facts of air travel—the globe has been shrunk, time and space have collapsed.

If one accepts that technology is not neutral, it follows that information technology must have attributes that are unique in the world view they impose and the experience of work to which they give shape. The flexibility, memory, and remote access capabilities of information systems create new management possibilities and, therefore, choices in the design of an application.

This argument suggests three general areas for management deliberation and action in the deployment of new information systems. The first concerns policies that shape the quality of the employment relationship. The second involves attitudes toward managerial control, and the third concerns basic beliefs about the nature of an organization and the role of management.

THE QUALITY OF THE EMPLOYMENT RELATIONSHIP

Because the computer mediation of work can have direct consequences for virtually every area of human resource management including skills training, career paths, the social environment, peer relationships, supervision, control, decision making, authority, and organization design, managers need to think through the kind of workplace they want to foster. They need to make design choices that reflect explicit human resource management policies.

For example, consider the automated collections system I described earlier. Although the system minimizes individual decision making, most managers I interviewed in that organization believe that collector skill and judgment are critical variables in the organization's ability to generate payments and have compelling financial data to support that view.

A management policy commitment to maintaining skill levels, providing challenging jobs, and promoting collector loyalty and motivation could have resulted in an information system that preserves the entrepreneurial aspects of the collector's job while rationalizing its administration with on-line record-keeping. But to assess the likely consequences of an approach to automation that strictly rationalizes procedures, managers need to understand the human logic of a job; in many cases, this human logic holds the clue to the motivational aspects of the job that should be preserved in the conversion to new technology.

What do managers do when faced with some of the more intrinsic features of information technology? First, they need to understand the kinds of skill demands that the computer mediation of work generates, and to construct educational programs that allow employees to develop the competencies that are most relevant to the new environment.

If a more theoretical comprehension of the task is required for effective utilization of the information system, then employees should be given the opportunity to develop this conceptual understanding. If an information system is likely to reduce the sense (if not the fact) of individual control over a task, is it possible to redesign the job to reinvest it with a greater self-managing capacity? As elements of supervision and coordination are loaded into jobs that have been partially drained of challenge, new learning and career development opportunities can open up. The astonishing quantity of information that is available can be used to increase employees' feedback, learning and self-management rather than to deskill and routinize their jobs or remotely supervise them.

New systems are often presented with the intention of providing "information resources" for more creative problem solving. Unless employees are actually given the knowledge and authority to utilize such resources in the service of more complex tasks, these systems will be undermined, either through poor utilization or more direct forms of resistance.

THE FOCUS OF MANAGERIAL CONTROL

Because of the many self-management opportunities the information resource makes possible, managers may have to rethink some classic notions of managerial control. When industrial work exerted stringent demands on the placement and timing of physical activity, managers focused on controlling bodies and stipulating the precise ways in which they should perform.

With the burgeoning of office work, physical discipline was less important than reading or writing and, above all, interpersonal behavior. Because people needed to learn how to behave with superiors, subordinates, and the public, managers began to control less what people did with their bodies and more what they did with one another—their communication, teamwork, meeting behavior, and so forth.

With computer-mediated work, neither physical activity nor interpersonal behavior appears to be the most appropriate targets of managerial control. Instead, patterns of attention, learning, and mental engagement become the keys to effectiveness and high-quality performance. Obviously, people have always had to "pay attention" to their work in order to accomplish it properly. But the quality of attention computer-mediated work requires is essentially different.

For instance, in almost all accounts of routine work, researchers report that employees are daydreaming and bantering with one another while they accomplish their tasks. Of course, they must pay attention with their eyes, but not so much with their brains. In contrast, people concentrating on a visual display unit may pay a very different sort of attention. If employees are to understand and properly respond to information, they must be mentally involved.

Managers can experiment to find how to make the most of people's attending and learning qualities as well as their overall engagement in the information environment. One observation that emerges from my current field research is that imposing traditional supervisory approaches on the computer-mediated environment can create considerable dysfunction. Supervisors and managers who concentrate on the physical and interpersonal behavior of employees working with information systems simply exacerbate tensions instead of creating an environment that nurtures the kind of learning and attention computer-mediated work makes necessary, and compensating for some of its less obvious but potentially negative attributes.

THE NATURE OF ORGANIZATION AND MANAGEMENT

With information technology, managers will do a variety of tasks that others once did for them. Because of this, we are likely to see a gradual shift in the overall shape of the organization from a pyramid to something closer to a diamond shape—with a diminishing clerical support staff, swelling numbers of professionals and middle managers, and a continually more remote, elite, policy-making group of senior managers.

While these considerations should be of central importance to management policy in the coming years, as a society we are sure to see a continuing challenge to the salience of work and the workplace in our daily lives. The traditional importance of occupational distinctiveness may be further eroded as what it means to "accomplish a task" undergoes a fundamental change. When a person's primary work consists of monitoring or interacting with a video screen, it may become more difficult to answer the questions, "Who am I" and "What do I do?" Identification with occupational role may diminish, while the transferability of on-the-job skills increases. Will this have implications for individual commitment to an organization and for the relative importance of work and non-work activities?

Information technology is also likely to introduce new forms of collective behavior. When the means of production becomes dependent on electronic technology and information flows, it is no longer inevitable to perform work in neighborhood centers, at home, or on the road. At the same time, electronic technology is altering the traditional structure and function of communication within the organization. Who interacts with whom in the organization? Can the neat chain of command hierarchy be maintained? Should it be? What does it take to lead or influence others when communication itself becomes computer mediated? Finally, who is likely to gain or lose as we make the transition to this environment?

These developments make it necessary to rethink basic conceptions of the nature of organization and management. What is an organization if people do not have to come face to face in order to accomplish their work? Does the organization itself become an abstraction? What happens to the shared purpose and commitment of members if their face-to-face interaction is reduced? Similarly, how should an "abstract" organization be managed?

If information technology is to live up to its promise for greater productivity, managers need to consider its consequences for human beings and the qualities of their work environments. The demands for a thoughtful and energetic management response go deeper than the need for a "friendly interface" or "user involvement." The underlying nature of this technology requires understanding; the habitual assumptions used in its design must surface. Managers' ability to meet these demands will be an important determinant of the quality of work in future organizations.

NOTE

1. "Social Effects of Automation," *International Federation of Automated Control Newsletter* Issue 6 (September 1978).

6

An Engineer's Critical Perspective on Technology

Steve M. Slaby

I believe in the vengeance of history,

in the vengeance of heaven for depravity

. . . .

"Darkness is coming,

  Darkness!"

It reeks of deepest hell.

Those who can breathe this stench

are not worth keeping alive!

When the world is a cadaver,

a cesspool of fog and chaos,

it is a sign of quality

to sink and drown.*

PROLOGUE

The ideas and critiques of technology that are presented in this chapter are the resources gathered by one professor of engineering to challenge the assumptions of students and colleagues. They should be placed in the context of my own influences in education, experience, family, and the social/political environment to which I have been exposed. Many of the comments on technology presented here also represent the public policy debate engendered by the rapid social and technological changes that took place roughly during the period of 1960 to 1975 that were of seminal importance to engineers and engineering students.

Industrial Detroit during the decades of the 1930s, 1940s, and early 1950s, like the industrial Midwest as a whole, was intimately tied to the blue collar working class. Most relatives, friends, and neighbors were workers who labored in the various automobile factories (Ford, General Motors, Chrysler) and job shops which were supported by this industry. During this period, Detroit also was a vibrant city that offered a diverse culture which supported an excellent public educational system and excellent libraries, which we as young students were taught to use and value. In addition to the normal basic subjects of reading, writing, and arithmetic, music programs were available to any student, including the free use of musical instruments and excellent, committed teachers. The city also supported extensive instruction in music and in the arts and crafts, allowing young people to attend, at no cost, major concerts presented by the Detroit Symphony Orchestra, to see first-class ballet, and hear world famous opera singers and classical instrumental performers of great renown. All of this was free to the public.

Junior high and high schools offered a combination of vocational education and college preparatory programs so that one could learn both in order to connect the eyes, mind, and hands; this was an invaluable educational experience which introduced me to the realities of technology and some of the impacts it had on my immediate neighbors and relatives. I clearly remember that on my block, one out of every four or five adults had lost one or more fingers in industrial accidents related to widespread factory technologies. In short, I was embedded in two cultures, the culture of music (art) and the culture of technology, which were related in a very dynamic and synergetic fashion, all within the confines of the world's major automobile-producing city at that time.

As an adult, during work on a Mechanical Engineering degree, I was "on the line" at the Ford Motor Company Rouge Plant. It was, from the 1930s to the early 1950s, perhaps the largest industrial-technological enterprise in the world located on one plot of land, where over 100,000 people were employed. The technologies at the Rouge Plant ranged from the production of pig-iron in huge blast furnaces to rolled steel to auto-window glass to the finished automobile. The Rouge Plant was, in effect, a largely self-sufficient technological "machine" possessing the capability of processing raw materials, steel fabrication and machining operations, and assembly line organization required to produce large numbers of automobiles each day. From those on-the-line duties I graduated to various hands-on machine and steel fabrication operations and ultimately to the engineering department in the Ford Motor Company.

During part of World War II I was a member of the engineering department of the Republic Aviation Corporation and I served in the Army Air Corps. My teaching career began at the Associated Colleges of Upper New York near Geneva. After leaving there I traveled extensively in northern Europe and was able to see the destructive effects of World War II weapons technology on the cities of Holland, Germany, France, and England. This had a lasting impression and led to a commitment to the peace movement. Graduate studies in the area of labor economics stressed the connection among technology, economics, and politics. Later, as an engineering professor, I felt there was a need to transform the parochial and regimented approach to engineering education followed in the traditional institutions of higher education.

My work in academia and private consulting for municipalities, small firms, pro-bono work with inner-city community groups, people's organizations working on appropriate technology, alternative energy projects in inner-city communities and "third world" countries in the Caribbean islands, and in Vietnam working with the National Science Center of Vietnam offered me further field opportunities to develop a broader perspective on technology and to obtain a clearer understanding of its impact on human beings and their societies. My education and experience caused me to question more deeply the whole concept and role of technology in human life and how it affected the human condition. Consequently, I came to firmly believe in the necessity of challenging my students to develop a critical and questioning approach and attitude toward what many consider to be the sacred cow of technology in engineering through such courses and seminars as "Technology and Society—Present and Future Challenges" and "Technology and Society—Problems in the Human Environment." It was clear that many of my colleagues considered this to be a form of Luddism.

Engineers are generally not noted as agents of social critique. Why do engineers generally refrain from raising probing questions about technology? Only a few became whistle blowers in the nuclear power and aircraft industries, and found that without support systems, they were quickly unemployed. Engineers are educated to be "anonymous." An author who felt compelled to be known only as "a Ph.D. in engineering from a leading school . . . who wishes to remain anonymous" wrote that

[E]ngineering education is controlled by big business and by government [and] the cultivation of an independent, critical outlook on life
and the inculcation of an ethical loyalty to society appears nowhere
in the picture.[1]

In order to challenge my students and my colleagues to question the
sacrosanct place of technology, I sought out some political and policy
commentary dealing with critical analyses of technology and its impact
on society which developed through the last few decades. Most of this
literature, it should be noted, has been produced by non-engineers. My
hope has always been to help students, engineers, and scientists to
confront the form of American technological domination that they are
helping to create.

INTRODUCTION

This chapter then deals with these ideas and feelings developed out
of this background on the impact of technology on our society and the
social, political, economic, psychological, moral, ethical, educational,
and natural physical environment. All of these are integrated and
determine our quality of life. Although known pejoratively, the Luddites
were quick to perceive this. They were a group of craftsmen in England
during the early nineteenth century who lost their means of livelihood
in the textile industry because of the introduction of textile machinery
like mechanized looms. These mechanized looms displaced much of the
hand labor normally used in the production of textiles and presented a
form of competition to the craftsmen which made it difficult for them
to maintain their trades. While historically, these craftsmen have been
depicted as the people who physically attempted to destroy the technology of their era because it threatened their economic security, what is
not stressed is that they also were concerned about the social consequences of the introduction of this innovative technology and about the
inferior quality of the textiles being produced by these new machines.
In other words, they were questioning the introduction of this technology and were critical of it because they were not part of the decision-
making process, the results of which had a negative impact upon them
and their families. Is one a Luddite just because critical questions are
asked about the introduction of technologies over which one has no
control? Quite the contrary, I firmly believe that it is crucial to question
authority if education and democracy and technology are to have any
meaning.

What we appear to have now is a condition of mutual dependency between technology and society requiring study from interdisciplinary vantage points. A number of questions must then be asked when we try to critically analyze the technology/society complex. Those questions revolve around the control of technology, how technology affects values, morals, and ethics, the role of people and history in relation to technological decisions and political power, and the role of education in a high-tech society.

The main purpose of this chapter is to explore the often overlooked implications of the impact of technology on society. Some of the analyses presented have been considered controversial, but if they stimulate critical thinking and responses they will have served their purpose. I begin with a definition of what is meant by technology—a word that has been used almost a dozen times already in this chapter.

DEFINITION AND MEANING OF TECHNOLOGY

From the traditional perspective, technology has been defined within the domains of tools, machines, and other mechanical hardware and electronic technical artifacts. This perspective has proven to be wholly inadequate, especially but not primarily in the context of a high-tech society. The deeper and fuller meaning of technology includes concepts that blend with and at the same time transcend its traditional definition. Technology includes systems which involve techniques of organization and control. As such, technology becomes an integral part of the political, economic, and social milieu, having political and psychological as well as sociological effects and implications. Technology analyzed in this way stresses predictability driven by ordered mechanisms and systems— whether they be technological, political, or organizational—to the exclusion of dissent. Order and control take precedence over all else in technology. Robert Merton sums this up when he relates technology to technique in general. In doing this, he broadens the concept of technology to a general phenomenon where technique is defined as a "complex of standardized means for obtaining a pre-determined result. Thus, technology so defined, converts spontaneous and unreflective behavior into behavior that is deliberate and rationalized."[2]

What is the effect of technology so defined? Merton further observes that

the irreversible rule of technique is extended to all domains of life [resulting in a] civilization committed to the quest for continually

improved means to carelessly examined ends. . . . Technique transforms ends into means. What was once prized in its own right now
becomes worthwhile only if it helps to achieve something else. And
conversely, techniques turn means into ends. Know-how takes on an
ultimate value.[3]

Robert Hutchins examined the political effects of technology concep-
tualized in this sense, and, in principle, agreed with Merton when he stated
that the normative elements of political philosophy have been driven
back into ethics, and "ethical principles in their turn have been removed
from the field of rational discourse." All that remains of political philosophy

is linguistic analysis [without] any normative elements. . . . Science
and technology cannot judge themselves. . . . But, when [scientists
or engineers] decide to conduct the experiment or manufacture the
weapon, they are . . . entering the realm of moral and political philosophy. They have abandoned their moral neutrality. The decay of
political philosophy means that politics is nothing but the exercise
of power. . . . Politics so conceived cannot help us find the means of
guiding and controlling science and technology.[4]

In 1969, Vice-Admiral H. G. Rickover, in a speech delivered at the
University of Georgia on "Automation and Society," sensed the point
Hutchins was making. He said:

Every citizen is duty bound to make every effort to understand how
technology operates and what are its possibilities and limitations. . . . A
free society centers on man. It gives paramount considerations to
human rights, interests, and needs. But once ordinary citizens come
to feel that public issues are beyond their comprehension, a pattern
of life may develop where technology, not man, would become
central to the purpose of society. If we permit this to happen, the
human liberties for which mankind has fought, at so great a cost of
effort and sacrifice, will be extinguished.[5]

In the process of technological development, especially under the free
enterprise philosophy, values are embedded in the technologies created
and implemented. These values accrue and subconsciously become "built
in." Once in place, the technology seems to exude its own values. Arthur
Loesser points out that, even in the quasi-cultural arena of piano making,

the technology to machine-produce these instruments drove changes in their distribution.

> Factory production involves problems that do not affect individual craftsmen. A factory must pay a considerable number of regular wages, . . . high ground-rent or taxes, and it . . . has money tied up in large amounts of materials. It can only meet these expenses by assuring itself a rapid, uninterrupted sale of its products. Inevitably, the head of a factory tends to regard sales as more important than production [since] it is clear that [sales] cannot be left to the inertia or the unguided whims of potential customers.[6]

Technology then tends to become more master than servant. Human beings are thereby in a subservient position to technology, fitting into the needs of technology rather than the other way around. Examples of this are obvious in the assembly line industries where people are really only cogs in the bigger machine. This can also be seen in the current computer craze sweeping through modern society. The external manifestations of the assembly line have seemingly been changed, but its basic character remains and actually is magnified: people chained to the small machine are required to meet the strict needs of the guiding software and system. On the old assembly lines of the past, workers were allowed more movement than just their fingers. Further, a *New York Times* article in 1988 contained a startling admission by John W. Bachman, chairman of the Securities Industry Association: "We don't know where the technology is taking us."[7] In other words, technologies are calling the tune in ever higher social levels of professional work.

The dichotomy of technology is that while it is created by human beings (and this creative experience is challenging, extremely stimulating, and interesting), once the inventions are implemented, they generally are not controlled by the creative agents. It is here that technology in effect begins to take on a life of its own as it affects large numbers of people who had no role in the creative or decision-making process. In other words, most technologies are imposed on people today. In spite of its promise of a better life, we cannot seem to escape technology's negative impact on quality of life: air and water pollution, acid rain, nuclear radiation, hazardous wastes, rampant urbanization represented by a continuing (almost geometrical) increase in world population to an estimated 10 billion people by the year 2050. In addition, the threat of a nuclear holocaust continues to face humanity in spite of the supposed end of the Cold War. There still exist at least 50,000 nuclear warheads in the world today and the proliferation of nuclear weapons technology is really not under control.

Most of those who do creative inventive work in technological development, such as engineers, scientists, and technologists, accept at face value the claim that technology and science are neutral and value-free. However, all inventors, engineers, scientists, and technologists bring into their work a significant part of their conditioned value system and this is reflected in the nature and results of their work. Value-free research in technology and science, with no strings attached, is a myth. Paul Goodman wrote

> that the claim that research is neutral, and it doesn't matter what one works on, is shabby, if we consider the heavy funding in certain directions. Social priorities are scandalous: money is spent on over-kill, supersonic planes, brand-name identical drugs, annual model changes of cars, new detergents, and color television, whereas water, air, space, food, health, and foreign aid are neglected. And much research is morally so repugnant, e.g., chemical and biological weapons, that one dares not humanly continue it.[8]

Langdon Winner agrees, arguing that "choices about supposedly neutral technologies—if 'choices' they ever merit being called—are actually choices about the kind of society in which we shall live."[9] Goodman further notes:

> The state of the behavioral sciences, if anything, is worse. Their claim to moral and political neutrality becomes, in effect, a means of diverting attention from glaring social evils, and they are, in fact, used—or would be if they worked—for warfare and social engineering, manipulation of people for the political and economic purposes of the powers that be.[10]

He goes on to argue that to claim that pure objectivity is working in the areas of technology and science is essentially a justification for the creation, production, and implementation of harmful and deadly products and systems, including weapons of mass destruction.[11] Engineers and scientists are hired to produce specific technologies, which they do not question. It is only a job. With very few exceptions, they accept the status-quo system which the technological order engenders. They go along to get along. Goodman, on the other hand, considers that a technician should be "a moral philosopher . . . able to criticize the programs given him to implement."[12]

The arguments of engineers and scientists that technology and science are value-free have developed into a mythology which masks and consolidates power. One has only to reflect upon the institutionalization of the power of military establishments in the United States or the former Soviet Union to gain an insight into how technology is controlled, and empowers those already in positions of power, and affects their sponsoring societies.

Another concept which must be challenged when discussing technology is the concept of a hierarchy of values—with science and technology at the top of that hierarchy. This idea implies that value choices are possible in relation to technology, and that is what occurs in most societies, and those choices are reflected in the order of social priorities. In dealing with this concept one enters the realm of social morality. If one could unequivocally define true values versus false values then one could extend his or her thinking to accept that true values lead to a true morality, and false values lead to a false morality. Hierarchical concepts deal with standards of right or wrong conduct and the setting of those standards is influenced by historical and cultural processes, among them the development of science and technology. In such a context, when we deal with morality, we experience double standards, such as when a government considers that it is not wrong to carpet bomb a foreign peasant society but that it is wrong for people to (perhaps violently) confront indifference to the desire and petitions for justice from their government.

Ralph Nader argued in 1967 that

> in so far as technology does things to us that we do not want to endure, to that extent can it be called out of control. As long as there is undue and parochial attention paid to the short range economic utility of product and process, at the same time that the short and long range biological consequences are treated with indifference or contempt, our society is going to plunge into deeper collective cruelties. [T]he lag between a framework of responsibility for the safety of the man-made environment and the increasingly far reaching impact of corporate decision-makers threatens to render the future significantly more challenging to our humane values than the past.[13]

Technology, therefore, is one of the dominant factors shaping human, social, political, and economic development and values. Its definition must encompass global concepts rather than those limited in scope and vision to purely mechanical items. Such limited ideas and visions can be destructive social myths which "reconcile contradictions in real-life actions. They are fictions with a deep symbolic truth for people who chose to believe in them."[14]

RESULTS OF THE MYTHS

Neutral, value-free technology as a guiding myth is directly and intimately related to power, ranging from the spectrum of physical to political, social, economic, and psychological power. This myth has led to a point in history where

> Every advanced country is over-technologized; past a certain point, the quality of life diminishes with new "improvements." Yet no country is rightly technologized, making efficient use of available techniques. There are ingenious devices for unimportant functions, stressful mazes for essential functions, and drastic dislocation when anything goes wrong, which happens with increasing frequency. To add to the complexity, the mass of people tend to become incompetent and dependent upon repairmen—indeed, unrepairability, except by experts, has become desideratum of industrial design.[15]

By contrast, in early stages of technological development, simple tools extended the physical power of the human being when used in combination to form a simple system. As technological development continued through the ages up to modern times, physical powers have expanded into the political, economic, social, and psychological realms. Looking back at the discussion of the definition of technology, I would argue that techniques have been developed in all these areas and have been organized into complex systems which in effect have become organizational technologies in their own right. Those technologies are directed toward influencing and controlling large numbers of people. I would also include direct physical force and the use of modern technological weapons and techniques for crowd and riot control which are able to generate fear—a very powerful deterrent against dissent. Control can also be exercised more subtly through psychological technologies like electronic and print media, biased educational techniques, and technology which create a regimented mind-set and value order, which tend to reflect and replicate the interests of the dominant status-quo power structure. [See Michael Carbone's chapter in this book for a fuller treatment of this idea in education.—Ed.] This can perhaps best be seen in the United States, where Madison Avenue technology has been very finely honed and implemented to this end.

A major result of this type of technological control is that it promotes a remarkable and empty homogeneity among the large mass of people in a country steeped in the rhetoric of "diversity." Henry Miller observed in his novel *Sexus*:

> We are accustomed to think of ourselves as a great democratic body, linked by common ties of blood and language, united indissolubly by all modes of communication which the ingenuity of man can possibly devise; we wear the same clothes, eat the same diet, read the same newspapers, alike in everything but name, weight and number; we are the most collectivized people in the world, barring certain primitive peoples whom we consider backward in their development. And yet—yet despite all the outward evidences of being close-knit, inter-related, neighborly, good-humored, helpful, sympathetic, almost brotherly, we are a lonely people, a morbid, crazed herd thrashing about in zealous frenzy, trying to forget that we are not what we think we are, not really united, not really devoted to one another, not really listening, not really anything, just digits shuffled about by some unseen hand in a calculation which doesn't concern us.[16]

I would argue that another example of how effective the development of these social and psychological technologies have become is the quick disappearance of the "Vietnam Syndrome" (a demand for a peace dividend) after the media hyped the "victory" of Desert Storm. Relatively few American people challenged or questioned the massive military expenditures saddled upon their backs during the 1980s and early 1990s. However, just after the Vietnam War, arguments were made to use the money which theoretically should have been saved by the ending of the war as a peace dividend to invest in the economic and social development of the United States. That it never materialized points toward the political impotence of public opinion and the corresponding power of the Pentagon/defense contractor revolving door and their influence on the media and Congress. I have written elsewhere of the cozy relationship between university research and the government and defense establishments in the Vietnam era. It would appear that the inbred nature of this power continues.[17]

Similarly, after the Gulf War and fall of the Eastern Bloc, a widespread demand for the peace dividend was renewed. However, successive administrations and Congresses continue to pass, with little debate, huge "defense" appropriation bills. Military expenditures in the United States alone amounted to about $2.2 trillion between 1980 and 1989. Techniques that were used to "put the Vietnam War behind us" and extol the "victory" of Desert Storm included the careful control of media technology by the military establishment the second time around. Further, part of this technology-media control was aided by the fact that our educational system has taught most young people in the United States little to nothing about the histories of the people of Vietnam and Iraq and the nature of the United States' involvement in those areas of the world over a long period of time.

This chapter has already explored how politics, power, values, and technology are intimately intertwined. Again, I want to emphasize that one of the main characteristics of technology is that it has a political dimension. For instance, David Noble has noted that

> Practitioners of science and technology, in following their own Muses, have always claimed to be servants of society as a whole. [T]hey customarily renounce all politics to demonstrate their disregard for power and influence. [However,] this posture . . . serves merely to insulate them and their activities from political scrutiny. [T]he very fact that scientists and engineers are in a position to learn [from experiments] and to use their knowledge for practical ends, to make decisions about the design and even the use of new technologies, indicates their close relationship to social power.[18]

The political dimensions of technology contain the concepts of rule, control, and physical and psychological domination. If nowhere else, this struggle to dominate and harness people to the needs of the machines has taken place in the charged arena of negotiation over workers' bodies on the factory floor:

> [I]ndustrial technology . . . shapes workers who are capable of exercising considerable control over their own spontaneous impulses (and so can conform to the behavioral demands of mechanized production). . . . Industrial workers were also required to turn their bodies into instruments . . . for producing calculated effects on material and equipment. . . . There is evidence that workers submitted to the physical rigors of factory discipline only when other alternatives had been exhausted.[19]

One of the critical roles of education therefore should be to deal with the origin and nature of power and its technological connection. This means taking a critical approach to the teaching of history. I have written elsewhere that the history of technology in particular requires a critical search for meaning and consequences. Thomas Jefferson wrote "that the study of history in particular, would teach the young to judge the actions and designs of men, . . . to know ambition under every disguise it may assume, and knowing it, to defeat its views." However, the "contemporary history of technology tends to read as a form of propaganda. The public, including many intellectuals, is [led to believe] that the continued unlimited application of undirected technology ultimately is going to solve most human problems."[20]

CRITICAL-HISTORICAL PERSPECTIVES ON THE HISTORY OF TECHNOLOGY

Kenneth Clark in a *New York Times* article in 1975 pointed out that our

highly developed technological society that has pioneered in space exploration continues to tolerate large-scale decay of the residential portions of its cities, deterioration of public education, and accelerated pollution and wastage of its natural and human resources. [The] crisis of inconsistencies in American life—the American dilemma— is primarily a crisis of moral ambivalence. It is an honesty-dishonesty dilemma that pervades all dimensions of our social, economic, political, educational and, indeed our religious institutions. . . . Reality, efficiency, and morality are defined as if they were synonymous: that [which] is real and moral leads to success. If this is found to be too abstract an approach even for pragmatic morality, then outright moral cynicism and hypocrisy are available as alternative approaches to personal success and effectiveness.[21]

The famous physicist Max Born expressed serious reservations about science and technology in a series of articles he wrote in 1965. He stated that his main occupation during his last years was concerned with "the social, economic, and political consequences of science, primarily the atomic bomb, but also other pathological symptoms of our scientific age, like rocket research, space travel, overpopulation, and so on."[22] In another article in this same series, Born spelled out in detail his reactions to his work as a scientist:

Science in our technical age has social, economic, and political functions, and however remote one's work is from technical application it is a link in the chain of actions and decisions which determine the fate of the human race. I realized that aspect of science and its full impact only after Hiroshima. But then it became overwhelmingly important. It made me ponder over the changes which science has caused in human affairs during my own time and where they may lead.[23]

Primitive technology developed by artisans was basically independent of science and grew very slowly. There was a sudden explosion of intellectual activity about three hundred years ago and modern science and technology were born. Since then, science and technology have "increased at an ever-growing rate, probably faster than exponentially, and are now transforming the human world beyond recognition." Born points out that although this scientific and technological explosion "is due to the mind, it is not controlled by the mind." He gives as examples, people crowded into cities who have lost all contact with nature, disappearance of wild animal life, instant communications making a reasonable politics impossible, the automobile making the whole countryside accessible to everybody but the roads are choked and the places of recreation spoiled. He states:

> The real disease lies deeper. It consists in the breakdown of all ethical principles which have evolved in the course of history and preserved a life worth living even through periods of ferocious fighting and wholesale destruction. It is enough to give two examples of the disillusionment of traditional ethics by technology: one concerns peace, the other war. In peace, hard work was the foundation of society. And man was proud of what he had learned to do and of the things he produced with his hands. Skill and application were highly valued. Today there is little left of this. Machines and automation have degraded human work and destroyed its dignity. Today its purpose and reward are cash. The cash is wanted for buying technical products produced by others for the sake of cash. In war, strength and courage, magnanimity toward the defeated foe and compassion for the defenseless characterized the idea of soldier. Nothing is left of this. Modern weapons of mass destruction leave no place for any ethical restrictions and reduce the soldier to a technical killer.[24]

Born was pessimistic and "cannot see any but a dark future for mankind."[25]

In contrast, Victor C. Ferkiss represents an answer to these critics of a technologically based society and responds to the argument that "man is a cog in the machine, or a product produced by it, or both" by pointing out that if this type of criticism is accepted, the alternatives are "revolt, withdrawal or despair." Ferkiss feels that "one can reject [this criticism] by denying that the facts are as stated, or that they lend themselves to the interpretations given them by critics of mass society." He argues further that one does not have to either deny or accept the indictment in the terms in which it is presented:

> it is possible instead to hold that the quarrel over whether or not industrialism has created a mass society threatening human freedom has been rendered meaningless by the continuing development of technology itself, that the industrial era is already in the process of being superseded by a new phase in human history and that industrial man, whatever his characteristics, is evolving into something different and superior—technological man.[26]

Ferkiss concludes that "if technological man comes into existence not only among scientists and technologists but in all walks of life in all advanced nations the existential revolution can become an instrument for liberation rather than destruction."[27]

In addressing Ferkiss's challenge, the key point in his statement above is the universality of the transformation. Looking at today's world one can easily conclude that precious few humans can be classified as "technological man" since the implications of the statement are that one has to be quite technologically knowledgeable to attain the title of "technological man." The reality is quite different. Simply using technology when one had little or no part in its creation, development, and dissemination makes one largely an illiterate consumer of imposed artifacts. In fact, quite the opposite of "technological man" develops because technologically illiterate people begin to develop a faith in the power of technology and become true believers in its efficacy. John McDermott has pointed out that "If religion was formerly the opiate of the masses, then surely technology is the opiate of the educated public today. . . . No other single subject is so universally invested with high hopes for the improvement of mankind generally and of Americans in particular."[28]

Neil Postman, in his recent writings, stresses that technocracies (like the United States) subordinate science and culture to technique and technology; and states that among the assumptions of a technocracy are the beliefs

> that the primary, if not the only, goal of human labor and thought is efficiency; that technical calculation is in all respects superior to human judgment; that in fact human judgment cannot be trusted

because it is plagued by laxity, ambiguity and unnecessary complexity; that subjective thinking is an obstacle to clear thinking; that what cannot be measured either does not exist or is of no value, and that the affairs of citizens are best guided and conducted by experts. ... The uncontrolled growth of technology destroys the vital sources of our humanity. It creates a culture without a moral foundation. It undermines certain mental processes and social relations that make human life worth living.[29]

The discussion that has taken place so far in this chapter has, I believe, provided a context for a brief critical analysis of the foundation of our new "Information Society."

INFORMATION VERSUS MISINFORMATION AND TECHNOLOGY

What is "information"? It is defined as: "to give form," "to represent," "to teach," "telling and being told something," "knowledge acquired in any manner; facts; data; learning, lore." What is misinformation? The definitions include: "wrong information," "false account or intelligence," "misleading information."[30] Definitions for the words *information* and *misinformation* are almost self-evident. However, access to huge amounts of information blurs the distinction between false and true "facts." Bluntly, people are subject to information/misinformation overload by modern electronic and print media technology. Our age has been referred to by many intellectuals and media specialists as the Information Age. Perhaps it might be more apt to refer to it as the "mythinformation"[31] age, where the computer and the video screen have become instantaneous purveyors and disseminators of these informations. The truth is an elusive ingredient in today's overkill atmosphere. Images, sounds, junk mail, junk newspapers, misquotations, distortions, hype, interviews, commercials, and mass advertising overwhelm nearly everyone near this onslaught. Some people do "tune out" in order to escape this external invasion of their psyche, senses, and brains. Some are hypnotized by the drone and become, in a sense, semi-comatose. But our minds, spirits, and values are all affected, consciously or subliminally, by this information/misinformation invasion no matter how we deal with it individually. How much can the human mind absorb and evaluate for accuracy and credibility under "pressure cooker" type conditions and the torrents of information/misinformation which bombards it virtually twenty-four hours per day? "The real pitfall is not to overvalue or undervalue information, or the amount of information available, but to be mesmerized and anesthetized by it."[32]

Tom Wolfe has doubts "whether electronic advances have made information more available [or] that there has been any information explosion." Is it in reality an implosion as suggested by Edward Tenner? "[T]he media scholar Brian Wilson could call the information revolution an illusion, a rhetorical gambit, an expression of profound ignorance, a movement dedicated to purveying misunderstanding and dissemination of misinformation."[33] The critical issue here is the fact that the have-nots in our society are most affected by the information implosion and that the middle class is also feeling the effects of this phenomenon. The argument is that the cost of having access to information, whether in electronic or print forms, has risen:

> New information technologies, even those that decrease in real cost, increase the cash and (equally important) time cost of information. We have more mailboxes to maintain and check. Fax and electronic mail are parallel channels with their own hardware and service expenses, and neither reduces the national overhead of postal and express shipping routes. First class postage has risen from 6 cents in 1970 to 29 cents in 1991.[34]

Tenner points out that print media prices have escalated, citing examples of the *New York Times* and *Wall Street Journal*. Both started at 15 cents in 1970 but have jumped to 50 cents and 75 cents respectively.[35] If one considers the price of books today, it is clear that the have-nots and segments of the middle class cannot afford to purchase many of them. The escalation has bordered on the obscene. Paperbacks, which for example sold for 95 cents in the 1970s, today command prices well in excess of $4 to $5. Hardcover books (especially technical and scientific publications) have gone beyond the means of affordability of those in the middle class and below.

Another phenomenon clearly related to the information implosion is the restriction of public access of community users to university and college libraries by charging high user fees. It should be noted that many of these libraries are subsidized, directly and indirectly, by the public through local, state, and federal tax exemptions, state and federal grants, and research grants (from which universities reap up to 70 percent in overhead charges). As an example, for the public to use my own university's library, the user fee schedule is as follows: $13 per week or $26 per month or $115 per year. This bars a very significant segment of the public from having access to the collections and information retrieval system installed there. This user fee arrangement is a great contributor to the information implosion especially taking place in communities in which colleges and universities have instituted such fees and in communities in which local libraries cannot afford sophisticated computer technology. Institutional and corporate users are also assessed user fees. For example, Rider College in Lawrenceville, New Jersey, just a few miles from Princeton University, is assessed $1,200 per year for five library cards used by their faculty for research access to Princeton's main library. Interestingly, Rider College, which is also a private educational institution, has free and open public access to its library, including Princeton University faculty and students.

I think George Orwell summed up our situation best when he wrote in 1937 of

the queer spectacle of modern electrical science showering miracles upon the people with empty stomachs. You may shiver all night for lack of bedclothes, but in the morning you can go to the public library and read the news that has been telegraphed for your benefit from San Francisco and Singapore. . . . What we have lost in food we have gained in electricity. Whole sections of the working class who have been plundered of all they really need are being compensated, in part, by cheap luxuries which mitigate the surface of life.[36]

CONCLUSION

Technology is a dialectical phenomenon in the sense that it is one of the greatest manifestations of the human mind and spirit. The creativity required to invent technological devices and systems is simply amazing, especially when one views technological development historically. And it is obvious that very few humans can survive, especially in today's technology-based world order, without it. Perhaps this is why science and technology have such potent social, cultural, and even spiritual prestige. For example, in his Christmas Message of 1954, Pope Pius XII stated: "The Church loves and favors human progress. It is undeniable that technological progress comes from God, and so it can and ought to lead to God."[37] This statement, in a sense, goes so far as to imply the deification of technology.

On the other hand, I have tried to examine the opposite side of technology and its profound negative impact on people and their environment. These negative effects are staring us in the face every day—provided we have not been totally anesthetized against recognizing and dealing with this reality. If one puts this into a religious context, as does Pius XII, then it could be argued that technology is both a social good and an evil. I strongly believe in critical thinking and analysis and have tried to encourage my students to adopt this approach to the living of life and questioning the authority and power of technology and those who dominate its development and dissemination. I have encouraged them not to become enamored of the artifacts of technology without carefully examining and evaluating them in a wider context; to put technology into a subservient position relative to human beings and life in general and not to permit technology to become an addictive drug. Addicts are controlled by their drugs.

EPILOGUE

I use computers regularly in addition to many of the other technologies which surround all of us. I also taught a course for many years dealing with computer-aided design, and used computerized information retrieval systems in libraries. I have personally found all of these technologies to have served useful purposes, but all of them have significant limitations. However, it is obvious from what I have argued that I am not a true believer in the heralding of technology as either a Savior or a Devil. I basically believe Mahatma Gandhi's philosophy when it comes to technology. He was once asked, "Are you against all machinery?" He answered, "emphatically No. [W]hat I object to is the craze for machinery."[38]

In a provocative article, John Buschman forcefully points out that systems and technologies have inherently political qualities which have social and economic consequences before any specific uses. The need for control and management of such large and complex systems imposes institutional and hierarchical patterns of authority and forms of power.[39] These are points made earlier in this chapter and unfortunately these concerns, in general, receive little serious attention in engineering schools, colleges, and universities. Buschman ends his article by stating that

It is not the effects of information technology that worry me, but rather the powers of the machine to set the limits of what is valuable, informative, socially worthwhile, and logical. In short, it is its "hidden curriculum" which may affect us the most. [We] need to raise and debate these questions in order to recognize alternatives and the kinds of choices.[40]

A significant question was also raised by Don Crabb in an article interestingly entitled "Can Software Render You Dumber?" He wrote that

"One of the perceived benefits of using a Mac[intosh computer] is that it is supposed to make you smarter, in ways both subtle and profound." But he questioned this assumption and expressed a concern

> about what really happens to our thinking as we become more dependent upon using machines for what we used to do in our heads. [He] hypothesized that using a Mac everyday could make us dumber, not smarter, as we allow our critical faculties to go unexercised while expecting our [computers] to give us answers we seek. [Software can be] so good at doing its own "thinking" that it can take an individual "out of the analysis loop." . . . We trust software all the time to give us reliable results, regardless of the manipulations involved. [One should] think about how such actions affect you personally and the way you interact with the machine. Most of us have forgotten that important stage of reflective thinking.[41]

In concluding this epilogue, I would again state that all of us, as responsible citizens and human beings, need to raise and debate these questions in order to recognize alternatives, consequences, and the kinds of choices involved. This is the only way that people can empower themselves to deal with the unabated and ever-burgeoning and uncontrolled technology to which we are subjected. We face a choice: technological fascism or people in control of their lives and destiny.

NOTES

1. *The Mute Engineer* (Princeton: Literary Publications, 1974) 105.

2. Robert Merton, foreword, *The Technological Society*, by Jacques Ellul (New York: Knopf, 1964) vi.

3. Merton vi.

4. Robert M. Hutchins, "Doing What Comes Scientifically," *Center* 2.1 (January 1969): 60.

5. H. G. Rickover, "Automation and Society," *Wall Street Journal* 10 March 1969: 16.

6. Arthur Loesser, *Men, Women and Pianos: A Social History* (New York: Simon & Schuster, 1954) 133.

7. "Wall Street's Souped-Up Computers," *New York Times* 16 October 1988, sec. 3: 1

8. Paul Goodman, "Can Technology Be Humane?" *Technology and Man's Future*, ed. Albert H. Teich (New York: St. Martin's Press, 1981) 337.

9. Langdon Winner, "The Political Philosophy of Alternative Technology," *Technology and Man's Future*, ed. Albert H. Teich (New York: St. Martin's Press, 1981) 385.

10. Goodman 337.

11. Goodman 338–54.

12. Goodman 339–40.

13. Ralph Nader, "The Engineer's Professional Role," *Journal of Engineering Education* 57.6 (February 1967): 450.

14. Jefferson Morely, "The Ballad of Fawn and Arturo," *Nation* 17 October 1987: 397.

15. Goodman 341.

16. Henry Miller, *The Rosy Crucifixion, Book One: Sexus* (New York: Grove Press, 1965) 126–27.

17. See "The GOP: Caught in the Revolving Door at the Pentagon," *U.S. News and World Report* 27 June 1988: 9–10; Molly Moore, "Military Revolving Door Quickens," *Washington Post* 3 July 1990: A21; Michael Shear, "Pentagon's 'Revolving Door' Still Open," *Los Angeles Times* 16 March 1989, sec. IV: 3; and Steve M. Slaby, "What Should We Ask of the History of Technology?" *History and Philosophy of Technology*, eds. George Bugliarello and Dean B. Doner (Urbana: University of Illinois Press, 1979).

18. David Noble, "Is Progress What It Seems to Be?" *Datamation* 15 November 1984: 140.

19. Shoshana Zuboff, *In the Age of the Smart Machine* (New York: Basic Books, 1988) 30–31; see 19–173 generally.

20. Slaby 114–15.

21. Kenneth Clark, "The American Dilemma," *New York Times* 16 February 1975: E15.

22. Max Born, "Recollections of Max Born: What I Did As a Physicist," *Bulletin of the Atomic Scientists* 21 (October 1965): 13.

23. Max Born, "Recollections of Max Born: Reflections," *Bulletin of the Atomic Scientists* 21 (November 1965): 4.

24. Born, "Reflections" 4.

25. Born, "Reflections" 4.

26. Victor C. Ferkiss, *Technological Man: The Myth and the Reality* (New York: George Braziller, 1969) 76.

27. Ferkiss 271.

28. John McDermott, "Technology: The Opiate of the Intellectuals," *Technology and Man's Future*, ed. Albert H. Teich (New York: St. Martin's Press, 1981) 130.

29. Quoted in Michiko Kakutani, "Technology's Erosion of Culture," *New York Times* 6 March 1992: C30.

30. *Webster's New Universal Unabridged Dictionary*, 2nd ed. (New York: Simon & Schuster, 1983).

31. Edward Tenner, "The Impending Information Implosion," *Harvard Magazine* November-December 1991: 34. (Langdon Winner is generally credited with first coining and exploring this concept.)

32. Tenner 34.

33. Tenner 34.

34. Tenner 32.

35. Tenner 32.

36. George Orwell, *The Road to Wigan Pier* (1937; New York: Harcourt, Brace & World, 1958) 89–90.

37. Leo Haigerty, comp., *Pius XII and Technology* (Milwaukee, WI: Bruce Publishing, 1962) 2.

38. M. K. Gandhi, *Industrialize and Perish* (Ahmedabad, India: Navajivan Publishing, 1966) 18.

39. John Buschman, "Asking The Right Questions About Information Technology," *American Libraries* December 1990: 1027.

40. Buschman 1030.

41. Don Crabb, "Can Software Render You Dumber?" *MacWeek* 25 May 1992: 39.

II

Critical Approaches to Information Technology in Librarianship: Applications

7

Issues in Censorship and Information Technology

John Buschman

Censorship is an issue on which librarians have a great deal of credibility. After all, for many decades now, the American Library Association's Library Bill of Rights has affirmed the responsibility of librarians to provide services and materials for and from all points of view, not to exclude materials for racial, nationality, political, social, or religious reasons, and to challenge censorship in the maintenance of those responsibilities.[1] There is evidence that librarians will carry this ethic into the era of electronic resources in libraries. For instance, in an article on the political persuasion of librarianship, William Birdsall noted that

> liberalism's concern for the free flow of ideas provided the philosophical basis for librarianship's most fundamental principle: intellectual freedom. . . . American librarianship's enthusiastic embracing of the concept of the utility of information and its effort to incorporate information science within its sphere is the logical result of this . . . foundation.[2]

The Library and Information Technology Association (LITA) Committee on Technology and Access has called for "information technology [to] be available in libraries throughout the United States to support: Productivity, . . . Literacy, . . . [and] Democracy" and has proposed changes in federal information policies to further those goals.[3] In fact, "so ingrained and self-evident is this theme that relatively few librarians have felt the need to explore its . . . origins."[4]

Professional librarians continue to resist censors in their traditional form: the "examiner of literature, plays, or other material, who may

prohibit what he [or she] considers morally or otherwise objectionable."[5]
But, as Lawson Crowe and Susan Anthes have pointed out, the electronic
environment gives rise to new challenges to our ethical commitments:

> It is ironic that the extraordinary development of information tech-
> nology, which has made . . . librarian[s] more effective, . . . also has
> the potential for misuse and frustration of the librarian's . . . ethical
> duty . . . to guarantee . . . access and to resist any policy or practice
> that limits or denies free access.[6]

I would suggest that censorship in the electronic age encompasses a
broader concept and field of play than the traditional definition of the
problem would imply.[7] To adapt another definition of the censor from
the language of psychoanalysis enables us to add another facet to what
we already understand about censorship. In addition to the classic
definition, censorship in the electronic age may also concern a "hypothetical . . . agency that represses . . . notions before they reach [public]
consciousness."[8]

Working within this expanded notion of censorship, this chapter will
explore five areas of censorship in relation to information technology and
libraries. The first area is what I refer to as clear and present instances.
Librarians will clearly recognize these as new wrinkles on traditional forms
of censorship. The remaining four areas are explorations of aspects of the
expanded idea of censorship. Each has definite connections to our traditional definition, but each requires a deeper inquiry as well. The role of
information technology in each area is examined, and the materials,
formats, or ideas that are censored or suppressed are identified. Librarians
must become aware of the deeper consequences of their professional
decisions to put information technologies in libraries, because such decisions endorse particular forms of power and social, economic, intellectual,
scholarly, psychological, and political values that accompany the machines.

PRESENT AND CLEAR INSTANCES

There are numerous (and even some famous) clear cases of traditional
forms of censorship of electronic resources. It is safe to say that a healthy
majority of professional librarians would oppose them. However, to imply
broad agreement on their unacceptability is not to brush them aside or
minimize them. They bear examination and reexamination so that librarians recognize and resist them in the future.

First, there have been instances of outright denial of information access. Dun & Bradstreet forced DIALOG to revoke the passwords to its databases for librarians of a labor union. This was specifically to deny the union the increased ability to manipulate company data.[9] In another instance, Stanford University sought to suppress a humor bulletin board on the campus network. This might seem trivial, but the issue went all the way to Stanford's president after it was challenged by the Computer Science Department and the Academic Council on Libraries, both of whom compared it to censoring library materials.[10] Installing dial-in catalogs and databases in public libraries has been questioned as essentially serving only the "person who's got a PC and therefore has a certain amount of money . . . [rather than the] library's mission . . . to serve the more needy."[11] Libraries in effect invest in resources which economically (or intellectually, if one chooses not to purchase a computer and modem) discriminate. A final example of this issue looms over the National Research and Education Network (NREN). A recent Congressional panel became concerned that the network "is being set up in a way that could deny access to a wide variety of prospective users. Some university officials agree . . . that without proper safeguards, access to the network could be controlled or restricted by one or more companies."[12]

There are instances of censorship of electronic content as well. For example, an issue arose with Prodigy, the joint IBM/Sears venture. Company officials commented on the e-mail part of the system, saying that they "prescreen messages that run on the 'public' parts of their system and would ban anything considered 'grossly repugnant to community standards.' "[13] Prodigy managers reserved the right to "edit" messages, while absolving themselves of responsibility by declaring them public domain after they were put on the network. For instance, "messages that might offend Prodigy's corporate sponsors can be eliminated."[14] Some, in fact, were eliminated when the Anti-Defamation League complained about anti-Semitic messages on the e-mail system.[15] Elsewhere, the University of Washington removed a picture file, which included pornography, from a campus computer. A shortage of disk space was cited, but the file was removed shortly after some negative newspaper publicity and after a similar file at another state university was questioned by auditors.[16] However, none of these problems are particularly recent. As far back as 1984 H & R Block notified a subscriber of its CompuServe system that messages with the word "gay" or "lesbian" would be deleted from the National Electronic Bulletin Board. In a familiar refrain, they cited the need for "certain standards of expression [to] conform to the tastes of our general audience as we perceive them." This was in response to messages about a gay-run vacation to Puerto Rico.[17] In perhaps a harbinger of things to come, local network managers now have programs which allow them

> to peer into directories of files stored on individual PCs, letting them read, rewrite and delete files from PC hard disks. [M]anagers [can] see what's being typed on the screens of as many as eight PCs at once [and even] seize control of PCs and run them remotely.[18]

Other current trends which clearly censor and deny access to materials are the related issues of fees for services and privatization. The American Library Association (ALA) saw early on that "the charging of fees . . . for information services, including those services utilizing the latest information technology, is discriminatory in publicly supported institutions."[19] As Steve Slaby pointed out in his chapter, the vast majority of libraries are publicly underwritten in some form. This is a controversy that has not abated, although as Henry Blanke has pointed out, there have been a series of "elaborate rationalizations for librarianship's accommodation to [such] market imperatives."[20] The charging of fees, as most librarians still recognize, inherently leads to differing amounts of access for different people: the information rich and poor.[21] The American Library Association's Commission on Freedom and Equality of Access to Information stated the ethical situation clearly:

> Marketplace forces that are propelled by the exotic and expensive new information technologies must be tempered by consideration for public interest and public need. . . . [A]n information need is not . . . synonymous with an information market. Neither is it in the national interest to permit the development of a two-tier society incorporating a permanent underclass of print and information illiterates. . . . [T]hose who are denied access to information resources in either traditional or electronic formats are in a very real sense denied thereby the opportunity for full and effective participation in modern democratic society.[22]

The driving force behind the fee issue is the privatization of information. Herbert and Anita Schiller succinctly characterize this phenomenon: "commercialization and privatization are means to institutionalize a process whereby information is restricted to those with the ability to pay."[23] The ALA Council just quoted went on to note that, as a result of privatization, "some major categories of government information are already accessible only electronically. This has profound consequences for libraries which have long served a social function to assure at least minimum citizen access to government information."[24]

Familiar to most librarians, this issue arose out of the Reagan administration's "war on waste" and resulted in the Office of Management and Budget's (OMB) Circular A–130 mandating "maximum feasible reliance on the private sector for dissemination of products and services."[25] Some dramatic rises in online costs for government information remarketed through private companies have resulted.[26] Generally, there has been a dramatic overall drop in government publications and increased attempts to control that information flow,[27] and private information companies have lobbied hard to continue to get more exclusive rights to remarket government databases.[28]

Lest librarians think that this issue is becoming another staple "cause" of the profession, consider what Bruce McConnell, the Bush administration's acting chief of information policy at the OMB, said of the NREN: "the government will seek to transfer ownership, operation, funding, or pieces of those, to the private sector. The key issue is not will we privatize, but when and how."[29] It is this future move which spurred Congressional and academic concerns over access to the network. Finally, access to the Internet is subsidized by the government as well,[30] and it may also be targeted for privatization. Again, future questions of control, access, and costs are at stake.[31] The closely related issues of user fees and privatization have revolved around information technology resources and the profits to be made from them. This is a form of censorship that, as Sue Jansen states in her chapter, "exercises its discipline at the cash register."

The examples noted in this section are still recognizable censorship issues that librarians would resist or have resisted. However, of equal or perhaps even greater concern are some of the newer facets of censorship in which information technology plays a key role. Four areas I would like to examine are: market censorship, privileged formats of knowledge, the fate of print culture attributes in the electronic context, and the electronic panopticon and fate of the historical record.

MARKET CENSORSHIP AND LIBRARIES

I would like to carry forward Jansen's identification and analysis of the concept of market censorship to identify its inroads in librarianship. To paraphrase Dallas Smythe, the modern act of censorship is not limited to governmental or citizen suppression of materials. It also rests in corporate decisions as to what will and will not be mass-produced and disseminated in the cultural arena. Since private corporations are accorded the same legal privileges as persons, it follows that they have similar responsibilities. And, since the means of mass communication are under private corporate control, it is accurate to think of their production and dissemination decisions, which are guided by their "reading" of the market, as censorship.[32]

At the same time, Ben Bagdikian has long warned of the dangers of information control and manipulation when ownership of media resources becomes centralized. He wrote in 1989 that

> A handful of mammoth private organizations have begun to dominate the world's mass media. . . . Moreover, each of these planetary corporations plans to gather under its control every step in the information process, from creation of "the product" to all the various means by which modern technology delivers media messages to the public. . . . Bookstores and libraries still offer miles of shelves stocked with individual volumes. . . . But if this bright kaleidoscope . . . was replaced by the corporate colophons of those who own this output, the collage would go gray with the names of the few media multinationals that now command the field. . . . Together, they exert a homogenizing power over ideas, culture, and commerce [and] have their own political agenda. [No one] has commanded as much power to shape the information on which so many people depend to make decisions about everything from whom to vote [for] to what to eat.[33]

Market censorship becomes a critical issue when centralized ownership severely restricts the number of players making competing production and dissemination decisions. The marketplace of ideas is narrowed, and the three conditions of freedom of information are threatened: the ability to watch or read anything available, diverse sources of information, and systems for access to it all. This pattern of ownership has already affected materials libraries buy. Multinational media corporation ownership of many of the journals to which libraries subscribe has driven the dramatic price increases that have wrecked many a budget.[34] It has also affected the content of books available to libraries as well. The case of the demise of Pantheon, a subsidiary of Random House (itself a division of the Newhouse empire), is illustrative. In the words of editors who resigned in the wake of the severe cutback in publishing schedules, Pantheon was "Newhoused" by the parent media company for publishing "books that involved risk—and not just to the bottom line, but politically, socially, culturally."[35] This is not farfetched since others in the publishing industry concurred, and noted that the reasons for the cuts did not withstand even a strict cost/benefit analysis.[36]

Market centralization and censorship can be identified in the electronic resources that libraries purchase as well. The lack of diversity in sources of information, technology, access, and the attendant narrowed market decisions as to what to produce and disseminate is following the pattern set in print and broadcast media. For instance, the major database vendors are becoming part of media conglomerates. DIALOG is owned by the Knight-Ridder newspaper chain.[37] BRS and Orbit are owned by Elsevier. Along with two other database vendors, these companies control over 90 percent of the sales and use of databases worldwide. IBM manufactures two-thirds of the world's computer hardware, and three companies control 80 percent of the world's market for workstations by now.[38]

Immediately after the October 30, 1991, Supreme Court decision lifting the ban on the Regional Bell Operating Companies' (RBOCs) entrance into the information provision business, they began adding to their holdings of electronic information resources. Ameritech acquired Notis and Dynix to add to their holdings of two other library automation systems, OCLC's LS/2000 and the Tacoma Public Library system. Ameritech now controls a significant portion of the library automation marketplace. US West announced plans to work with France's Minitel system to offer electronic mail, a videotext gateway, and an electronic document interchange service. Pacific Bell already had a joint project with San Francisco Public Library to provide modem access to CD-ROMs and eventually electronic books.[39]

There are indications that the publishing of electronic books will be dominated by similar corporate control as well. Xerox is testing a book-on-demand electronic system and IBM has developed interactive media/text products. Thomson Corporation (owner of Gale Publishing and Warren, Gorham & Lamont) recently purchased the ISI database along with a handful of newsletters and over forty journals. Among those producing, testing, or looking into electronic books are Bertelsmann, Sony, Sharp, Time-Warner, Rupert Murdoch, Simon & Schuster, and Whittle Communications.[40]

That this centralization of ownership has and will continue to affect content and access is beyond question. For instance, while DIALOG was a subsidiary of Lockheed, its president stated flatly that "we can't afford an investment in databases that are not going to earn their keep and pay back their development costs [i.e., the] humanities."[41] As early as 1977, the director of the Division of Science Information of the National Science Foundation noted that the shift toward electronic and nonprint distribution was driven by "major elements comprising the U.S. information economy" and not by libraries.[42] This has gone on unabated and continues to shape electronic content as acknowledged by a scientist at AT&T's Bell Labs: "information has progressed from intrinsic knowledge to a commodity. . . . Marketplace forces . . . drive the development and introduction of new information products."[43] There is a remarkably unified example of this which also illustrates new depths of corporate moxie. A representative of Elsevier, one of the prime culprits in journal inflation, cited rising journal costs to demonstrate the need for electronic journal publishing ventures and licensing—which Elsevier is of course pursuing.[44] In his chapter for this volume, John Haar examined the potential profits—and dangers to libraries—in this arrangement.

Second, my coauthor and I examined DIALOG's database offerings in 1990 and found that, of the twenty-five categories of databases, seventeen were of primary use to the business and economics areas.[45] CD-ROM publishing has been affected as well. Only 13 percent of the 2,212 titles available in 1992 are related to history or the arts. As early as 1989, those areas only represented 4 percent; in 1990, less than 7 percent; and less than 10 percent in 1991. The market had to become saturated with products related to business and economics first before these products became marginally profitable and marketable.[46]

As a final example, privatized government databases are subject to market censorship as well. Apart from the cost/fee/access issue, Marc Levin raises the question of what happens to public access when private contracts with the government run out, or those companies change hands. He asks, "Is the American public willing to place the future of federal information services in the hands of the lowest commercial bidder?"[47] There is also cause for concern over "creaming": private contractors servicing only profitable or easy customers with only the profitable government databases, and dropping the rest.[48] In effect, classic market mechanisms will censor some government information. Even the GPO Gateway bill (Senate version) only specifies cheap electronic access to the Congressional Record and the Federal Register, and perhaps "dozens" of others.[49] The Council on Library Resources best summed up the entire marketplace censorship issue when they stated: "Uncritical adherence to the concept of information as a commodity will distort the agendas of institutions and disciplines alike. [T]he information needs of society cannot be defined by the market alone."[50]

PRIVILEGED FORMATS OF KNOWLEDGE AND CENSORSHIP

I would next like to turn to a form of censorship closely allied to market censorship, albeit not as apparent. I refer to this new form as privileged formats of knowledge (versus lower-status formats). Insofar as librarians have allied themselves with information technologies, and those technologies embody and represent higher status and privileged forms of information (because of their affiliation with science), then information technologies represent higher-status, privileged formats of information. This analysis goes well beyond the mere social cachet of a technology. It is grounded in the Frankfurt School of Critical Theory, which long ago established the analysis and critique of the elevation of scientific reason over other forms of learning and knowing.

Briefly, Herbert Marcuse, in a summary of the Frankfurt School analysis, found that "scientific, technological rationality became reason [itself] divorced from the validating 'ends' set by philosophy. [It] expressed and extended the specific rationale of the . . . ever more effective mastery of the environment."[51] Jurgen Habermas picked up this thread and linked it to capitalist economics. Essentially, the need for continuous expansion among the advanced industrial economies would drive an escalation of technical control over nature and, administratively, over people. "In this system, science, technology, industry, and administration interlock. . . . [Scientific] technological rationality . . . as a value . . . does not have to be justified, . . . it has a preferential status as against all other values."[52] Educational scholars have subsequently identified a consequent distinction between high-status (scientific and measurable) and low-status (humanistic) knowledge in the culture of schooling and in curricula.[53]

The development of information technology is an extension of the privileged status of scientific rationality. Historically the computer is linked to the science-technology-industry-administration cycle. The origins of the computer are firmly rooted in the processes started with industrialization. "The computer represents only the latest . . . version of a long line of 'control technologies' that have emerged to satisfy an industrial(izing) society."[54] Specifically, information technologies developed out of the classic framework of the World War II military-industrial complex. The language of information, as John Durham Peters notes, has "never strayed far from a mix of management, military, and machines [jargon]. . . . Information is the stuff of science, and science is (rightly) where [it] has taken strongest root."[55] But the connection goes a step further. Like scientific rationality, technologies in general, and information technologies in particular, have become autonomous, severed from their original purposes, with inherent economic, political, power, and value consequences prior to any specific application.[56] If there was any doubt, note that along with a healthy measure of social prestige, information technologies are firmly aligned with socio-economic clout as well. A ten-year review of studies "point[ed] to computer ownership and availability of school-based instruction as primary determinants of [children's computer] competence. And these in turn are strongly correlated to income and affluence."[57]

As a format of information and knowledge, information technologies are an extension of the privileged status of scientific rationality. I would suggest that, in opting for these resources, librarians are accepting the privileges of this format of information and moving away from lower-status formats—most obviously print. There is no need to repeat some of the evidence. It will suffice to refer back to the purchasing patterns noted in the introductory chapter and the illustrations of the content of online and CD-ROM databases. As a privileged format, library electronic resources are receiving heavy library investments, and they are primarily in service to the content needs of the science-technology-industry-administration cycle. However, there are other ways in which high-status formats and access affect libraries.

First, while librarians hold high hopes for the potential of the NREN, the network was supported by Congress originally as a necessary and critical step to solve the "Grand Challenges [of] problems in science and engineering with broad importance in economics and research."[58] In the subsequent environment of increasing demands on the network, "the quantitative sciences are going to have an easier time justifying their need for this than the humanities or the non-quantitative sciences." That would include library applications as well.[59] High-status formats will continue to be allied with privileged forms of knowledge.

Second, the information technology-based fee services libraries offer almost exclusively benefit businesses. This arrangement amounts to publicly subsidized data services for only one segment of the public. While libraries rarely make a profit (or much of one), their "return" on offering this service is a "gain" in credibility and prestige in the business community.[60] Apparently, the mere affiliation with computer formats, content, and the business community is ample reward for librarians.

Third, there is a developing pattern of money targeted specifically for these high-status formats. For instance, in the course of an audience discussion at a recent conference, a director of a state university library in the Northeast reported that her state's legislature would only allocate new

library monies for technology-related projects. Historically, library automation developed from grants and matching federal funds to large universities. Now, in order for small libraries to automate, they are urged to
pursue private funds. This flow of money replicates the pattern of computer resources benefiting those who already have socio-economic power.
For example, Apple Library of Tomorrow awards have gone to high school
and public libraries in affluent communities like Berwyn, Pennsylvania
and Liverpool, New York, the Louisville Public Library, Yale University's
Sterling Chemistry Library, the University of Alaska Library, and the
Library of Congress. In each of these instances, Apple furthered technological investments already in place.[61] DIALOG funded two years of full
and open access to its databases for all students and faculty at Earlham
College to gather information on patterns of unfettered database use, and
in the process, Earlham received an endowment from an alumnus to
continue support for online searching.[62] As a privileged format in libraries,
information technologies draw financial backing.

Fourth, Haar wrote that our investments in electronic reference sources
can skew collection patterns since they affect what patrons use. Electronic
reference sources become the *de facto* benchmarks for collection building
(as their print counterparts have been). They also potently generate
patron demand for certain resources as a higher-status form of access. I
would argue that the evidence suggests this analysis is still essentially
correct. Presently, CD-ROMs are the electronic medium of choice, and
most of the ones libraries buy are still periodical indexes. The result is
more awareness of periodical literature and less use of "underindexed"
monographs. If collection development librarians respond in the conventional way, then monographic budgets will be reduced, and the money
will follow demand. The high expense of electronic reference sources,
coupled with their high status and bias in favor of serials information,
amounts to a decision to cut book purchases. "The real choice may be
whether to buy ease of bibliographic access at the expense of constricting
[new] acquisition[s]."[63]

This has proven to be remarkably accurate. As noted in the Introduction, Paul Gherman's outline for Virginia Tech's Library follows just this
pattern, with one new twist: cuts will go deeper in order to purchase access
rather than more subscriptions. The same pattern was duplicated at
Central Michigan University Library when the effects of CD-ROM
purchases were studied in 1989.[64]

Finally, to complete the picture, it is easy to show the decline in library
investment in lower-status formats of information. While library investment in electronic formats continues to grow as noted in the Introduc-

tion, academic libraries are slashing book and journal budgets, and collecting and preserving less.[65] The budget woes of public and state library systems are a regular feature of newspapers and the *Library Hotline*. The results have shown up in cuts in hours, collections, services, and in the case of the Los Angeles Public Library, a proposal from the librarians to work for free to address a budget shortfall.[66] This lack of investment in print resources is affecting book production. The last available figures show an overall drop of 17 percent in new American titles.[67] Meanwhile, scholarly publishers continue to produce more titles, while selling fewer volumes per title. University presses face the loss of subsidies and the consequent shift toward publishing fewer titles, shorter runs, and more (potentially) profitable manuscripts.[68] In one of the more egregious examples of institutional investment in high-status formats allied with privileged knowledge, the New York Public Library announced plans to open a Science, Industry, and Business Library "without walls" in Manhattan at a public cost of $18.5 million. This came on the heels of $25 million in system-wide budget cuts and cutting after-school services to children.[69]

ELECTRONIC SUPPRESSION OF PRINT CULTURE ATTRIBUTES

The attributes—forms of learning and rationality—of print literacy do not carry over into electronic formats unchanged. This is perhaps the most complex facet of our expanded notion of censorship, but it is one that bears examination since it is of broad intellectual and scholarly concern. As libraries consistently move toward electronic formats, their availability continues to grow. There are six refereed electronic journals in existence, industry plans for electronic books, and over 300 projects worldwide to digitize book texts—mostly classics. The library literature predicts the end of the book format, the end of libraries as book warehouses, and the coming of "virtual" libraries that never sleep.[70] Put at its most basic, this new digitized text does not serve print literacy, and may in fact suppress the conditions necessary for it. A brief review of what some scholars see as the attributes of print culture is in order before we consider the disruptions of digital text.

In an admirable summary of the basic points of scholarly agreement, Sven Birkerts identifies the salient features of print culture:

> The order of print is linear, and bound to logic by the imperatives of syntax. It requires the active engagement of the reader [in] an act of

translation. . . . The print engagement . . . pass[es] from the privacy
of the sender to the privacy of the receiver. [It] posits a time-axis [in]
the turning of pages, not to mention the vertical process through the
page. [P]rinted material is static—it is the reader, not the book, that
moves forward. The physical arrangement of print . . . accords with
our traditional sense of history. Materials are layered; they lend
themselves to rereading and to sustained inquiry.[71]

Those last points are important (as will be seen in the final section of
this chapter) and they bear reinforcing. Print societies "cannot [easily]
discard, absorb, or transmute the past. [They] are faced with permanently
recorded versions of the past [making] historical enquiry possible [and]
encourag[ing] skepticism . . . about the legendary past [and] about received ideas."[72]

I have offered beginning analyses of some forms of censorship in the
electronic era, and expanded the notion of censorship as an analytical
tool. However, *even if the information technology environment were perfectly
neutral* (which it is not), *digitized text would still suppress attributes of print
culture*.

To begin, Peters observes:

The resistance of [printed] texts to interpretation, and their power
to engender many and conflicting readings, evaporates when they
become information. . . . Information lacks history [and] when a
library is thought of as containing information, then . . . the obsoles-
cence of texts is natural. . . . Information's value is given in relation
to time [and] new "information" does not enlarge or transform old
information, but makes it obsolete. [T]exts preserve meaning across
all the ravages of time.[73]

Neil Postman has argued that "when a medium of communication has
the power to disembody words, to split them away from their original
source, the psychological and social effects of language are forever
changed." He goes on to contend that the "information environment"
shifts social organization and "intellectual predispositions" away from the
hard work of learning literacy as the fundamental building block of
rationality.[74]

Information technology frames language as merely a conduit for information. When language culture becomes embedded in a binary code, the
nature of knowledge changes to conform to the machinery that stores it.
That new format of knowledge is a commodity critical to economic and

productive power. Further, the language of information technology promotes certain kinds of images, metaphors, and ways of thinking. The
result, as C. A. Bowers states, is a

> sender-receiver model of thought and communication . . . [where]
> the human authorship of the knowledge is obscured. What moves
> through the conduit of language takes on the appearance of objec-
> tivity [and] misrepresents how knowledge is humanly constructed
> over time in culturally specific ways and continually reconstructed
> as it is communicated to others.[75]

As opposed to printed texts, digital text is a reified format of information.

Information technology is, as Roger Shattuck noted, actually the
interactive convergence of three older technologies: print, photography,
and telegraphy.[76] This convergence is coming together in electronic texts
with pictures and sound developed as interactive media. As such, they
will not be merely digitized text, but another medium altogether whose
effects would be analogous to those of the broadcast media. Their very
appeal is to the generation reared on MTV.[77] Scholars see communication
and socialization influenced by broadcast media and information technology in a variety of ways: these forms of communication are inherently
non-rational, they change the nature and basis of human contact, they
homogenize vocabulary, they profoundly affect privacy taking place as
they do over public airwaves and networks, they influence the psychological development of the self, and many thinkers see that "changes in
information storage and access are bound to impinge upon our historical
memory."[78] Ella Taylor questions whether "we may lose the linguistic
autonomy and analytic distance that enable us to assess our world" in this
new environment.[79]

Finally, texts as a broadcast-like multimedia product become part of
something bigger, which has its own communicative messages and priorities. In an excellent analysis updating a work of communications scholarship, Jay Rosen states:

> In an electronic environment, where everyone is saturated with
> messages, sending another message won't amount to much. . . . The
> point is not to deposit your messages . . . but to somehow activate
> the layers of meaning already . . . there. . . . Our minds are no longer
> separate cognitive spaces. They are each a part of the electronic
> commons. . . . The way you communicate . . . is not to send messages
> (or compose texts). Instead you fashion a "package of stimuli" that

will "resonate" with what is already and continuously communicated. . . . It is not that print is dying, and with it abstract sequential thought. . . . These statements are true, but they fail to account for what else is happening: . . . the search for the "responsive chord" is crowding out all other impulses.[80]

In sum, there is ample reason to be concerned about digitized text and its future development as a broadcast-like medium. There is a body of scholarship, from which this review only skims, which is strongly suggestive that these developments will censor the historical, intellectual, social, and psychological attributes of print culture. Even divorced from ownership and power issues (which no technology ever is), information technology still does not have neutral effects in this cultural arena.

THE ELECTRONIC PANOPTICON AND THE HISTORICAL RECORD

Library literature strongly points in the direction of a truly "virtual" library institution in the future. One of the most complete "visions" of this appeared in a recent *Library Journal* article. Essentially, to escape the "print prison" librarians are urged to endorse the work of

gathering a single comprehensive collection, including all extant current, past, and future scholarly publication. . . . Of course, both the collection and apparatus [of distribution] would be electronic [and] accessible anywhere, using the worldwide communications structure that presently exists. . . . No substantial technical problem lies in the way of [this] accomplishment.[81]

Framed in this way, as purely a technical issue, the "virtual" library masks many underlying issues. Once and for all, library decisions about format and collections are connected to larger contexts—that is the essence of this volume. Our decisions are never of concern only within the hothouse atmosphere of librarianship, and the proposal in *Library Journal* is no different. For instance, Colleen Roach has pointed out that the "worldwide communications structure that exists" is deeply biased in favor of the power and values of Western, industrial nations, and that attempts to inject some equality in that structure met with sustained resistance from the United States and UNESCO.[82]

If this vision of a single, comprehensive national source for all digitally stored text is even partially accomplished—for instance, with 50 percent of all new monographs and journals stored electronically in three or four centers by the year 2010—then I believe we are in danger of two potential and related forms of censorship that have some current precedents: the electronic panopticon and manipulation of the digital historical record.

The concept of the electronic panopticon has been explored by all of the scholars that will be noted in the remaining paragraphs of this section and this historical overview of the idea is drawn from all of them. Briefly, the electronic panopticon is an adaptation of an architectural design by Jeremy Bentham. Bentham designed a prison structure which allowed a central guard cell to observe many prison cells from one vantage point—without being seen. While as a practical matter prisoners could never be watched at all times, this arrangement had precisely that effect since prisoners could never know if and when they were being observed from the central, unseen guard cell. While this design idea was carried out in a prison, Bentham noted its generalized applicability to other social institutions (schools, factories, etc.). Michel Foucault analyzed this concept as functioning like a "machine" for the purpose of exercising discipline and social power. The advent of information technology has, of course, technically realized many of the panoptic machine's observational possibilities, and freed it from its pure architectural function. It also has made possible the exercise of panoptic power (observation and discipline) on a mass scale.

That this danger is very real is easily demonstrated. The electronic invasion of privacy is an extremely sensitive issue, and there are a wide range of ways in which it is getting more intrusive. For instance, computer overlays of demographic and financial data make possible very specific direct targeting of advertising to people. It will even get as specific as a city-block demographic and financial map of the nation when the 1990 Census data become available to marketers.[83] Government and corporate information gathering on individuals has been described as having "laser-like precision and sponge-like efficiency. We're not even aware of most monitoring." Even local government records are electronically available to those with a computer and modem—allowing a fairly complete data picture to be constructed of any given individual.[84] Block modeling is a computer program which evaluates employees "on the basis of their relations with other employees," and it is constructed from not particularly sensitive data.[85]

In another example, Citicorp put together a Point of Sale Information Service meant to link data on individual supermarket shoppers with their specific product purchases. Not only would food manufacturers know the demographic data of their customers, they would also know their names and addresses and specific products purchased. The consumer payoff is a discount for allowing the data collection. Citicorp gathered an information data bank on over 2 million households from over 400 supermarkets, although their goals were more than twice those amounts.[86] My own observations indicate that these data-gathering programs in supermarkets continue to expand. Kevin Robins and Frank Webster have outlined our "surveillance society" in the tracking of cable television channel selections to electronic banking transactions.[87] There are many other kinds of examples too numerous to mention here.

Electronic supervision of work dramatically shifts power to management, as Shoshana Zuboff observed in her chapter, and can lead to electronic Taylorism.[88] In the education field, teachers were among the first to adopt

> panoptic control [since they] considered data to be essential for measuring the progress of students. This same penchant for . . . efficient teaching procedures, and for collecting data . . . has led to viewing the management of the instructional process as one of the major challenges in computer application [in schools].[89]

All of these developments take place in a country where "no laws exist . . . that are directly comparable to the all-encompassing data protection laws of such countries as Great Britain, Germany, or France."[90] And, needless to say, the Reagan and Bush administrations have created a hostile environment for individual civil rights and regulatory restraints on corporations, and in turn, have run roughshod over constitutional restraints on executive and governmental power.

It is not at all farfetched to extend these dangers to libraries. After all, electronic text delivery to the "virtual" library presupposes centralized storage, control, and monitoring. There will at least need to be accounts and records kept for copyright considerations. There will be a far more extensive data trail on who reads what, and where and when, in the digital text environment. There are indications now that the U.S. government is limiting the encryption of some electronic texts so that, when they are sent, they remain more easily monitored.[91] (See also Gray's chapter.) There exist right now forms of electronic supervision in libraries, that is, programs to monitor the ongoing work of copy catalogers.[92] Tom Gaughan, editor of *American Libraries*, visited OCLC and mused on the possibilities of their telephone system, which monitors the number of calls handled, average wait, and the abandon rate (people who hang up). He "wondered if there's a library in the country with a phone system slick enough to measure the abandon rate of telephone reference queries."[93] I have wondered elsewhere if it is realistic for professional librarians to expect to slip through this kind of supervision, given its presence in libraries and extensions to other forms of professional work.[94]

There are programs designed to process and compare texts in order to catch plagiarism. This has been described as a "misconduct machine" designed specifically with the idea of *searching out* "behavior not consistent with accepted practices."[95] Lastly, electronic signatures, or small data tags to be worn by people, are designed to track their movements and provide instant electronic identification. Applied in libraries, they "could protect against theft, while speedily entering transactions" at an enormous cost of loss of privacy.[96] Clearly broader social forms of the electronic panopticon have the potential to take root in librarianship. I now turn to consideration of libraries' role in the preservation of the historical record.

Eugene Provenzo originally supported what he termed the Post-Gutenberg era. However, after reflecting on the uses to which information technology power has been put, he has reconsidered. Along with other scholars, he has recognized the dangers of an electronic panopticon, but he goes one step further. He notes that digitized culture becomes very vulnerable to manipulation of its historical record. Precedents for this abound in the broadcast media. Two very recent examples will suffice. The media scholar Todd Gitlin has written about an interview he did that was televised on a network news program during the Gulf War. The interview was severely edited and, juxtaposed with cut-in images and voice-over characterizations, made Gitlin appear to support the war.

> The result was a badly misleading impression [and] a simplistic piece about "complexity" [of the new anti-war protests]. People who disdain television [and] know "the news" is selective and . . . "constructed" . . . all took the statement I was shown making at face value.[97]

Another case was the Massachusetts governor's campaign of 1990. A portion of an interview with one candidate was excerpted, the picture enlarged and distorted, and broadcast in a commercial by the opposing candidate to great effect.[98] Such media manipulations are so well known—the selective and edited nature of broadcast pictures and words—that they have created widespread public cynicism about the media.

However, it is the ability to extend these manipulations into the storage of the digital historical record which is so disturbing. Jurgen Habermas wrote in 1963 that "the negative Utopia of technical control over history would be fulfilled if one were to set up a learning automation as a central system of . . . control which would answer questions cybernetically."[99] It is just this chilling possibility that Provenzo sees in digitized culture:

> We are faced . . . with a new type of literacy—one that is subject to greater control and manipulation than was the case in typographic culture. . . . Anyone who has used a word-processing system . . . knows how easy it is to transform information in a digital context. One word can be automatically substituted for another, a name changed, a date altered, an idea corrupted without any record of what the original source said. . . . The alteration of digitally stored photographs in our era is [also] quite practical [as they are] easily restructured and reformatted. [This] represents a major problem in terms of the integrity of historical documents, and the extent to which we can trust the information from such sources in the future. . . . The ability to alter the past has always been potentially possible in analogue culture. It has tended, however, to be enormously time-consuming and relatively easy to detect. [Now, with digitized text and photographs,] as Orwell . . . predicted, . . . history becomes a function of the future and changing ideologies and political opinion.[100]

I would only add that history would also function for those who would own and control those digitized sources.

Has librarianship given the full consequences of the "virtual" library adequate thought? The privacy of patrons to gather and read materials *may* be forever altered, and the historical record *may* become a fluid and manipulable concept. In such a case, libraries would no longer function as a place of civic and social memory. To envision the "virtual" library as purely a technical problem to be surmounted is to irresponsibly overlook some of the dangerous censorship possibilities of the electronic era and continue to court high-status formats and their attendant power structures.

CONCLUSION

This examination of censorship issues is not to suggest that librarians are unwittingly or wittingly ushering in an era of unfettered domination of people through information control and censorship. However, the progression from cases of clear electronic censorship, to market censorship of electronic resources, to privileged formats, the fate of print culture in a digital environment, and the electronic panopticon and fluidity of the digitized historical record, does suggest that the issues are deeper than a simplistic review would represent. That hypothetical agency suppressing notions and formats from public consciousness exists in some cases, and is a very real potential in others. Each of these newer forms of censorship has a broader social precedent, and some have rudimentary equivalents already in place within libraries. Technologies embody power relationships, and censorship is about the power to monitor and control what and how people read, see, and thus think. Library information technologies are not exempt from these broader implications.

NOTES

1. Reprinted in Jean Key Gates, *Introduction to Librarianship*, 2nd ed. (New York: McGraw-Hill, 1976) 255–56.

2. William F. Birdsall, "The Political Persuasion of Librarianship," *Library Journal* 1 June 1988: 77–78.

3. "Information Technology and Libraries: Federal Roles," *LITA Newsletter* Winter 1991: 9–10.

4. Ronald J. Heckart, "The Library as a Marketplace of Ideas," *College & Research Libraries* 52 (November 1991): 491.

5. *The American Heritage Dictionary of the English Language* (Boston: Houghton Mifflin, 1971).

6. Lawson Crowe and Susan H. Anthes, "The Academic Librarian and Information Technology: Ethical Issues," *College & Research Libraries* 49 (March 1988): 129–30.

7. I have previously explored this idea in a more basic and different form in "Self Censorship and Information Technology," a paper presented as part of a panel presentation on "Self Censorship in U.S. College and Research Libraries," 6th ACRL Conference, Salt Lake City, 14 April 1992.

8. *Webster's New Collegiate Dictionary* (Springfield, MA: G. & C. Merriam, 1977). Sue Curry Jansen nicely explores this concept in more depth in her book *Censorship: The Knot That Binds Power and Knowledge* (New York: Oxford University Press, 1988): she argues that the

> definition of the term [should be] much broader than definitions which have currency in Liberal free-speech theory. [Rather, the idea of censorship should be extended to encompass] socially structured proscriptions or prescriptions which inhibit or prohibit dissemination of ideas, information, images, and other messages . . . by political, economic, religious, or other system of authority. It includes both overt and covert proscriptions and prescriptions. . . . I am more interested in the socially structured silences of political capitalism which almost never receive sustained public attention but nevertheless render some ideas and then authors unpublishable. . . . To this end, I have cut a far wider theoretical path than do researchers working within the paradigms of Liberal free-speech theory. (221–22)

9. Brian Campbell, "Information Access and Technology," *LITA Newsletter* Summer 1988: 11.

10. Carl M. Kadie, BITNET communication, 6 May 1992.

11. T. R. Reid, "Computer Access System Brings the Library Home," *Washington Post* 2 September 1989: A3.

12. David L. Wilson, "High-Speed Network for Research Stirs Controversy," *Chronicle of Higher Education* 4 March 1992: A22.

13. *Newsletter on Intellectual Freedom* January 1992: 18.

14. Willard Uncapher, "Trouble in Cyberspace: Civil Liberties At Peril in the Information Age," *The Humanist* 51 (September-October 1991): 6.

15. *Newsletter on Intellectual Freedom* January 1992: 18.

16. *Newsletter on Intellectual Freedom* March 1992: 61–62.

17. Peg Byron, "Computer Service Deleting Gay Messages," *New York Native* 27 July 1992: 3 (reprinted from the 26 April 1984 issue).

18. John R. Wilke, "For Network Managers, Snooping Gets Easier," *Wall Street Journal* 23 March 1992: B1.

19. Quoted in Barbara Smith, "A Strategic Approach to Online User Fees in Public Libraries," *Library Journal* 1 February 1989: 33.

20. Henry T. Blanke, "Libraries and the Commercialization of Information: Towards a Critical Discourse of Librarianship," *Progressive Librarian* 2 (Winter 1990/91): 12.

21. A good summary of the issue may be found in Ronald D. Doctor, "Information Technologies and Social Equity: Confronting the Revolution," *Journal of the American Society for Information Science* 43 (1991): 216–20.

22. Quoted in Nancy L. Eaton, "Freedom and Equality of Access to Information: The Lacy Commission Report," *Library Trends* 39 (Summer/Fall 1990): 117.

23. Herbert Schiller and Anita Schiller, "Libraries, Public Access to Information, and Commerce," *The Political Economy of Information*, eds. Vincent Mosco and Janet Wasko (Madison: University of Wisconsin Press, 1988) 163.

24. Quoted in Eaton 117.

25. Quoted in Nancy C. Kranich, "Information Drought: Next Crisis for the American Farmer?" *Library Journal* 15 June 1989: 22.

26. See Kranich; Frances Seghers, "Computerizing Uncle Sam's Data: Oh, How the Public is Paying," *Business Week* 15 December 1986: 102–3; and Patricia Glass Schuman, "Making the Case for Access: ALA Needs You!" *RQ* 29 (Winter 1989): 166–72.

27. See Donna A. Demac, "Hearts and Minds Revisited: The Information Policies of the Reagan Administration," *The Political Economy of Information*, eds. Vincent Mosco and Janet Wasko (Madison: University of Wisconsin Press, 1988) 125–45; Jansen 169–70; and R. Kathleen Molz, "Censorship: Current Issues in American Libraries," *Library Trends* 39 (Summer/Fall 1990): 31–33.

28. See Schiller and Schiller; and Patricia Glass Schuman, "Cynicism, Euphemisms, and Seductive Hyperbole About Privatization," *American Libraries* February 1992: 189.

29. Quoted in David L. Wilson, "Debates on Access, Expense, and Management Rage Over Development of High-Speed Computer Network," *Chronicle of Higher Education* 15 April 1992: A25.

30. Wilson, "Debates" A25.

31. Elizabeth Caskey, BITNET communication, 8 May 1992.

32. Dallas W. Smythe quoted in Jansen 165.

33. Ben H. Bagdikian, "The Lords of the Global Village," *Nation* 12 June 1989: 805, 807.

34. Bagdikian 812, 815; Schuman, "Cynicism" 189; and Patricia Glass Schuman, "Reclaiming Our Technological Future," *Library Journal* 1 March 1990: 36.

35. "Newhoused," *Nation* 19 March 1990: 369.

36. John Buschman and Michael Carbone, "A Critical Inquiry into Librarianship: Applications of the 'New Sociology of Education,' " *Library Quarterly* 61 (January 1991): 25–26.

37. Bagdikian 815.

38. Schuman, "Cynicism" 189; and Schuman, "Reclaiming" 35–36.

39. See Nancy Melin Nelson, "Dynix: Baby Bell Ameritech: Data Research and 'The' Network," *Information Today* May 1992: 47–48; S. Michael Malinconico, "Information's Brave New World," *Library Journal* 1 May 1992: 37–38; Joseph A. Webb, "Supreme Court Allows RBOCs to Provide Electronic Information," *Information Today* December 1991: 9; and Reva Basch, "Books Online: Visions, Plans, and Perspectives for Electronic Text," *Online* July 1991: 22.

40. See Malinconico 38; Bruce Flanders, "Multimedia Programs to Reach an MTV Generation," *American Libraries* February 1992: 135–36; Nathaniel Lande, "Toward the Electronic Book," *Publishers Weekly* 29 September 1991: 28, 30; and "Thomson Pays $210M for Electronic Database, Journals," *Publishers Weekly* 20 April 1992: 6.

41. Quoted in Schiller and Schiller 161.

42. Quoted in Schiller and Schiller 151.

43. Quoted in Blanke 10–11.

44. Nancy Melin Nelson, "Academic Networks: Publishers Consider Opportunities in Library Technology," *Information Today* December 1991: 12.

45. Buschman and Carbone 27.

46. Paul Nicholls, "United States History on CD-ROM: A Buyer's Guide," *CD-ROM Professional* May 1992: 72–73.

47. Marc A. Levin, "Government For Sale: The Privatization of Federal Information Services," *Special Libraries* 79 (Summer 1988): 213; see 210–13 generally.

48. Kranich 25; and Levin 212–13.

49. "Make Way for Gateway," *American Libraries* July/August 1992: 545.

50. Quoted in Schiller and Schiller 162.

51. Herbert Marcuse, "On Science and Phenomenology," *The Essential Frankfurt School Reader*, eds. Andrew Arato and Eike Gebhardt (New York: Continuum, 1982) 469–70.

52. Jurgen Habermas, "Theory and Practice in a Scientific Civilization," *Critical Sociology: Selected Readings*, ed. Paul Connerton (New York: Penguin, 1976) 340.

53. Michael J. Carbone, "Empowering the Liberal Arts: Analysis and Paradigms From Critical Theory," *Quarterly Journal of Ideology* 12.3 (1988): 4–5; and Stanley Aronowitz and Henry A. Giroux, *Education Under Siege* (South Hadley, MA: Bergin & Garvey, 1985): 92.

54. John Durham Peters, "The Control of Information," *Critical Review* 1.4 (Fall 1987): 6.

55. John Durham Peters, "Information: Notes Toward a Critical History," *Journal of Communication Inquiry* 12.2 (1988): 19–20.

56. Milton Mueller, "Technology Out of Control," *Critical Review* 1.4 (Fall 1987): 25–27.

57. Doctor 219–20.

58. David L. Wilson, "Gigabits Aside, People Can't Seem to Agree on Best Use of Planned High-Speed Network," *Chronicle of Higher Education* 15 April 1992: A25.

59. Wilson, "Debates" A21.

60. Although I know of no study which demonstrates this point nationwide, each new report on such services in libraries directly states this or it is directly implied in the way the services are marketed. Among many examples, see Michael Rogers, "Library Searching Powers Attract Private Firms," *Library Journal* 1 April 1992: 36; Julie L. Nicklin, "Many Institutions Conduct Research for Companies for a Fee, But Others Assail the Practice," *Chronicle of Higher Education* 19 February 1992: A29; Alice Sizer Warner, "Librarians as Money Makers: The Bottom Line," *American Libraries* November 1990: 947–48; and Steve Coffman and Helen Josephine, "Doing it For Money," *Library Journal* 15 October 1991: 32–36.

61. Thom Gillespie, "High-Tech Libraries of Tomorrow—Today," *Library Journal* 1 February 1991: 46–49; see also Ernest A. Muro, "The Library Automation Marketplace," *Library Technology Reports* July-August 1990: 457; and Dwight F. Burlingame, "The Small Library and Fund-Raising for Automation," *Library Hi Tech* 7.2 (1989): 49–51. The statement on state legislature funding priorities came during the discussion of the panel presentation on "The New Information Technologies" at the American Library Association Annual Conference, San Francisco, 28 June 1992.

62. See Judith Axler Turner, "Earlham College Tests Value of Mass Use of 'Dialog' Data Base," *Chronicle of Higher Education* 26 September 1990: A15; and David L. Wilson, "Earlham's Access to Data-Base Service Endowed by Alumnus," *Chronicle of Higher Education* 23 October 1991: A19–20.

63. John M. Haar, "The Reference Collection Development Decision: Will New Information Technologies Influence Libraries' Collecting Patterns?" *Reference Librarian* 22 (1988): 118.

64. May M. Moore, "Compact Disk Indexing and Its Effects on Activities in an Academic Library," *Journal of Academic Librarianship* 16 (November 1990): 291–95.

65. See Julie L. Nicklin, "Rising Costs and Dwindling Budgets Force Libraries to Make Damaging Cuts in Collections and Services," *Chronicle of Higher Education* 19 February 1992: A1, A28; Liz McMillen, "Recession Pushes Libraries to Cut Back on Acquisitions of Literary Archives," *Chronicle of Higher Education* 19 February 1992: A29–30; and Julie L. Nicklin, "Libraries Drop Thousands of Journals as Budgets Shrink and Prices Rise," *Chronicle of Higher Education* 11 December 1991: A29–30.

66. See, for example, "Where is the Library?" *International Herald Tribune* 28–29 December 1991: 6; "Open Letter From Connecticut State Librarian," *Library Hotline* 16 December 1991: 2–3; "National Coverage of Financial Plight of Libraries," "Montgomery County Cuts," and "Cuts in Library Hours Prompt Student Sit-In," *Library Hotline* 25 February 1991: 1–2.

67. Chandler B. Grannis, "Title Output In 1990 at a Record Low," *Publishers Weekly* 20 September 1991: 31–32.

68. See Sanford Thatcher, "Scholarly Monographs May Be the Ultimate Victims of the Upheavals in Trade Publishing," *Chronicle of Higher Education* 10 October 1990: B2–3; and Julie L. Nicklin, "Many University Presses Are Forced to Put New Emphasis on the Bottom Line," *Chronicle of Higher Education* 18 March 1992: A31–33.

69. "NYPL Takes Major Step to Aid Regional Economic Development," *Library Hotline* 16 December 1991: 1; and Richard F. Shepard, "The Libraries, Squeezed by Hard Times, Shut Children Out," *New York Times* 14 July 1991: E20.

70. See Lande; Basch 14; David L. Wilson, "Testing Time for Electronic Journals," *Chronicle of Higher Education* 11 September 1991: A23–24; Raymond Kurzweil, "The Future of Libraries Part 1: The Technology of the Book," *Library Journal* January 1992: 80, 82; Raymond Kurzweil, "The Future of Libraries Part 2: The End of Books," *Library Journal* 15 February 1992: 140–41; Harold Billings, "The Bionic Library," *Library Journal* 15 October 1991: 38–42; Michael Rogers, "Library of Congress Unveils High-Tech Lab," *Library Journal* 1 May 1992: 26, 28; Kathryn M. Downing, "An Electronic Publishing Primer," *Publishers Weekly* 19 April 1991: 44–46; Charles Robinson, "The Public Library Vanishes," *Library Journal* 15 March 1992: 51–54; and Eldred Smith, "The Print Prison," *Library Journal* 1 February 1992: 48–51.

71. Sven Birkerts, "Into the Electronic Millennium," *Boston Review* 16 (October 1991): 15.

72. Jack Goody and Ian Watt, "The Consequences of Literacy," *Power and Ideology in Education*, eds. Jerome Karabel and A. H. Halsey (New York: Oxford University Press, 1977) 470.

73. Peters, "Information" 19–20.

74. Neil Postman, *Teaching As A Conserving Activity* (New York: Dell, 1979) 30–31; see 29–106 generally.

75. C. A. Bowers, *The Cultural Dimensions of Educational Computing: Understanding the Non-Neutrality of Technology* (New York: Teachers College Press, 1988) 42–43; see 37–44 generally.

76. Roger Shattuck, "From the Swiss Family Robinson to Narratus Interruptus," *Boston Review* 17 (May-July 1992): 22.

77. See Rogers, "Library of Congress"; Kurzweil, "Part 2"; Flanders; and Beverly T. Watkins, "Videodisks Add 'Dimension of Emotion' to Ethics Education," *Chronicle of Higher Education* 4 March 1992: A22–23.

78. Birkerts 19; see also Jascha Kessler, "Epimetheus—or, A Reflection on the 'Box,'" *Boston Review* 17 (February 1992): 13–14; Ella Taylor, "Virtual Reality," *Boston Review* 16 (December 1991): 18–19, 22; George Scialabba, "Extra-Sensory," *Boston Review* 17 (February 1992): 16–17; David Hellerstein, "Computers on the Couch" (interview with Sherry Turkle), *Esquire* December 1985: 360–65; Susan E. Davis, "Twilight Zone of the Tech World," *Washington Post* 22 August 1989: Health sec. 8–9; and John Markoff, "Some Computer Conversation Is Changing Human Contact," *New York Times* 13 May 1990: 1, 20.

79. Taylor 22.

80. Jay Rosen, "Playing the Primary Chords," *Harpers Magazine* March 1992: 23.

81. Smith 50–51.

82. Colleen Roach, John Buschman, and Mark Rosenzweig, "Towards a New World Information and Communication Order: A Symposium," *Progressive Librarian* 3 (Summer 1991): 6–15.

83. Paul Farhi, "For Business, Census Is a Marketing Data Motherload," *Washington Post* 17 March 1990: C1–2; and Robert J. Samuelson, "Computer Communities," *Newsweek* 15 December 1986: 66.

84. John Markoff, "Remember Big Brother? Now He's a Company Man," *New York Times* 31 March 1992: E7; see also "Sellers of Government Data Thrive," *New York Times* 26 December 1991: D2; and Donald R. Katz, "We Know All About You," *Esquire* July 1990: 51–52.

85. Scott A. Boorman and Paul R. Levitt, "Big Brother and Block Modeling," *New York Times* 20 November 1983: F3.

86. Fred R. Bleakley, "How a Terrific Idea For Grocery Marketing Missed the Targets," *Wall Street Journal* 3 April 1991: A1, A12.

87. Kevin Robins and Frank Webster, "Cybernetic Capitalism: Information, Technology, Everyday Life," *The Political Economy of Information*, eds. Vincent Mosco and Janet Wasko (Madison: University of Wisconsin Press, 1988) 57–62.

88. Shoshana Zuboff, *In the Age of the Smart Machine* (New York: Basic, 1988) 315–61; and Shoshana Zuboff, "Problems of Symbolic Toil," *Dissent* Winter 1982: 51–61.

89. Bowers 18.

90. Michael Rogers Rubin, "The Computer and Personal Privacy, Part III: the Regulation of Computer Records in the United States," *Library Hi Tech* 27 (1989): 11.

91. David Bellin, letter, *New York Times* 22 April 1992: A24.

92. A. J. Anderson, "The Electronic Supervisor," *Library Journal* 15 October 1989: 55–56.

93. Tom Gaughan, "The Corporate Culture of OCLC," *American Libraries* October 1991: 894–95.

94. John Buschman, "Information Technology, Power Structures, and the Fate of Librarianship," a paper presented as part of a panel on "The New Information Technologies: Hidden Agendas, Institutional Power and the Fate of Librarianship," American Library Association Annual Conference, San Francisco, 28 June 1992.

95. Philip J. Hilts, "Plagiarists Take Note: Machine's on Guard," *New York Times* 7 January 1992: C1, C9.

96. Tom Gaughan, "Luddites of the World, Unite!" *American Libraries* November 1988: 912.

97. Todd Gitlin, "On Being Sound-Bitten," *Boston Review* 16 (December 1991): 16.

98. Anne W. Branscomb, "Common Law for the Electronic Frontier," *Scientific American* September 1991: 157.

99. Habermas 345.

100. Eugene Provenzo, "The Electronic Panopticon: Censorship, Control and Indoctrination in a Post-Typographic Culture," ms. *Literacy Online*, ed. Myron Tuman (Pittsburgh: University of Pittsburgh Press, 1992 forthcoming) 171, 174–75, 179–80.

8

The Civic Role of Libraries

Carolyn M. Gray

INTRODUCTION

Citizen involvement in the democratic process must be based on knowledge of the workings of the federal, state, and local governments. Information policy formulated to support the basic principles and values of American society can help us examine issues in relation to (1) the stewardship and control of resources upon which we are dependent; (2) the organization of work in society; (3) the exchange and distribution of the products of that work; and (4) the governance of decision making. The public library in the United States is an important bulwark in the maintenance of an informed and involved citizenry.

This essay reviews the civic role of libraries; describes the two primary models of citizenship and relates these models to library service; reviews the major technological and political trends that impact the civic role of libraries; and suggests a policy framework for addressing these trends. The focus of this essay is the impact of information technology on the civic role of America's libraries. There have been a number of political and technological trends which impact open access to information. Recent developments that are examined include: the passage of the High Performance Computing Act of 1991, commonly referred to as NREN (the National Research and Education Network); the decision by U. S. District

This chapter is based in part on two of the author's works: "Information Technocracy: Prologue to a Farce or a Tragedy," *Information Technology and Libraries* (March 1987): 3–9; and "The Civic Context of Electronic Citizenship," *Citizen Rights and Access to Electronic Information: The 1991 LITA President's Program Presentations and Background Papers*, ed. Dennis J. Reynolds (Chicago: Library and Information Technology Association, 1992) 141–49.

Judge Harold H. Greene to lift the restrictions on the expansion of the regional Bell operating companies into information services; the pending House "WINDO" or Senate "Gateway" legislation; and the 1992 proposed revision to the Office of Management and Budget (OMB) Circular A–130. All of these developments have the potential to radically alter the civic context of information delivery.

THE CIVIC ROLE OF LIBRARIES

The philosophical roots of the civic role of libraries are traceable to Thomas Jefferson's day. The public library is a place where, in Jefferson's words, "the energies of the individual can be harnessed toward constructive social goals." As Edward Everett, past president of Harvard College, said in 1858 at the dedication of a new building for the Boston Public Library, "The American way was to make the care of the mind from outset a part of the public economy, the growth of knowledge a portion of its public wealth."[1]

During the past quarter century, the National Assessment of Educational Progress has documented a decline in civic knowledge and values among America's youth.[2] This trend is particularly disturbing because of the growing pluralism among Americans and the growth in public policy issues that are complex and potentially divisive (e.g., health insurance, educational reform, trade policies, welfare policy, etc.). The decline in civic knowledge and growing pluralism put pressure upon public institutions such as libraries to strengthen their civic role within the community.

Technology and the information explosion are having both positive and negative effects on citizens' access to information. The editors of *Civitas* outline a number of trends which are changing citizens' relationship to the policy process. The trends which are particularly relevant to the civic role of libraries include: (1) greater access to information on policy issues; (2) more information, making it difficult to assess what is relevant; (3) greater use of technology to facilitate access; (4) technology creating a false sense of involvement; (5) greater social diversity; (6) erosion in the sense of community; (7) influence of mass communication on citizens' understanding of public policy issues; and (8) segmentation of the policy process.

At this important juncture in the development of information services for the twenty-first century, it is important for us to reconfirm the civic role of libraries. This chapter suggests important roles libraries and librarians can play in exercising and promoting the responsibilities and rights of citizens in a participatory democracy. These are not new, but they are explored in an effort to frame the civic context for discussing information access in an electronic environment. Knowledgeable participation in-volves: acquiring and processing information; assessing one's involvement and stake in an issue; making decisions regarding governance; developing and using standards helpful in evaluating a position, such as the United Nations' Declaration on Human Rights; communicating ideas to others, including decision makers, leaders, and officials; and cooperating with others to reach mutual goals.[3]

Some of the civic roles libraries might assume to help engage citizens in the maintenance of democratic values include: collecting and making accessible information by and about government relevant to a free society; preserving historical information by and about government; providing public space for training in democratic principles; facilitating literacy training (basic literacy, civic literacy, information literacy); offering voter registration in public libraries; and supporting diversity within the com-munity (language and ethnic).

Because access to the full range of both print and electronic information technologies is so essential to effective participation in a modern demo-cratic society and a free economy, librarians must assume an active political role to ensure that libraries are assigned a higher place on the societal agenda.

Since the days of Madison and Jefferson, Americans have recognized freedom of information to be an essential component of the democratic process. Freedom of information implies that access to government infor-mation shall be both unrestricted and free of charge. For groups as diverse as environmentalists, scientists, librarians, labor unions, human service advocates, and consumer rights organizations, as well as private citizens, freedom of information is relevant. A lack of concrete information may have adverse effects upon the ability of any such group to bring about change, to conduct research and accurately report findings, and to advise the public of potential danger, or good.

MODELS OF CITIZENSHIP

Before moving into a discussion of the impact of information technol-ogy on libraries, a brief description of two models of citizenship is pre-sented in an effort to clarify how citizens are served by libraries. In the American tradition there are two primary philosophical positions on the meaning of citizenship. They have been described as follows:

Citizens have obligations (the classical republican tradition). This view holds that citizenship necessarily implies certain responsibilities or duties to serve the common good. In this view, citizens ought to be motivated by a devotion to civic virtue, which places the common good before private interest. . . .

Citizens have rights (the liberal-democratic tradition). This view holds that the rights of citizenship are important primarily because they enable citizens to protect themselves from the government and to advance individual liberty and interests. It emphasizes that whether or not one assumes some or all of the traditional obligations of citizenship is a matter of choice.[4]

Within the classical republican tradition the concept of civic virtue implies a foundation of knowledge and skills about the ideals and workings of constitutional democracy. Armed with requisite knowledge and skills, citizens develop a reasoned and informed commitment to participating in constitutional democracy. The Founders of the American Republic drew upon the traditions of Aristotle, Cicero, Machiavelli, Montesquieu, and Rousseau in developing a concept of civic virtue which asks citizens to "subordinate their private interests and elevate their personal obligation to work on behalf of the common good."[5]

It is out of this classical tradition that library service values have evolved. It is from this tradition that the great public libraries were founded and have continued to flourish. We can see this tradition reflected in another quote from Edward Everett's dedication speech at the Boston Public Library:

Hitherto the system of public education, excellent as it is and wisely supported . . . does but commence the work of instruction and carry it to a certain point; well advanced, indeed, but far short of the goal. . . . It disciplines the faculties and forms a taste for the acquisition of knowledge, on the part of our young men and women, but it provides no means for their exercise and gratification. . . . But to-day our honored city carries on and perfects her work. The trustees . . . have never failed to recommend a first class public library . . . for whose accommodation you destine this noble building, as the completion of the great system of public education . . . where Boston men and women, children of a larger growth, may come to acquire the additional knowledge which is requisite for the most successful discharge of the duties of the various callings of society.[6]

The Founders also drew upon a second model of citizenship evolving out of the seventeenth- and eighteenth-century writings of Locke and

Hobbes, the liberal-democratic tradition. This liberal-democratic perspective emphasizes "the chief end of government to be the prime protector of the individual rights of citizens in a democratic republic."[7]

It is out of this liberal-democratic tradition that the Library Bill of Rights and concepts of intellectual freedom have developed in the library community. Many of the librarians active in issues related to intellectual freedom follow in this liberal-democratic tradition. Their perspectives are largely shaped by the concept of citizen rights. As we seek to develop information policies to help us cope with societal trends and our changed democratic environment, perhaps we should strive, as the editors of *Civitas* have suggested, to achieve a dynamic equilibrium among these competing values. This dynamic equilibrium between the classical republican and liberal-democratic traditions is created when "individual rights are viewed in light of the public good and the public good includes the basic protection of individual rights."[8] The traditions of American libraries have long embraced the concept of library service as supporting the public good. Librarians' emphasis upon intellectual freedom, diversity, and individual rights is a more recent phenomenon. The Library Bill of Rights was first codified some fifty years ago.

Whether we see tension or equilibrium between these two traditions, it is important for us as citizens to be able to identify and understand their ingredients. Armed with that understanding, we can have a positive impact on the development of public information policies that support civic values which advance the common good and protect individual rights. The civic obligation to promote the common good is necessary to ensure the stability and continued existence of the political community. The public good is enhanced by many public sector activities, but beyond basic services, long-range questions arise concerning the relative responsibility of the government, voluntary nonprofit organizations, and private business. We have developed a matrix of roles and responsibilities in the delivery of information services without a clear consensus of what is necessary to support the public good.

Of particular concern to libraries is the First Amendment protection of the right to free speech, assembly, religion, and the press. All of these "rights" are related both to personal and public freedom which ensures the common good of the democratic political community. The state is obligated to protect the individual against infringement by a coercive majority, and these intellectual and academic freedoms are especially guarded by the library community. The civic culture of the library community embraces the right of citizens to speak, read, inquire, think, express, learn, and teach without arbitrary constraint. It is this freedom which ensures the means for citizens to make rational political choices among real alternatives on the basis of reliable knowledge.

EMERGING PROBLEMS OF INFORMATION TECHNOLOGY

These concepts of the civic role of libraries and the rights and responsibilities of citizenship serve as a backdrop for an examination of relevant information technology trends. For the past two decades, writers such as Theodore Lowi have warned that "As a result of information technology, man's power over his environment will increase greatly and his susceptibility to manipulation will rise proportionately."[9] As a nation, we are faced with important policy issues related to developments in information technology being implemented by the federal government. As librarians, we need to involve citizens in policy formulation relating to the collection, transfer, and dissemination of government-held information through public awareness campaigns and other educational programs. The issues involved include the right to privacy, the freedom of information, First Amendment rights, Fourteenth Amendment rights, and the provision of information by the government.

Some disturbing developments illustrate the importance of addressing these issues in relation to information policy formulation. The free flow of information about the workings of the American government is being restricted by a number of recent trends: (1) the privatization of public information; (2) the reduction in the number of government documents printed; (3) the exemption of electronic information from the provisions of the depository library regulations; (4) the subversion of the Freedom of Information Act; and (5) the circumvention of the Privacy Act by government agencies.

The privatization of public information is the process whereby information gathered at the public's expense is sold to a private company, which in turn markets the information for its own profit. Access is thus limited to those who can pay. Citizen access to public information is a right that is being threatened by the very nature of the technology which has led to the "information explosion." The 1966 Freedom of Information Act (FOIA), as amended in 1974, clearly defines the right to access information collected at government expense. That right includes access to any document, file, or other record in the possession of an executive agency of the federal government, subject to nine specific exemptions.[10]

The following, taken from the March 1984 *Congressional Record*, illustrates the trend toward the privatization of public information: "The

Patent and Trademark Office has signed agreements with private companies for the automation of agency records at no cost to the Government. One aspect of these agreements requires the agency to deny Freedom of Information Act requests for the records in automated form."[11] Another example in 1985 was the introduction of the OMB Circular A–130, which is a policy advisory from OMB to all federal agencies concerning the management of government information resources. As first issued, Circular A–130 was used to raise prices on or eliminate many free publications, and to promote the privatization of the dissemination of government information.

However, on April 29, 1992, OMB published a notice in the *Federal Register* asking for public comments on proposed revision of its OMB Circular A–130. As James Love, director of the Taxpayer Assets Project in Washington, notes, the April 1992 draft is a major improvement from the 1985 circular or any of the previous attempts to revise it.[12] The best new features of the circular are its decreased emphasis on privatization, the much more generous mandate to use computer technologies to disseminate government information, and OMB's statement that the pricing of government information should be no more than the cost of dissemination. However, the OMB contends that federal agencies do not have to give electronic information products and services to the federal depository library program. There are 1,400 federal depository libraries, including most major research libraries. Libraries provide free access to thousands of government publications. By law all federal agencies are required to provide copies of paper products to this program. OMB's proposal, which does not appear to be legal, is a major change in philosophy, and it should be criticized strongly. Technology should not act as a *de facto* sunset clause to this program, which is so important in the maintenance of an informed citizenry.

The reduction in the number of government documents put out by the Government Printing Office (GPO) means there are reduced sources of important information. According to the American Library Association's (ALA) Washington office, one in every four of the government's 16,000 publications has been eliminated since 1982. Since 1985, the OMB has consolidated its government information control powers, particularly through Circular A–130. The Paperwork Reduction Act places federal agencies under the directive from the OMB to reduce the number of publications. Such inadequate information resources can lead to major miscalculations in the formulation of federal policy. Examples include data about early childhood immunizations, prescription drug use, the consumer price index, and hazardous waste cleanup.

The exemption of electronic information from the Federal Depository Program is another development, with major implications for public access. The growing tendency is for federal agencies to utilize computer and telecommunications technologies for data collection, storage, retrieval, and dissemination. Though electronic technologies promise great opportunities, they carry with them the triple specters of monopoly control, invasion of privacy, and limitation of access to government-held information. This growing tendency of federal agencies to utilize computer and telecommunications technologies has resulted in the increased emergence of contractual information collected at taxpayer expense, higher user fees for commercial firms to disseminate government information, and the proliferation of government information in electronic formats only. Electronic products and services have begun to be distributed to federal depository libraries, offering some glimmer of hope that public access to government information will be increased. It is only when all appropriate electronic products and services are distributed freely to federal depository libraries that public access to government information will be assured. Proposed legislation seeks to address the provision of GPO electronic documents to the public.

The ALA's Washington office reports a glaring example of the trend toward privatization and limitation of access to government information is a move by OMB to discontinue making their circulars available through the Depository Library Program. OMB maintains that the circulars—which are key documents if the public is to understand federal regulations and requirements for public and private organizations—are for administrative purposes only, not subject to depository requirements. Now the public and libraries can get access to the circulars through an expensive electronic product available from the National Technical Information Service.[13]

The Federal Depository Library Program is a manifestation of the public value Americans have placed upon information. One of the chief methods of ensuring a free flow of information by and about the federal government has been through a strong nationwide network of depository libraries dating back to the middle of the nineteenth century, and the granting of free access to these materials. No provisions requiring free access are made for documents published in electronic form. Technological advances allow for electronic storage and retrieval of information, intensifying the complexity of information access for an open democratic society. Members of the library community have requested that the scope of the depository program be expanded to include access to electronic databases created by the government. Maintenance of "free" access to government information regardless of the format is the key issue. In response to pressures from librarians, professional associations, and individual citizens, Congress appointed an Ad Hoc Committee on Depository Library Access to Federal Automated Data Bases. The final report of that committee, published in 1984 and entitled *Provision of Federal Government Publications in Electronic Format to Depository Libraries*, presents a good overview of the issues, as well as providing specific recommendations.[14]

Current legislation in the form of the House "WINDO" (Wide Information Network for Data Online) and the Senate "Gateway" bills seeks to ensure access to electronic formats, but as of this writing that legislation has not been passed. HR 2772 introduced by Rep. Charlie Rose (D-NC) proposes a network to be managed by the GPO which would act either as a gateway to dozens of federal databases or to provide GPO online system for direct access to taxpayer-supported databases. Rose proposes that WINDO should be affordable to citizens and provided free to federal depository libraries.

According to a fact sheet put out by the ALA's Washington office, the WINDO/Gateway is envisioned as a one-stop shopping way to access government databases using a single system, complementing rather than supplanting other agency efforts to disseminate information. It would not be an exclusive method of dissemination. Its purpose is to make it more convenient for the public to obtain low-cost access to government information.

A significant trend affecting access to information is the subversion of the Freedom of Information Act by executive orders, directives of the OMB, and the curtailment of funds to federal agencies to support FOIA compliance requirements. Looking back over the years since the FOIA was passed, we see that its implementation has gone awry. When hostile to a particular concept, an administration can subvert a law which promotes that concept. Not until 1966 did citizens win the statutory right of access to federal agency documents with the passage of the FOIA. The FOIA passed with broad bipartisan Congressional support. However, agencies of the executive branch showed little regard for the bill either when it was enacted or during the seven years following passage. Congress expressed displeasure with the treatment of the FOIA by government agencies and moved to strengthen the bill in 1974.[15]

The 1974 amendments to the FOIA require agencies to furnish information either without charge or at a reduced rate when the agency determines waiver or reduction of the fee to be in the public interest. Research shows that federal agencies have unclear or nonexistent fee waiver regulations, and in fact, that fee waivers are seldom granted. In the twelve years of the Reagan and Bush presidencies the trend toward charging fees has increased. Even with these limitations, other research shows that open government policies have positively affected administrative behavior. Everett Mann has pointed out that freedom of information policy established by the FOIA does not flow from an express, constitutional right to know, although there is some controversy surrounding the question of whether a public right to know is political rhetoric or an unenumerated constitutional right protected under the Ninth Amendment. In a 1980 case, *Richmond Newspapers, Inc. versus Virginia*, the majority of the Supreme Court concluded that the First Amendment gave the public a right of access to criminal trials. This ruling rests on the traditional importance of citizen scrutiny of the judicial trial process. Justice William J. Brennan argued that the theory of citizen participation in self-government also supports the right, and that this right is not confined to access to courtrooms. In another concurring opinion, Justice John Paul Stevens pointed out that in this case the court recognized for the first time a protected right of access to important government information.[16]

In spite of these precedents and laws, access to unclassified government information has decreased. In a 1984 series in the *Boston Globe*, Ralph Gelbspan found that "The Reagan Administration, while denying it is pursuing any formal policy, has moved systematically over the last three years to restrict or cut off access to a wide range of traditionally public information." He cites three broad areas of concern: (1) the reclassification of previously open information as secret; (2) restrictions seeking to control communications by scientists under government contract; and (3) the noncompliance by federal agencies with Freedom of Information requests.[17]

An example of the use of FOIA materials was reported in the *Washington Post*. The owner and publisher of the *Santa Fe New Mexican*, Robert McKinney, fired his managing editor and criticized a series of articles detailing safety and environmental hazards at Los Alamos National Laboratory, the largest employer in the Santa Fe area. The series contained thirty-two articles published during six days in February 1991. The series, based in part on documents obtained under the FOIA, stated that cleaning up 1,800 sites of possible contamination near Los Alamos would cost $2 billion over a twenty-year period. The articles further stated that the lab releases large amounts of chemical and radioactive contamination into the environment daily, although the risk to public health is slight or nonexistent.

Lab officials did not cite inaccuracies in the series or ask for corrections. But the *New Mexican* published critical opinion pieces by the director and former director of Los Alamos. In late August 1991, Los Alamos released a 308-page internal evaluation highly critical of its failure to comply with safety and environmental regulations, essentially confirming much of what had been in the paper's February series.[18]

The "right to know" is closely associated with the concepts embodied within the FOIA. Within the library literature, the right to know and freedom of information are often discussed as if they were one. There are some important distinctions to be drawn. Most importantly, as noted earlier, the FOIA is specifically and exclusively related to the public's right to know information in custody of the executive branch of the federal government. Individual states have also enacted statutes which provide for public disclosure of state-level government information. On the other hand, the phrase "right to know" is used for its rhetorical appeal. As Steven Shiffrin points out, "the phrase captures several major themes in First Amendment law. . . . The phrase conjures up the citizen critic responsible for democratic decision making and a vigilant press acting as public trustee in gathering and disseminating vital information."[19] The American library community also sees itself as a public trustee in gathering and disseminating information. But, does the public have a constitutional right to know anything that speakers, private companies, or private citizens are unwilling to provide? Shiffrin goes on to note that "To date, there is no judicial authority for the proposition that the public or the press has any First Amendment right to information voluntarily withheld by private actors."[20]

The Privacy Act of 1974 was passed in response to public concern about databases of information being maintained by government agencies. The law provides an individual with the right of access to any files concerning him maintained by government agencies (except law-enforcement and national security files). If an individual believes that information about him is incorrect or incomplete, he may file an injunctive relief to correct the file. Information in government files is not to be used for any purpose other than the original intent without the consent of the individual. Benefits may not be denied to individuals who refuse to disclose their social security numbers. No agency may maintain records describing the exercise of rights protected under the First Amendment.[21]

In spite of the Privacy Act, government agencies continue to gather much information about individuals. The nature of the technologies being used makes monitoring more difficult and increases the danger for invasion of an individual's privacy. David Burnham, writing in the *New York*

Times, reports, "The Reagan Administration has sharply reduced the number of Federal employees working to protect individuals from improper use of public and private records, according to a report by the Government Accounting Office."[22] In fact, the National Security Agency (NSA), with a staff approaching 40,000, according to John P. Barlow, poses more of a threat to privacy than most people realize. Readers may have noticed passing references to restrictions on "encryption" devices in recent news stories. Although the NSA is constrained from domestic surveillance, it is pursuing policies which make it easier for individual privacy to be invaded in an electronic environment. Encryption may be the only reliable method of conveying privacy to the inherently public domain of electronic networks. The NSA views encryption algorithms as weapons of war and enforces a policy which holds that if a device or program contains an encryption scheme which NSA cannot break fairly easily, it will not be licensed for international sale. This policy has the effect of limiting the development of encryption devices because of the global environment of computer technology. The effect on the individual is that if you use computer networks, you cannot be assured of any degree of privacy.

The privatization of public information, the reduction in printed government documents with a related limitation on access to electronic information, and the subversion of laws enacted to protect both access to public information and individual privacy are trends which prompt this author to suggest the need for increased public involvement in information policy formulation.

TELECOMMUNICATIONS TRENDS AND ACCESS TO INFORMATION

Another major development, though not specifically related to government information, but certainly related to the impact of technology on the civic role of libraries, is a recent decision by Judge Harold Greene of the U.S. District Court for the District of Columbia. The question is, under what condition should the regional Bell operating companies (RBOCs) be allowed to provide information services? This dates back to the breakup of the Bell system in 1982 through an antitrust decision, presided over by Judge Greene. Judge Greene has continued to preside over issues resulting from divestiture, and prohibited the RBOCs—newly created in 1984—from entering unregulated businesses such as electronic publishing or the manufacture of telephone equipment, because of the RBOCs' dominant power in their local service areas. While this dominance over local telephone service is eroding, most telephone customers are still able to obtain local service from only one company. Judge Greene modified these restrictions in 1988 to allow provision of information "gateways" and limited electronic information, but not true content services.

More recently, Judge Greene, in a July 25, 1991, ruling, reluctantly lifted the restrictions, because he felt a 1990 decision of the U.S. Court of Appeals for the Ninth Circuit had left him no choice but to do so. He stayed the order pending appeal, but a subsequent appeal to the Supreme Court to reinforce the stay was rejected. The RBOCs are free to develop true content services. They will probably begin with directory services, but no current legal constraints prevent their entry into a broader information market. [See citations related to this in Chapter 7.—Ed.]

In the library community the sentiment is probably stronger for opposing RBOC entry into the area of information provision. However, some librarians in rural areas have argued forcefully that sophisticated information services will never reach rural libraries or residents of rural and sparsely populated areas until the phone companies are permitted to provide them. Some rural libraries incur a long-distance charge to connect to a value-added network for online database searching because no local node exists—a problem severe enough that certain state library agencies and library networks subsidize the higher costs for rural libraries to participate in online networks. Some have argued that libraries should work with phone companies and negotiate favorable arrangements to make library services available to the public via phone company gateways.

The National Telecommunications and Information Administration (NTIA) issued a report in October 1991.[23] In general, NTIA's recommendations propose further deregulation of the telecommunications industry. However, NTIA also recommends that the concept of universal service (the basic telephone service package) should be expanded to include certain advanced features such as touchtone dialing and access for the hearing impaired.

Another development with the potential to significantly alter the information environment for libraries is the emerging national public network. The High-Performance Computing Act (S. 272, PL 102–194), signed into law on December 9, 1991, establishes the National Research and Education Network (NREN) through an upgrading of the federal backbone portion of the Internet, together with related activities. The NREN is a high-capacity computer network designed to link research and educational institutions, libraries, government, and industry in every state. Though not the ultimate broadband network that will reach every home, the NREN is a powerful incentive to marketplace development of a truly ubiquitous network.

Mitchell Kapor and Jerry Berman have suggested that the development of the NREN can be a testbed for the National Public Network. They see a National Public Network emerging over time from the phone system, cable television, and a variety of computer networks. They offer a number of recommendations that include reasonable policy directions of particular interest to the library community. Their recommendations adapted with a library slant include:

1. *Universal access.* Get the network to everybody—in their homes, in their libraries, in their offices, in their schools—throughout the country in rural and urban areas. This requires pricing for universal access.

2. *Competition among carriers.* The network must be a site where competitive energy produces innovation for the public benefit; it should not be a refuge of monopolists.

3. *Create an open platform for innovation.* Equitable access to the network must be available to information providers to facilitate a wide variety of information services. This requires an open architecture (non-proprietary) platform, with low barriers to entry.

4. *Make the network simple to use.*

5. *Develop standards of information presentation.* The library community has been at the forefront in the development and adoption of standards of information presentation. That understanding of standards should be used to assist the National Public Network in the development of a suite of standards for the exchange of richly formatted and structured information, whether as text, graphics, sound, or moving images.

6. *Promote First Amendment free expression by affirming the principles of common carriage.* In a society which relies more and more on electronic communications media as its primary conduit for expression, full support for First Amendment values requires extension of the common carrier principle to all these new media.

7. *Protect personal privacy.*[24]

PUBLIC POLICY: A FRAMEWORK

The convergence of print media with the electronic media and computer technology is creating an environment that allows bureaucrats to limit the public's access to government-held information. There are no longer printed documents for some types of information. With the installation of word-processing, text-editing, and electronic photocomposition equipment in government agencies, the creation and storage of government documents is becoming electronic in nature. The evolution of the National Public Network presents threats and opportunities for universal access to information.

We must have an understanding of information technology issues if we are to retard the forces which can prevent the maintenance of an environment where informed, timely debate about critical policy issues can take place. One of the issues of policy formulation is the traditional economic conflict between equity and efficiency. The stakes are high for companies in the information-processing field. Information entrepreneurs stand to make huge sums of money in the purchase, repackaging, and sale of government information. In the development of information policy we must develop a strategy that balances equitable access with the need to encourage private sector investment in information technology.

With the convergence of print media, computer technology, and communications technology, information policy issues become critical to the maintenance of an informed, free democratic society. The three-way division of power in the federal government has provided a system of checks and balances; until recently, a network of safeguards had protected the collection, transfer, and dissemination of information in American society. Regulations differed because of the nature of the media and the development of technology. In the past, the print media, especially newspaper journalism, were separated from the electronic communications media. Even with the emergence of broadcast journalism, there were still fundamental differences in the media and healthy competition among them. The limited spectrum for broadcasting dictated some forms of regulation. The Communications Act of 1934 established the Federal Communications Commission (FCC), which, in the public interest, was empowered to regulate interstate and foreign communication by wire and radio. The fundamental differences between printed sources and broadcast media have been blurring ever since the establishment of the first data communications network. Ithiel de Sola Pool expressed this convergence in the following manner:

No longer can electronic communications be viewed as a special circumscribed case of a monopolistic and regulated communications medium which poses no danger to liberty because there still remains a large realm of unlimited freedom of expression in the print media. The issues that concern telecommunications are now becoming issues for all communications as they all become forms of electronic processing and transmission.[25]

The recent Judge Greene decision regarding the right of the regional Bell operating systems to deliver electronic information services confirms the admonition of the eminent de Sola Pool.

The consequence of doing nothing about information policy formulation threatens the very fiber of the democratic process, because access to information in this country determines, to a large extent, the quality of the decisions which citizens make. For good or ill, the fragmentation of information policy formulation strengthens the role of private industry. We must develop a mediated agreement between the varied private interests and the public welfare in the development of information policy. Rapidly changing technologies, and the concomitant emergence of new economic interests, serve to create a diversity of interests resulting in a fragmentary approach to the formulation of information policy.

To understand policy directions for the future it is helpful to examine some of the information policies developed by the federal government in the past twenty years. During the mid-1960s issues of privacy relating to government-collected information came to the national attention with the *Griswold vs. Connecticut* case. With that case, the Supreme Court began the process of developing a new legal definition of privacy. Nine years of Senate hearings, House hearings, and public debate regarding the invasion of privacy by government agencies ensued before the Privacy Act of 1974 was enacted. The development of computerized data banks by the federal government made potential abuses so threatening.

In 1966, the Freedom of Information Act was enacted under pressure for more open government. Amendments in 1974 clarified the scope of the act and the requirement for compliance by federal agencies. The Paperwork Reduction Act of 1980 established the Office of Information and Regulatory Affairs and the Federal Information Locator System (FILS) within the OMB. FILS is intended to be used by federal agencies to determine whether data sought have already been collected. The act requires all agencies to have a senior-level official who coordinates information activities, including: (1) an inventory and review of information systems; (2) a check for duplication of functions within agencies; and (3) an impact assessment of the burden of paperwork of proposed legislation affecting the agency.[26]

A directive from the OMB, entitled Improving Government Information Resources Management, has as one of the stated objectives a review process to determine if federal information centers perform a necessary government function, duplicate a private sector service or another government operation, and/or operate on a full-cost recovery basis. "The Paperwork Reduction Act has provided a framework through which information, broadly defined, is viewed as an economic resource to be managed effectively and efficiently."[27]

The OMB review process is a policy which encourages, and even, under certain economic conditions, mandates, the privatization of public information. To eliminate duplication of services offered by the private sector, reviews have concentrated upon information centers of the Department of Education, the National Library of Medicine, Federal Information Centers of the Department of the Interior, the Department of Labor's Occupational Safety and Health Administration Technical Data Center, and the information centers of NASA. In 1982 alone, twenty-six federal agencies were targeted for the review process. No provision for free public access to the information once it has been transferred to a private sector provider is made.

Under the OMB review policy in 1985, the Securities and Exchange Commission (SEC) issued a request for proposal for a pilot test of an electronic filing, processing, and dissemination system. The SEC is seeking a system to handle the multiple disclosure forms which publicly held companies are required by law to file. These forms represent some of the most heavily used information collected by the government at public expense. The SEC has said that the company chosen to run the system will be required to make a certain amount of basic information available at low cost.[28] As in the case of the Patent and Trademark Office, there is no assurance of reasonable access to the forms by individual citizens or public interest organizations. Finally, a promising piece of legislation introduced in December 1991, and still pending, is the Improvement of Information Access Act, HR 3459, introduced by Rep. Major Owens (D-NY). This act would require federal agencies to store and disseminate information products and services through computer networks, and set the price of information products and services at the incremental cost of dissemination.

THE ROLE OF GOVERNMENT AND CITIZENS

No legislative action has tied together the laws and regulations regarding the print, communications, and electronic media. The only indication by Congress of a need for coordination of issues regarding information policies that have been developed occurred ten years ago with Senate Bill 3076, introduced on March 4, 1976, which would have required that all reports accompanying proposed legislation include an information impact statement; the bill was never passed. Representative Owens's bill (HR 3459) updates the earlier Senate version.

Public laws continue to bring into existence commissions that relate to specific aspects of information policy. Laws have covered privacy, wiretapping, electronic funds transfer, federal paperwork, and the records and documents of federal officials. The executive branch has responded in much the same way as Congress when faced with information policy issues. Our government does not seem equipped to meet the immediate pressures generated by technology and citizen demands.

Broad input into the policy-making process is desirable. "Our challenge is to ensure that the changes in society, caused by changes in technology, are consistent with the principles that have framed our society for the last two centuries."[29] Librarians, along with citizen groups, should take the lead by informing the public of the problems and offering constructive solutions to the legislature. Public interest groups with which librarians can align themselves include the Consumer Federation of America, the Alliance for Public Technology, the Electronic Frontier Foundation, and the Computer Professionals for Social Responsibility. States such as Ohio are attempting to develop model information policy programs, which may in turn be adopted by other states, for the new technologies affect more than just federal information.[30] These model state programs could serve to put information policy formulation on the national agenda. It should be noted that the recent spate of bills related to information technology are being proposed in large measure on "economic competitiveness" grounds.

Taking into account the pluralistic nature of our political process, we must frame an agenda with two very broad policy categories: (1) the legal foundation of information dissemination and access; and (2) the economics and management of information. An independent commission should be established to coordinate activities, work with Congress to create the necessary legal foundation, and work with the private sector to resolve conflicts arising from competing interests. The National Commission on Library and Information Science (NCLIS), an independent agency which advises the executive and legislative branches of government on policy, though having a more narrow focus, has served some of the functions being proposed. Given adequate funding and support, NCLIS could be charged with the coordinating role of establishing a national information policy agenda.

As Lewis Branscomb suggests, a discussion of information policy rationales should start with the expected social returns. He sees the following important benefits from additional public investment in information infrastructure: "[1] a smarter, more capable society . . . [2] a more productive society . . . [3] a more creative society . . . [4] a more equitable society . . . [and] [5] a wiser, more caring society."[31] A broad information policy agenda to address these social returns should include: (1) formulate information collection, storage, access, and dissemination policies to balance governmental needs against economic, political, and social costs; (2) establish principles which promote efficiency and provide adequate safeguards against the invasion of individual privacy for the intra-governmental transfer of information; (3) develop a more rational disclosure policy on the part of government agencies; and (4) establish principles and enabling strategies for the creation of a truly ubiquitous National Public Network.

Actions by the executive branch are shaping national information policy without any rational plan or public input. As Wilson Dizard has noted:

Despite the advances in consumer rights practices in recent years, decisions on the consumption of communications and information still tend to be the exclusive province of the bureaucracies—public and private—involved. At a time when we need to take actions to strengthen communications and information patterns in this country through the end of the century, an important element in the decision process is often missing—the views of the individual consumers.[32]

The complementary nature of government and the private sector can exist only through a spirit of cooperation that will lead to the achievement of the overall objectives of an open information society. Dizard proposes an information grid which will deal with public needs, available technology, and economic resources. The information grid gives the private sector responsibility for the development of technology in a competitive market. Society develops a set of social goals to establish information technology needs. The public sector's role is limited to providing fiscal incentives for applications of technology to meet the social goals which could not otherwise be met on economic grounds. Within this construct, the public sector must also assure the availability of communication and information services. This cannot be provided equitably in a competitive marketplace without the establishment of an information elite.[33]

The Electronic Frontier Foundation recommends launching a national public network. Their initial strategy, which does not require replacing all copper wire with fiber optic cable, calls for adopting the basic rate ISDN (Integrated Services Digital Network, a telephone company offering available so far only in limited applications) technology as a national standard for interim deployment of integrated voice, data, and video services. The Computer Professionals for Social Responsibility (CPSR) organization is also working on citizen design of a national public network. Its initial strategy is to educate the general public to the importance of the issues involved. CPSR feels public libraries would be likely sites for (as well as active participants in) such regional education.al meetings.

As librarians, we must perfect our political and technological skills, so we may fully participate in the ongoing debates and help frame a rational information policy agenda to ensure that citizens and politicians understand the importance of these issues for the maintenance of an open democratic society. We must not leave the system of knowledge generation, diffusion, and use to the "play of the marketplace."

NOTES

1. Edward Everett, *Orations and Speeches on Various Occasions*, vol. III (Boston: Little, Brown, 1879) 610.

2. *CIVITAS: A Framework for Civic Education*, Charles N. Quigley, Editorial Director: Charles F. Bahmueller, General Editor *National Council for the Social Studies Bulletin*, No. 86 (Calabas, CA: Center for Civic Education, 1991).

3. *Civitas* 43.

4. *Civitas* 611.

5. *Civitas* 162.

6. Everett 605–6.

7. *Civitas* 12.

8. *Civitas* 12.

9. Theodore Lowi, "The Information Revolution, Politics, and the Prospects for an Open Society," *Government Secrecy in Democracies*, ed. Itzhak Galnoor (New York: New York University Press, 1977) 49.

10. *Freedom of Information Guide* (Washington, DC: WANT Publishing, 1984).

11. "Electronic Filing of Documents With the Government: New Technology Presents New Problems," *Congressional Record*, House (14 March 1984): H1614–H1615.

12. James Love, "The April 29, 1992, Proposed Revision to OMB Circular A–130," an Information Policy Note distributed electronically by the Taxpayer Assets Project, 23 June 1992.

13. *Less Access to Less Information By and About the U.S. Government; XVII: A 1991 Chronology: June-December* (Washington, DC: American Library Association, Washington Office, December 1991).

14. U.S. Congress. Ad Hoc Committee on Depository Library Access to Federal Automated Data Bases, *Provision of Federal Government Publications in Electronic Format to Depository Libraries* (Washington, DC: Joint Committee on Printing, 1985).

15. Tom Riley and Harold C. Rellyea, eds., *Freedom of Information Trends in the Information Age* (London: Frank Cass, 1983).

16. Everett E. Mann, "Freedom of Information Act," *Encyclopedia of the American Constitution* (New York: Macmillan, 1986) 781.

17. Ralph Gelbspan, "U.S. Tightening Access to Information," *Boston Globe* 22 January 1984: 1, 20; "When Scientists Get Aid From U.S.," *Boston Globe* 23 January 1984: 1, 20; "Reagan's Revised Information Act Under Scrutiny," *Boston Globe* 24 January 1984: 1, 16.

18. Howard Kurtz, "After Nuclear Series, Paper Melts Down: New Mexico Publisher Fires Editor, Faults Articles on Los Alamos Lab," *The Washington Post* 5 October 1991: A7.

19. Steven Shiffrin, "Right to Know," *Encyclopedia of the American Constitution* (New York: Macmillan, 1986) 1592.

20. Shiffrin 1593.

21. Dennis J. Mahoney, "The Privacy Act of 1974," *Encyclopedia of the American Constitution* (New York: Macmillan, 1986) 1457.

22. David Burnham, "Cuts Found in U.S. Work on Privacy Issues," *New York Times* 23 September 1984: 28.

23. U.S. National Telecommunications and Information Administration, *The NTIA Infrastructure Report: Telecommunications in the Age of Information* (Washington, DC: Government Printing Office, 1991).

24. Mitchell Kapor and Jerry Berman, "Building the Open Road: The NREN as Testbed for the National Public Network," *Building Information Infrastructure* (Cambridge, MA: Harvard College, 1992) 199–217.

25. Ithiel de Sola Pool, *Technologies of Freedom* (Cambridge, MA: Belknap, 1983).

26. Dennis D. McDonald, "Public Sector/Private Sector Interaction in Information Services," *Annual Review of Information Science and Technology* 17 (1982): 83–97.

27. McDonald 89.

28. Patricia Schuman, "Social Goals vs. Private Interests: Players in the Information Arena Clash," *Publishers Weekly* 23 November 1984: 56–58.

29. Michael Rogers Rubin, *Information Economics and Policy in the United States* (Littleton, CO: Libraries Unlimited, 1984).

30. Jerry Mechling, "A State-Level View of Information Infrastructure: Aligning Process and Substance," *Building Information Infrastructure* (Cambridge, MA: Harvard College, 1992) 31–45.

31. Lewis M. Branscomb, "Information Infrastructure for the 1990s: A Public Policy Perspective," *Building Information Infrastructure* (Cambridge, MA: Harvard College, 1992) 21.

32. Wilson P. Dizard, Jr., *The Coming Information Age: An Overview of Technology, Economics, and Politics* (New York: Longman, 1982).

33. Dizard.

9

Librarianship, Technology, and the Labor Process: Theoretical Perspectives

Michael F. Winter

TANGLED WEB: THE TECHNOLOGICAL NETWORK

Technology influences everything we do, and powerfully affects all aspects of work. Combining with social, economic, and cultural forces, it permeates all aspects of our daily lives. In its humbler periods it offered digging sticks, arrowheads, baskets, and simple plowing devices, and the knowledge required to make and use them; in modern times it ranges from printing, word processing, and database management to modern telecommunications, biotechnology, weapons, and transportation systems. In the information professions, we are increasingly involved with a wide range of technological developments in a variety of media and formats which are found throughout the society, although the major applications are in bibliography, documentation, and information retrieval. To use the convenient shorthand phrase coined by Patrick Wilson, our emphasis here is on technology designed for use in the "bibliographic sector."[1]

Librarians and other information workers increasingly spend much time keeping up with recent developments in this area, with the accent on making them usable in libraries and information centers. The need for this is certainly legitimate, but at the same time it has the unfortunate if unintended consequence of concealing a range of critical and theoretical issues, and the impact that these have on professional work. This chapter attempts to address some of these issues by reflecting on the larger significance of technology and its impact on librarianship. Its goal is to clarify and hopefully lead to a better understanding of some of the broader implications of working in libraries in our time. More narrowly, it focuses on librarianship as a form of organized work, showing evolving forms of task organization, and changing forms of control.

A few caveats are in order. Too often, "technology" is uncritically used to mean "computers" or "computerization." Obviously there is so much more to technology than computers that this is hardly worth noticing, were the confusion not so common. A related problem that we wish to avoid almost as much is the tendency to assume that the only technology worth mentioning is "high technology," or the technology of contemporary research and development. This is a little more subtle, and thus perhaps more damaging. Certainly it is tempting to reduce the whole field to its more visible contemporary forms, but this is hardly appropriate for a larger understanding of the issues.[2] But perhaps the most serious problem of this kind is the tendency to assume that technology "advances" in a simple unilinear fashion, with one device simply and effortlessly replacing its predecessor. Technological "progress," like the developmental patterns shown in the slow and uncertain growth of scientific thought, appears if anything to be more nearly in the form of overlapping spirals than straightforward linear progressions; and at times shows even a disconcertingly circular pattern as the old reappears alongside the new.

That these quite general points apply to libraries and information centers is clear enough to casual observation, and is in any case confirmed by recent discussions of the roles of technologies in libraries and in the history of scholarship.[3] We are surrounded, Walt Crawford argues, by "unnatural objects" that we use to help us accomplish various tasks, and in libraries we find a number of these: books, periodicals, microforms, audio and video tapes and discs, and of course all kinds of computer hardware and software, processing numbers, words, text, and images, and storing them in a variety of formats. All these are highly significant current forms of technology. The fact that some of them, such as books and journals, have ancient histories should not be allowed to obscure this fact. Further, "current" carries no necessary implication of "recent." While some technologies are both current and recent (videocassette, CD-ROM), some are current and ancient (books), and still others are fairly recent but obsolete (punched cards). Still others, which for obvious reasons would be impossible to name, are virtually obsolete even before they are available, since they never fully emerge from the research and development process.

Aside from this shifting and intermittent pattern of durability, the technological development of the bibliographic sector, like other areas of social and cultural change, reflects larger patterns of historical, socio-economic, demographic drift; these larger patterns seldom show anything

like a straightforward linear path. The now famous decline in the quality
of paper, which occurred in the early nineteenth century as paper manufacturing changed from cloth fiber to wood pulp, and which has caused so
many preservation problems in today's larger collections, was partly driven
by the need to find a manufacturing material economical enough for mass
production. The desire to tap a new market for printed materials, and the
need of those readers for more affordable items, simultaneously worked to
encourage the industrial innovation that led to a new product. Obviously,
"innovation" here led us in more than one direction; in a sense, it led us
backwards and forwards at the same time. A different example illustrates
the same point. One of the limitations of the computerization of printed
material is that the need for shareability and the demands of distribution
still link the machine-readable record to printers, one of several reasons
why the much-heralded revolution in electronic publishing is not mate-
rializing with any great speed. We like our printers, but as Crawford points
out, they can be "noisy, expensive, and low quality," and they remind us
that we are still highly dependent on the older technology of printing and
its associated system of hard-copy distribution.[4] Another reason, which
cannot be considered further here, is that publishers and other information producers with substantial capital invested in the technology of print
are very unlikely to abandon that investment until its returns begin to
diminish.[5]

The library and the librarian, then, are situated in a web of networks of
many different technological devices and systems, some quite venerable,
some middle-aged, some young, and some born only yesterday. Nowhere
do we see any simple pattern of development, with the newer always neatly
and efficiently replacing the older. What we see instead is a complex set
of overlapping and interwoven patterns, with some of the most ancient
technologies thriving side by side with the newest and performing with
equal or greater efficiency. For this reason it is not always easy to see how
technological developments have affected the work of librarians and other
bibliographic sector workers, but it forms our point of departure.

HIGH TECH, HIGH STRESS: SOME TYPICAL
APPROACHES TO TECHNOLOGY IN
LIBRARIANSHIP

But this is not the point of departure, apart from the examples already
cited, in much of the existing literature on technology. This literature
draws a considerably foreshortened picture of the network, with the most
current, high technology occupying most if not all of the picture. The

analytical impulse seems to have been eclipsed by the dazzle of the discovery of automation and microelectronics. To read these accounts, one would think that the technology of print, to say nothing of writing, had virtually disappeared, and that electronic access were our only problem. There is little sense of a complex overlap of technologies with which we began. History and social context seem to disappear, and are replaced by an exclusive emphasis on "techniques and technology."[6] The driving goals of much of this literature, it would seem, are to persuade and exalt rather than to understand or analyze.

Peter Hernon, in an emblematic example, focuses on the "exploitation" and "utilization" of machine-readable technology in handling government documents, with a clear accent on managerial approaches.[7] But also one finds an interest in mobilizing political sentiment in favor of computerization; here the rhetoric of advocacy heats up nicely.[8] These examples show a duality of focus that is very common in the literature. On the one hand, we are told that various technologies will help us to manage our work and do it better or more efficiently; on the other, we are stridently urged to adopt them, and even scolded for holding up progress. In these cases messianic zeal has perhaps gotten the better of us. Indeed, judging from its tone, the function of much of this literature seems to be expressive or emotional, providing an outlet for the awe, admiration, and the frustration that many feel when confronted with high rates of innovation. Perhaps these trends are responses to the high stress levels allegedly induced by living and working in a postindustrial society; in any case, they provide little in the way of basic analysis and description that would help us understand the consequences of technological change in our work.

OCCUPATIONAL ROLES AND ORGANIZATIONAL RESPONSES

Some library literature comes closer to our mark, and it gives us some useful directions. It is mainly concerned with the introduction of the newer information technologies and their impacts in two major areas. One of these is in the area of work roles; the other, in the area of the formal organization of the library.[9]

If there is an overriding concern, it is with the effects of innovation, which have two simultaneously occurring, and unfortunately rarely compatible tendencies. On the one hand, technological change has the potential to alter both work roles and organizational settings. For many obvious reasons—conservatism and high startup costs being only two of the more evident—this often leads to a rejection of innovation. Thus, we often use newer technologies to enable us to accomplish what we have already been doing all along, rather than significantly altering our work roles and our organizations to fit the innovations.[10] On the other hand, technological innovation, at least in libraries, tends to transfer routine and repetitive work to other workers or to providers outside the organization altogether (e.g., to a shared bibliographic utility which provides cataloging records or interlibrary loan services). This has the effect of taking away routine tasks and at the same time opening up the field for the assumption of many more. The simultaneous contraction and expansion of the field of work is, if it occurs quickly enough, exhilarating and liberating, but also very disconcerting, and it should not be surprising to find this phenomenon occasioning a good deal of ambivalence. We are often glad enough to get rid of the repetitious, but when we throw out the routine along with it, this can be quite a different matter, for we lose the cultural milieu that surrounded the routine.

All of this alerts us to a sense of malaise and its probable causes; but moving beyond requires another approach. I suggest that this is because the two areas of work roles and organizational settings are both rooted in, though not reducible to, a more fundamental notion—the notion of the labor process. Conceptually, the labor process is prior to the emergence of identifiable occupational groups, and prior to the organizations which form the typical settings where these occupations are found. Thus the labor process needs at times to be uncovered, or perhaps discovered, as a root phenomenon. At the same time it is of course true that the analysis of the labor process by no means explains everything. My point is rather that it provides an essential clarity about everything else, because it is fundamental.

TECHNOLOGY AND WORK: SOCIOLOGICAL PERSPECTIVES ON THE LABOR PROCESS

We look here to sociological literature in the same general spirit outlined in John Buschman and Michael Carbone's essay on the sociology of education.[11] The general idea revealed in this literature is that technological change, specialization, and innovation have the combined effect of altering the labor process in many ways, although the trend plays out very differently in different occupations, and, alternatively, in different sectors of the economy. In fact, its effects vary according to numerous other factors, which we cannot discuss in detail here. In some cases, this alteration redefines the tasks enough so that it makes more sense to reassign them to different groups of workers. But the alteration of the labor process has many different consequences, and thus part of the challenge is to understand how this has affected librarianship, historically and otherwise. The study of the labor process is rooted in classical political economy, and received its first and perhaps most elaborate formulation in Marx's first volume of *Capital*. Its more contemporary form issues largely from Harry Braverman's work in the 1970s, in which the Marxian theory is redefined for a later period of development.[12] Originally, the major concern was with the introduction and design of technology in industrial factories. Besides reducing the dependence of capital on labor in an immediate sense, the presence of "automation"—in this earlier use of the term—enhanced managerial control by permitting the breakdown of the labor process into increasingly smaller and finer components of production, transferring the knowledge—and to that extent, the control—of the production process as a whole from labor to management. Thus, what appears to be a politically neutral process of introducing new methods for increasing productivity is at the same time a definitive transfer of power.

The classical application of labor process theory is in the area of industrial and postindustrial production. The reason is that profitable markets give managerially dominated capital special incentives for exploiting and controlling certain types of labor more thoroughly than others, and the more potentially profitable the market, the more keen the incentive. (Thus, the value-added distribution of information products in commerce, industry, and more generally in research and development is particularly open to this kind of exploitation.) But it is also applicable with modification outside these areas, since labor process patterns found in the core sectors create a slow ripple effect across the occupational structure. This is partly because productivity standards developed in the profit sector are applied outside of it; but it is also in part because managers everywhere tend to adopt the culture of corporate life, and imitate its methods. In some professional fields, like law and medicine, the incentives to transform professional work are almost as significant as they are in manufacturing, and in these areas there are predictable advances in the corporate and technocratic invasion of work routines.[13] In others, like librarianship, potential profit margins are too low to attract aggressive colonization, but nonetheless librarians' work routines are inevitably affected by managerial decisions to use certain technologies. Thus labor process analysis suggests that the almost ceaseless activity of "technology transfer," or the continual introduction of new forms of technology into the workplace, has the cumulative effect of consolidating managerial control.

Professional or collegial control, on the other hand, does not disappear, any more than production workers in the older sectors of the economy totally lose control, but it tends to be confined to certain areas of work as the labor process as a whole falls under administrative jurisdiction. Decisions to adopt new technologies, and budgetary and long-range planning, for example, are generally administrative or managerial prerogatives, while issues of continuing education, choice of emphasis in professional development, peer review, and governance are more likely to be controlled by librarians. I emphasize this because it is easy to make the false assumption that professional control and a general increase in managerially engineered domination are incompatible; quite the opposite is true. Indeed, one powerful reason for management in the nonprofit sector to innovate is precisely because it serves as a useful check against the spread of professional authority in the organization.[14]

Technology, History, and the Labor Process

The historical record shows that librarianship has been altered in several major ways in response to important innovations, some of these occurring long before the industrial revolution. (See Table 1.) In each of these cases there is a clear alteration of the labor process in response to a basic innovation. In the later periods—roughly corresponding to the social changes brought about by the Industrial Revolution—this alteration is made much more complex by the accompanying effects of growing differentiation within the division of labor. There are a large number of these, but we concentrate here on shifting patterns of control over work, and on the appearance of administrative and managerial elites. Our purpose here is twofold. The first is to show that the work process of librarianship has been powerfully affected by prevailing technological forms of production, even though librarianship, as a service occupation, appears remote from anything resembling manufacturing and factory production. The second is to show that the effects of technology include, in more recent times, the ascendance of administrative elites who maintain and consolidate control over the labor process in libraries by judicious choice and implementation of technological innovations.

Emergence of Scribal Culture

The earliest technologies we refer to as "scribal," since they required substantial if not exclusive participation of key workers in the written production of the text. The technology of librarianship is, at this stage,

Table 1
Historical Period, Technology, and Labor Process

Period	Technology	Labor Process
Prehistoric	Oral	Recollective
Ancient & Medieval	Scribal	Productive
Modern	Print/Microform	Organizational
Contemporary	Telematic	Electronic Networking

merged with the technology of production, or with what would later be identified with printing and publishing.[15] This scribal period begins with the earliest collections of tablets in the ancient Near East, continues through the rise and fall of the great Mediterranean civilizations with their papyrus and vellum codex collections, and does not end until the late European Middle Ages, with the spread of movable-type printing.

As long as it was, however, it follows a much longer period in which oral culture dominated human life, and itself no doubt represents a major cultural transformation, and thus a revolutionary transformation of the labor process of those charged with the preservation of human records in the form of poems, songs, prayers, stories, myths, accounts of creation, arguments, and preliterate philosophical theorizing. Indeed, in ancient Greece the invention of writing was greeted by many with great skepticism and regarded as a threat to the crucial intellectual work of memory and speech. Anecdotal evidence for this can be found in the emphasis placed by the Greek poets and later by Socrates and other philosophers on oral discourse and their comparative neglect of writing, which became much more important in the Platonic and Aristotelian schools which followed them. But since it seems eccentric to refer to ancient singers of tales in preliterate societies or to sophists in newly literate ones as librarians—even though they must have performed some of the functions later assigned to that occupation—it is convenient to begin a historical overview with the technology of writing, copying, and the production and distribution of the handwritten book.[16]

The early keepers of tablets, scrolls, and manuscript books were often generalists, as we might expect from the relative simplicity of the technology they employed, and performed a variety of tasks now reserved for specialists. In addition to copyists they were also teachers, editors, critics, grammarians, translators, political advisers, priests, and even heads of state. One can see the dominance of writing in many if not all of these related roles, for it is natural that an expert working as a copyist might be called upon as a critic, a commentator, a grammarian, or an editor, especially since the standardization of language that we take for granted today existed only in an embryonic form. The political component is not quite as obvious, but if in modern times the ability to write often reflects social advantages, in the earlier parts of this period it is almost synonymous with political power. Since writing was largely confined to elites, and also because political and religious institutions were not sharply differentiated, scribes were often priests or government officials. The common thread uniting these diverse activities is the idea of authority, which is prominently associated with writing, written texts, and those who produced and had charge of them.[17]

The librarians of this period were of course also preoccupied with preservation, classification, and cataloging, but the labor-intensive character of book production, along with a high cost of materials, kept the sizes of most collections quite small. In the ancient world, several hundred tablets, scrolls, or codices qualified as a significant collection; and the largest libraries of the time would not be remarkable at all by more modern standards. At the same time, user populations were also small, and many knew their collections well enough to dispense with the organizational technology which is essential in larger libraries. In some ways the most purely scribal phase of this period of librarianship does not occur until the European Middle Ages, after the remnants of an ancient Greco-Roman book industry had more or less disappeared, placing an even greater burden on libraries and librarians in the process of text production. But while this is of considerable importance to the development of the occupation as a whole, it is not attributable to technological variation alone.

From Scribal Culture to Print Culture

It is of course the spread of movable-type printing that provides the next technological revolution, separating the librarians and the libraries of the late medieval period from modern times. With movable-type printing librarianship found itself poised on the edge of industrial mass production, and the attending "information explosion" of books, pamphlets, and periodical publications occasioned the first major crises of control.[18] As librarians lost their ancient affiliation with copying, block printing, and other laborious forms of book production—which later emerged as a cluster of new occupations, eventually spawning specialized spheres of printing, editing, and publishing—they profited from a new sense of urgency in the demand for their services. As their numbers increased along with the output of the burgeoning publishing industry, so also did their specialized expertise, and consequently their ability to control library collections, and thus to resist the influence of powerful patrons.

The early printed text was partly a work of art, and thus librarians of the early modern period had many of the functions of the modern-day museum curator. But as fine printing gave way to the mass-produced volumes of the industrial period, many librarians of necessity became less concerned with texts as physical objects and more concerned with the problems of library users. By the nineteenth century, problems of locating library materials, and the organizational concerns of classification, cataloging, and bibliography, at least for a time supplanted traditional problems of preservation. For this reason many of the great achievements in this area date from well after the invention of printing. Anthony Panizzi at the British Museum, Melvil Dewey at Columbia and other institutions, Herbert Ammi Cutter and other figures made monumental advances in classification, cataloging, indexing, and related areas, all aimed at improving access to materials for an increasingly numerous and socially diverse group of library users. As user populations and collections increased in size and complexity, new organizational needs called for more and better-educated librarians, and encouraged further specialization. Libraries as organizations became larger and more highly bureaucratized. Along with this, a greater sense of specialization and interdependence promoted cohesion among librarians. Collegial control began to emerge, along with an expanded network of professional expertise.

Toward the end of the nineteenth century, three of the more critical events in the development of collegial control in librarianship occurred; all were related to the technological revolution of movable-type printing. Each in its way emphasized a sense of belonging to the occupational group, and supported librarians' efforts to control their work routines and to secure their territory from outside encroachment. First, within librarianship numerous specialties appeared, eclipsing to a large degree the ancient ideal of the librarian as generalist. As the specialties developed, they became virtually autonomous occupational groups in their own right. Second, numerous national professional associations were established. Notable among these were the American Library Association, founded in 1876, and the Library Association of Great Britain, founded in 1877; the Canadian and German Library Associations followed in 1900. (Following these were many more specialized professional associations, providing more impetus for further specialization.) Third, it is impossible to overestimate the importance of the first professional schools in the formation of an intellectual spirit and the transmission of professional knowledge.

Eventually, the schools emerged from "general library education" and began to provide more specialized training in information science, documentation, preservation, and many other areas. In all these developments we see the trend of increasing specialization, following the original technological development.[19]

At the same time, however, and perhaps somewhat paradoxically, that professional control increased, managerial control over the labor process appeared in its first really systematic form. In scribal culture, there is a relatively simple domination of political, religious, and cultural elites; but in print culture, mass-production techniques permit such an extraordinary expansion of collection size and such a remarkable growth in the numbers of librarians required to deal with them that we find the first formation of administrative and managerial elites in the form of library administrators sharply differentiated from librarians. Along with the growth of publication output comes the modern form of librarianship as an occupation, which simultaneously shows high levels of collegial control and the formation of administrative elites whose function, increasingly, is to rationalize work by introducing innovations developed largely elsewhere.

FROM PRINT TO AUTOMATION AND TELECOMMUNICATIONS: EMERGENCE OF TELEMATICS

When we speak of "professionalism" as a type of collegial control over work routines, we often assume a kind of timeless present in which "professionalism" has always existed. Of course the kinds of occupations which are presently professionally or collegially controlled have, in many cases, been with us for centuries, but they have undergone frequent alterations in history, and their autonomy, as it is today, may be dated from relatively recent times.[20] Thus, even though medicine, law, the clergy, and librarianship have all existed in one form or another since ancient times, their contemporary collegial forms, and their freedom from client control, are in large part products of the Industrial Revolution. In the case of librarianship this is clearly shown in the emblematic importance of intellectual freedom and the circulation of ideas, both traditions clearly rooted in the liberal tradition of early industrial society and the political culture of print technology.[21]

Aside from politics and ideology, professional schools, associations, and collegially organized workplaces continue to support the autonomy and control over work grounded in the development of modern professional groups in the industrial period. At the same time, complete autonomy has for some time been checked by the administrative authority found in bureaucratized organizations. This begins, as we mentioned above, in the industrial period, and continues to gather speed in the age of high technology. More recently, the older liberal political influences have been challenged by the application of new technologies, and by the cumulative effects of increasingly complex work organizations. The key development here is the alliance of the computer with telecommunications. The expansion of automation and the contemporary combination of automation with telecommunications technology—dubbed "telematics" by French commentators—have threatened these to some extent. At the same time, telematics, by promoting a more open and potentially expanded information environment, provides many new opportunities for professional work.[22]

There are several factors at work here. One is that automation and telecommunications, first separately and later when combined as telematics, bring new clusters of occupations into the picture. New technical specialists abound, from software and hardware consultants to specialists in computer graphics and computer-aided statistical analysis. Sometimes these duties and roles are performed by librarians, but just as often these workers are recruited externally. As a result the labor process of librarianship, even for librarians who are traditionally trained, shows a shift to mastering electronic networks and interconnected databases of various kinds, along with a corresponding deemphasis on traditional bibliographic classification and control. A second factor is that telematics inevitably brings new managerial orientations, often shifting resources away from traditional areas of librarianship into high technology.

Telematics also permits a greater economy of scale in the sharing of resources, giving rise to extensive interconnected networks of library materials and expertise, which in turn permit expanded delivery of information services. Along with this comes a new administrative elite in libraries. Cosmopolitan, oriented toward national and international networking trends, and frequently remote from professional concerns and routine organizational problems, these elites are often openly allied with outside interests, such as legislative bodies, foundations, boards of trustees, and other administrative networks. Not surprisingly, contemporary library administrators often lean toward the elite corporate culture that controls telematic technology than to the technology of print, but they are also allied with publishing. Nonetheless, librarians find themselves more directly enmeshed in the technological network, with its often chaotic mix of the old and the new, and thus are not free to disengage in this fashion.

Somewhat more remotely, corporate capital's domination of the information industry threatens the autonomy of publishing, and along with the rise of a materialistic marketing ethos, exercises a chilling effect on the spirit of inquiry that has flourished in intellectual communities for centuries.[23] The effect on librarians is indirect, but real. If libraries continue to be largely parasitic on the publishing industry, corporate control of the latter sphere will have an inevitably limiting effect on the work of librarians, and perhaps on their overall professional vision. The reason for this is that librarians and libraries are now part of a much wider distribution network of information products, and for the most part are not involved in production. Unless librarians can make major shifts in collection practices, and turn away from mainstream publishing, they will be limited by what that industry is willing to produce. But there is a silver lining to this cloud: the appeal of libraries as new markets is limited by relatively low profit margins in both publishing and the library as a distribution network. (Far more promising from this profit-maximizing point of view are the expansion of cablecasting, narrowcasting, and the growth of interactive video systems, and thus it is reasonable to suppose that the most active incursions of big capital will be made in these areas instead.)

Many of the above are limitations, but there are opportunities in sight as well as trials. Many of these represent major transformations of the dominant labor processes of earlier periods. (See Table 1.) Indeed, as we mentioned earlier, the high stress levels we experience in information work issue not only from these limitations, but also from the proliferation of new areas of work that inevitably accompanies rapid technological change. For example, the cumulative effect of combining scribal, print, and telematic technologies in contemporary libraries means that librarians in the late twentieth century face many more formats than ever before, and frequently face them simultaneously. This requires a fascinating but often chaotic combination of skills from manuscript librarianship, descriptive bibliography, classification, and cataloging based on nineteenth- and early twentieth-century controlled vocabularies, and contemporary distributed database networks dominated by uncontrolled vocabularies.[24] In addition, librarians in larger libraries and library networks today need to deal with mainstream publishing, a prolific population of microforms, ephemera, a large output in small press items and government publications, and computerized files of many kinds. And the librarian of today is expected to master applications of automation which are unrelated to traditional bibliographic issues; these include word processing, data collection and analysis, database management, telecommunications processes, and desktop publishing.

DESKILLING, RESKILLING, AND THE
TECHNOLOGICAL TRANSFORMATION OF WORK

So far we have focused on the role of major technological innovations in altering the labor process, and on the fact that new technologies affect patterns of control within occupations. (Not major themes here, but clearly of enough importance to merit separate treatment, are the mediating influences of bureaucracy and organizational structure, which qualify but do not supplant the combined influence of professional groups and administrative elites.) But there is obviously an as yet unaddressed concern here, and that is how new technologies affect typical skill levels. (As with the questions of control, the roots lie in core industrial labor, but it has been extended to services and professions as well.) Since this is a widespread concern, we offer here an assessment.

Although there is no doubt that innovation does reduce skill requirements for many jobs—causing what is often referred to as "deskilling"—there are also cases in which the opposite is true, and areas in which there is little or no significant change. Thus, "deskilling" is somewhat misleading if applied across the board; but there is no convenient phrase simultaneously expressing all the possibilities. In librarianship, one can find examples of downward movement, but these are often accompanied by an at least partly compensating upward movement: "deskilling," in other words, is often followed by "reskilling." Indeed, this pattern of cyclical movement, as opposed to a simple net decline, may be one of the marks differentiating professional and managerial labor from working class occupations, where there have been long-term declines in skill requirements.

Again, although Marx was originally the champion of the view that capital seeks not only to eliminate human labor through technological innovation, but also wherever possible to lower the skill levels of remaining workers, Braverman took the analysis a good deal further and argued that the twentieth century had witnessed a systematic "degradation" of work.[25] Most sociologists steer clear of Braverman's moral and political agenda, but nonetheless have pursued a more neutral version of the same point by analyzing occupations in terms of long-term declines in skill levels.[26] While much of the analysis focuses on traditional working class occupations, some writers have specifically addressed the issue of deskilling in professional work, and it is this aspect that most affects us here.[27]

None of these writers has, however, looked at librarianship in any systematic way, and so there are few research findings to guide us. But there are hints that enable us to draw a sketch if not a finished picture of the situation. This picture, necessarily incomplete though it is, supports the cyclical "deskilling/reskilling" thesis much more than it provides any overall evidence for wholesale decline of skill levels. In the material that follows here we focus on some standard areas of librarianship which indicate that in the core areas of the field some deskilling has been followed by significant reskilling. (Although our focus is on professional workers, the situation of the paraprofessional, where very substantial upgrading of skill levels has occurred, seems even more clearly to follow this pattern.)

Technical Services

Technical services (usually including but not always limited to cataloging, acquisitions, and circulation) is a cluster of functional specialties which most closely follows the "production" or classic industrial model of labor process analysis. In these fields the use of large batch-process database management systems has dramatically lowered professional-to-support staff ratios, and transfers much traditional work from the professional to the paraprofessional or clerical worker. These trends are perhaps clearest in cataloging. Michael Gorman, for example, estimates that as much as eighty percent of output can in many large libraries be derived as copy from external utilities.[28] But although this means that it is no longer necessary for catalogers to produce this copy for large stretches of output, it does not necessarily spell deskilling, since there is more time for analysis of a wide range of marginal and highly specialized formats that earlier generations were unable to address. This holds for other technical services librarians as well. Also, if these professionals are present in fewer numbers, the ones remaining have much more supervisory responsibility than previously, since they are now free to coordinate paraprofessionals.[29] Finally, and perhaps most importantly, this shifting nature of the labor process in these areas permits them to pursue solutions to problems in the development, design, and critique of information systems.

Collection Development. At first glance collection development and management might seem to be completely different, but this is only partly true. The reason for this is that the same advances in batch-process information management that permit the development of bibliographic utilities for cataloging records are readily applied to the creation of acquisitions databases. Once these subsystems are established, the work of many different types of ordering plans, while technically possible without automation, are so much less labor intensive that they no longer require as much professional expertise. For bibliographers, this routinizes the selection of much mainstream material, and transfers much of what used to lie at the core of selection to a semiautomatic process. At the same time, the expanding network of cataloging databases provides verification tools that are highly accessible to paraprofessional and clerical workers.

All this leaves the selector free to enter many hitherto largely inaccessible areas: marginalia, grey literature, ephemera, preservation, and other areas previously reserved for special collections librarians. It also frees the bibliographer to become more involved in the subject area, to pursue collection evaluation, refine core lists, checklists, and other bibliographies, and to become more "user group" oriented, and thus to assume greater responsibility for a larger range of functions. Far from presaging deskilling, this cluster of changes in the labor process of the bibliographer has rather the effect of suggesting the bypassing of traditional functional specializations.[30]

Public Services

In public services the uses of skill and the delivery of service are centered in the crucial, typically face-to-face relationship between the provider and the client. Of course, there is an indirect sense in which this is true even in the "backstage" operations of technical services, but it is in reference and instruction that the contact achieves its most direct and its most visible "frontstage" form.[31] Nonetheless, paraprofessionals engage increasingly in face-to-face contact with library users, conduct interviews, answer reference questions, and provide point-of-use instruction. To this extent they occupy ground formerly held by librarians. But these developments are far from reflecting any decline in librarians' levels of skill and expertise, because there are so many new demands for higher levels of public services contact on the part of professionals whose attention is increasingly drawn into the use and understanding of new databases, new approaches to the storage and retrieval of information, and the appearance of automated networks linking systems of retrieval that were previously unconnected.

There are a number of examples that could be produced to illustrate this trend, but the one that comes most readily to mind is the area of online searching. Brian Nielsen, in an analysis that directly addresses this issue, argues that online searching leads to increased complexity of interaction with users, promotes subject specialization, delineates machine-readable reference work from paraprofessional service, and gives the librarian increased control over the interaction with the user.[32] The fact that the focus of Nielsen's analysis is on the early phase of (highly mediated) online service is not as problematic as it may at first seem to those who would argue that the author's thesis would have to be highly modified in the compact disk era. There is some truth to this, but it seems obvious, now that we are well into the age of "user friendly systems," that these call for a different range of new skills from librarians. If there is a shift here, it is not from a greater to a lesser level of skill on the part of librarians; it lies rather in the emergence of a new type of advisory role, where the librarian assumes the role of a kind of troubleshooting informational consultant, giving the user a sense of the larger patterns in the overlap and confusion of the sources. Thus, when the user becomes temporarily overcome or dazzled by the proliferation of formats and the variety of catalogs, bibliographies, indexes, and databases that many libraries today contain, the librarian can clarify goals, suggest strategy, assess progress, spot dead ends, recommend alternative paths, and in general work from a map far too large for the average user to be able to read unassisted.

CONCLUSION: SUMMARY AND POINTS OF DEPARTURE

Since we have come some distance in this analysis, and have perhaps taken a few unfamiliar turns, a summary and concluding statement may be useful. We began by arguing that in order to understand the importance of technology for librarians it is necessary to recognize its broader social context. This helps avoid some common errors, which we may conveniently group here as reductionism and oversimplification: technology is not reducible to any one of its more visible or fashionable forms, and specific technologies develop within the complex matrix of history and culture, which makes it difficult and at times impossible to judge their continuing influence, or indeed even to tell them apart. The lamb of the old lies down in disconcerting ease with the lion of the new. We suggested that technological development, like the development of scientific thought, does not proceed in any clearly unilinear or progressive fashion, but shows instead an uneven and irregular pattern of diffusion—it is, perhaps, less like a ladder with its clear succession of rungs leading the climber from lower to higher levels, and more like a complex overlapping, ingrown, and sparsely marked tangle of paths. Librarians and library users thus face a confusing tangle of technologies.

Understandably, this generates a certain amount of wonder and stress, and we find these reactions common in the professional literature. And while it makes sense to look at technology in terms of its practical impact on what services librarians can provide, and to look as well on the impact it has on the work roles of librarians and libraries, we have argued here that the analysis needs a more fundamental ground than either of these can provide, if the discussion is to move beyond these initial responses to the insecurity engendered by an environment of almost ceaseless technological innovation. This fundamental ground is found in the root relationship between technological change and the labor process. When we do this we discover that some of the confusion of technologies, organizations, and work can reduced by looking at the gradual development, over long historical periods, of basic style of work in librarianship as responses to the sea changes of social life that are triggered by major technological innovations. Thus in the drift from one dominant technological form to another, a process in which everything seems to be at least partly preserved, and nothing completely lost, we find a clue to understanding changes in the labor process of librarianship.

We also argue that although librarianship has undergone some very visible and dramatic changes, particularly in response to the introduction of printing, automation, and somewhat later at the telecommunications stage, it tolerates labor process change without wholesale or uniform deterioration of skill levels. This is probably because in librarianship the evolution of the labor process shows a drift away from the details of production, where the emphasis is on easily identifiable elements of physical labor, toward a more intangible, and to that extent analysis-resistant, range of cognitive and intellectual skills. It is, in other words, relatively easy to divide, subdivide, and thus rationally organize and control productive labor, much of which has shifted to nonprofessional workers in libraries, but much more difficult and in many cases impossible to do this where the main tasks are those of understanding, interpretation, research, evaluation, communication, and the application of abstract principles.

In terms of the ratio of professional to nonprofessional workers in libraries, librarianship's numbers may be declining, especially in technical services, but the overall impact seems if anything an upgrading rather than any downgrading of required skills. Indeed, it appears to flourish in an environment which is highly mixed from a technological point of view, and generally shows an ability to use technological developments to consolidate control over collections, work routines, ethical issues, and service policies, and maintains control in basic areas of governance.

At the same time, library administrators have acquired a collective identity and a reference group that is largely outside the library and to a considerable extent outside librarianship, reflecting the fact that automation, telematic technology, and other recent developments originate largely in the research and development circles of big government and big business. Library administrators, in other words, are perhaps less involved in the day-to-day control of libraries as organizations, having ceded these routine tasks to deputy and assistant directors or to management teams, but by virtue of their relationship to the developers of new technologies and others outside of libraries, they exert considerable general influence over libraries as organizations through budgeting, general planning, and the decision to adopt and implement new technologies.

The present situation is always the hardest to grasp. If we look at the clues presented here, however, there does appear, despite the proliferation and accumulation of technologies, a common pattern that at least partly unites the different things that librarians do in the era of the electronic network. If the librarians of the past concentrated on the representation of knowledge through recollection and recitation, or on the production and preservation of texts through writing, or again on the bibliographic organization of the masses of printed texts that began to overwhelm us in the early modern period, then the librarian of today is in a way an unconscious synthesis of all of these. Of course, not every librarian equally embodies this synthesis, but it lies beneath the many specializations, and at the same time provides both the foundation for referral outside one's specialty and the general framework of value underlying the work.

Survivals abound. The present-day children's librarian, for example, and the librarian who specializes in folklore, or deals in popular culture or multimedia, recall and to some extent preserve some of the traces of the earliest period. (Indeed, this is even true for librarians active in such seemingly disparate fields as musicology, ethnology, and oral history.) Manuscript librarians, archivists, and specialists of the handwritten and block-printed book, some of which are produced by contemporary small presses in literature and the arts, continue in the scribal tradition, as do those scholars and bibliographers who work with what historians call "primary sources." And all librarians, irrespective of their contemporary specialty of format, subject, user group, or library type, cannot escape participating in the culture of print—a culture dominated by rational discourse, evidence, and the ideals of persuasion with its emphasis on scientific bibliography, controlled vocabularies, and systematic, hierarchical classification systems.

And yet most librarians today are doing something different, something that has not been done before, and thus are not merely the sum of these historical parts. What precisely is this? Here we return to the imagery of the consultant, the adviser, and the map reader; and we emphasize as well an element of synthetic intellectual vision. The distinctively contemporary aspect of librarians' work has to do with a cluster of skills, values, and habits of mind that are rooted in the act of finding meaning through imaginative interpretation: of formats, of tools and sources, of user groups, of bodies of literature, of partly overlapping subjects and topics of concern, of provenance, and most of all, of the paths of acquisition, access, control, and application that form the networks of contemporary information products and services. In this contemporary version of librarianship's labor process, the earlier components recede somewhat in favor of an ability to serve as a kind of cognitive cartographer of emerging worlds of knowledge. Naturally some librarians will be better at drawing the maps, and some more adept at reading them or explaining them to the user, and in this there is something approaching a natural division of labor. This turn toward the interpretive in the labor process of librarianship is of course substantially rooted in the highly pluralistic, mixed-format environment of a contemporary library, with its locally distributed, decentralized, and enduser-accessible information technologies, none of which can be understood and applied without considerable reflective intellectual effort.

NOTES

1. Patrick Wilson, "Bibliographical R & D," *The Study of Information: Interdisciplinary Messages*, eds. Fritz Machlup and Una Mansfield (New York: Wiley, 1983) 389–97. The term "information sector," which comes to mind along with Wilson's "bibliographic sector," is too broad—it includes timekeeping, calculating, early telecommunications devices, and other technologies of information transmission that lie outside librarianship. For a sense of the breadth of the range, see Herbert Ohlman, "Information: Timekeeping, Computing, Telecommunications, and Audiovisual Technologies," *Encyclopaedia of the History of Technology* (London and New York: Routledge, 1990) 686 ff.

2. Buckland effectively avoids these common traps as follows: "Information technology . . . is commonly used to denote electronic computing and communications technology. However, we define information technology as any technology used in handling information. There seems no logical basis for defining it otherwise. Information technology thus includes pen, paper, card, microfilm, and any other nonelectronic as well as information technologies." Michael Buckland, *Information and Information Systems* (New York: Praeger, 1991) 69.

3. Walt Crawford, *Current Technologies in the Library: An Informal Overview* (Boston: G. K. Hall, 1988). In what follows I rely on material previously published in my review of this volume in *Library Acquisitions: Practice and Theory* 13 (1989): 458–59. For more detailed historical evidence, see Michael Stuart Freeman, "Pen, Ink, Keys, and Cards: Some Reflections on Library Technology," *College and Research Libraries* 52.4 (July 1991): 328–35. See also Michael Buckland, "Library Materials: Paper, Microform, Database," *College and Research Libraries* 49 (1988): 117–22. And for an ambitious and successful attempt to cover the history of scholarship and do justice to widely differing technologies of information recording and retrieval, see Tom Macarthur's *Worlds of Reference* (New York: Cambridge University Press, 1986).

4. Crawford 17.

5. This and other points addressing this question can be found in Scott Bennett, "Current Initiatives and Issues in Collection Management," *Journal of Academic Librarianship* 10.5 (November 1984): 257–61.

6. Buckland, *Information* xiii, 181 ff.

7. Peter Hernon, ed., *New Technology and Documents Librarianship* (Westport, CT: Meckler, 1983) xii–xiii. A similar approach, covering a general range of library applications and relying on a large body of similar literature, can be found in Lawrence Woods, *The Librarian's Guide to Microcomputer Technology and Applications* (White Plains, NY: Knowledge Industry Publications, 1983).

8. Bruce Morton, "Attitudes, Resources, and Applications: The Government Documents Librarian and Computer Technology," *New Technology and Documents Librarianship*, ed. Peter Hernon (Westport, CT: Meckler, 1983) 44. Many examples favor special library settings, but some attempt more general conclusions; see, for example, Rodrigo Magalhaes, "The Impact of the Micro-Electronics Revolution in Library and Information Work: An Analysis of Future Trends," *Unesco Journal of Information Science, Librarianship, and Archives Administration* 5.1 (January-March 1983): 2–11.

9. See, for example, W. A. J. Marsterson, *Information Technology and the Role of the Librarian* (London: Croom Helm, 1986); and Basil Stuart-Stubbs, ed., *Changing Technology and Education for Librarianship and Information Science* (Greenwich, CT: JAI Press, 1985). The first of these two provides numerous examples of literature that falls into one or both of these major areas. For an analysis that touches on both points and at the same time urges major reorganization, at least for academic and research libraries, see Michael Gorman, "The Ecumenical Library," *The Reference Librarian* 9 (Fall/Winter 1983): 55–64; and, by the same author, "The Organization of Academic Libraries in the Light of Automation," *Advances in Library Automation and Networking* 1 (1987): 151–68.

10. Marsterson 50–51.

11. John Buschman and Michael Carbone, "A Critical Inquiry into Librarianship: Applications of the 'New Sociology of Education,' " *Library Quarterly* 61.1 (1991): 15–40.

12. For historical background, see Andrew Feenberg, *Critical Theory of Technology* (New York: Oxford University Press, 1991) 16, 25–30; and for a general overview and critique of Braverman and other more recent formulations, see Stephen Barley, "Technology, Power, and the Social Organization of Work," *Research in the Sociology of Organizations* 6 (1988): 33–80.

13. For a study of medicine in this light, see Paul Starr, *The Social Transformation of American Medicine* (New York: Basic Books, 1982).

14. On the development and nature of occupational control in the professions generally and in librarianship, see the present writer's *The Culture and Control of Expertise: Toward a Sociological Understanding of Librarianship* (Westport, CT: Greenwood Press, 1988) 12, 13 ff, where I argue there that the same general relationship holds between professional authority and bureaucratic domination.

15. Texts were acquired by means other than copying, trade and war spoils providing two of the more common means. Also, strictly speaking, this statement about printing and publishing is an exaggeration, since in republican Rome there was a commercial book trade and publishing establishment, even if somewhat haphazardly organized until Caesarean times. But by the early medieval period, or the end of the Latin West, this had largely disappeared, as book production and circulation fell into religious hands. See L.

D. Reynolds and N. G. Wilson, *Scribes and Scholars: A Guide to the Transmission of Greek and Latin Texts*, 3rd ed. (New York: Oxford University Press, 1991) 2–3, 23–24 ff.

16. For material on the earliest period, see H. Curtis Wright, *The Oral Antecedents of Greek Librarianship* (Provo, UT: Brigham Young University Press, 1977). In our essentially Western or Mediterranean sequence, the dominance of oral civilization is long in the past. Nonetheless, as ethnohistorians have shown, the analysis and understanding of oral culture is crucial for understanding many more contemporary preliterature societies. See, for example, Jan Vansina, *The Oral Tradition: A Study in Methodology* (Chicago: Aldine, 1961).

17. For general background, see Jack Goody, *Literacy in Traditional Societies* (Cambridge, UK: Cambridge University Press, 1978); and, by the same author, *The Logic of Writing and the Organization of Society* (Cambridge, UK: Cambridge University Press, 1986) 63, 65, 83 ff, 116–17. A useful review of the scholarly debate on the impact of literacy on ancient society can be found in William V. Harris, *Ancient Literacy* (Cambridge, MA: Harvard University Press, 1989) 40 ff.

18. The importance of the "culture of print," as a French historian puts it, is by no means restricted to these examples from publishing, but also includes many applications bringing print into the lives of even the marginally literate—mass-produced signs are only the most obvious example—beginning in the eighteenth and nineteenth centuries. Roger Chartier, ed., *The Culture of Print: Power and the Uses of Print in Early Modern Europe*, trans. Lydia G. Cochrane (Princeton, NJ: Princeton University Press, 1989).

19. In the United States, formal education originated at Columbia College in 1887; others quickly followed. Formal training for librarians appeared at about the same time in Germany, Italy, and Sweden. (France, though strong in archives administration, did not follow this trend until 1932, when librarianship was added to the curriculum of the Ecole des Chartes.) Information science curricula were not incorporated into library schools until the period between the two World Wars, partly in response to the development of microform technology and the beginnings of automation.

20. Even occupations which today enjoy considerable freedom from external influence were once strictly controlled by powerful patrons. See A. M. and P. M. Wilson, *The Professions* (1933; London: Cass, 1964), and Terence Johnson, *Professions and Power* (London: Macmillan, 1977).

21. The connection between the technology of printing and the ideology of intellectual freedom in its various forms is made by Ithiel da Sola Pool, *Technologies of Freedom* (Cambridge, MA: Harvard University Press, 1983). We cannot reproduce the subtlety of the argument here, but note in passing that the technology of telecommunications, in contrast, is much more highly regulated than the technology of print.

22. The term "telematics" is a translation of the neologism "telematique," coined by Simon Nora and Alain Minc in *The Computerization of Society* (Cambridge, MA: MIT Press, 1980).

23. For a general discussion of publishing's transformation from the sphere of the cultivated gentleman to the sphere of big corporate capital, see, for example, Lewis Coser, Charles Kadushin, and Walter Powell, *Books: The Culture and Commerce of Publishing* (New York: Basic Books, 1982).

24. Not all automated databases fit this pattern, but there is a trend in this direction. See, for example, R. R. Larson, "The Decline of Subject Searching: Long-Term Trends and Patterns of Index Use in an Online Catalog," *Journal of the American Society for*

Information Science 42 (1991): 197–215. For a modified view which reviews several relevant studies, see M. Marlene Martin, "Subject Indexing in the New Ethnographic Bibliography of North America," *Behavioral and Social Sciences Librarian* 11.1 (1991): 13–26.

25. Harry Braverman, *Labor and Monopoly Capital: The Degradation of Work in the Twentieth Century* (New York: Monthly Review Press, 1974). For examples of literature which appeared in response to Braverman, see Michael Burawoy, *Manufacturing Consent: Changes in the Labor Process under Monopoly Capitalism* (Chicago: University of Chicago Press, 1979); and Dan Clawson, *Bureaucracy and the Labor Process: The Transformation of U.S. Industry, 1860–1920* (New York: Monthly Review Press, 1980).

26. Paul Attewell, "The Deskilling Controversy," *Work and Occupations* 14.3 (August 1987): 323–46; Barley 33–80; and Kenneth I. Spenner, "Deciphering Prometheus: Temporal Change in the Skill Level of Work," *American Sociological Review* 48 (December 1983): 824–37.

27. Marie Haug, "Deprofessionalization: An Alternative Hypothesis for the Future," *Professionalization and Social Change*, ed. Paul Halmos (Keele, UK: Keele University Press, 1973) 195–212; by the same author, "The Deprofessionalization of Everyone?" *Sociological Focus* 8 (August 1975): 197–213; Nina Toren, "Deprofessionalization and its Sources: Preliminary Analysis," *Sociology of Work and Occupations* 2 (November 1975): 323–37.

28. Gorman, "Ecumenical" 55–64. Gorman also points out, however, that this average figure conceals great variation from field to field. For example, in certain area studies fields, like Latin American studies, the amount of available copy is rather low, while in the English language literatures of the natural sciences, it approaches 100 percent. See Gorman, "Organization" 165. From this we conclude that not all areas are uniformly affected.

29. For empirical evidence, see Ruth Hafter, *Academic Librarians and Cataloging Networks* (Westport, CT: Greenwood Press, 1985).

30. Thus, the partial eclipse of the library as a functionally differentiated organization, and the increasing importance of "user group," "subject," and so on. Gorman, "Ecumenical" 55–64.

31. This distinction is based on the comparison of work as a form of social activity to a dramatic production, a favorite theme of role theorists such as Erving Goffman. See, for example, *The Presentation of Self in Everyday Life* (Garden City, NY: Doubleday, 1959), and other works by the same author.

32. Brian Neilsen, "Online Searching and the Deprofessionalization of Librarianship," *Online Review* 4 (September 1980): 213–23. The summarizing language is from Winter, *Culture* 52.

10

The Politics of Electronic Information: A Reassessment

John Haar

An electronic revolution is altering the ways librarians and patrons find, use, store, and even think about information. The revolution alarms and bewilders us because it often demands that we confront complex and confusing questions for which we feel ill-prepared: which sources do we buy? how do we pay for them? how do we make them accessible to patrons? We can also discern that it will require an overhaul of long-established and comfortably familiar systems designed for selecting, acquiring, cataloging, and circulating print materials. Yet however unsettling the changes, we can readily embrace the revolution's rich promise: the provision of more information to more people than ever before.

Our efforts to cultivate the electronic revolution's potential benefits should occasion reexamining fundamental concepts of information, such as what it is and to whom it belongs. It is argued in some quarters that information is but an economic commodity, a product whose value rises and falls in tune with marketplace rhythms. While few would deny that information has an economic value, libraries have traditionally recognized that it also possesses an integral social and political value that makes it far more than an ordinary article of commerce.

The extent to which the promise of electronic resources will be realized is directly dependent upon how we as a society choose to treat the information they supply. If we regard information holistically as a commodity of broad economic, social, and political dimensions, we increase the likelihood that new information tools will radically enhance access for everyone. Should we treat information solely as an economic item, we promote the power of electronics to control, restrict, and limit access, helping to assure that the promise is denied.

Questions of access are vital to libraries; access is our primary function. We act as intermediaries between producers of information, whose interests are often (as in the case of "trade" publishers) narrowly economic, and consumers of information, whose interests are ordinarily of a broader social or educational character. Our success in performing our primary function is contingent upon our ability to satisfy both the entrepreneurial demands of those from whom we acquire information and the needs of our users to obtain information with as few impediments as possible. If many—though by no means all—information producers are self-interested, that is, profit-oriented, then libraries can be said to represent the public interest. The public interest in this case means free and open access to information in all its forms, such access being vital to any democratic society. Because information is power, unequal access implies a fundamental inequality of opportunity and a consequent diminishing of democratic values. Optimally, libraries act to equalize access and opportunity.[1]

As intermediaries, however, our ability to serve the public interest is compromised by our relationship with self-interested information producers. The terms of our transactions with producers govern in large measure the terms of our transactions with our users. If we consider a source prohibitively expensive, we deny it to our patrons or provide it on a cost-per-use basis. Copyright law may prevent us from sharing other libraries' resources free of charge. Producer-imposed user fees can cause us to restrict entry to an online database only to users within our immediate library community.

Attempting to balance the conflicting interests of information producers and users has always been a part of our mission, but the proliferation of electronic resources promises to test our ability to contend with these opposing forces as never before. Products now on the market have already enabled us to expand our patrons' range of information choices exponentially. Yet they also give us fair warning that our latitude in controlling and disseminating the information we purchase is steadily contracting.

ONLINE SEARCHING: BENEFITS AND PROBLEMS

Both the benefits and detriments of electronic information sources became—or should have become—apparent as libraries widely employed online search services in the 1970s.[2] Accustomed to one-dimensional indexing and abstracting tools, we were taken with the ease and relative precision of searching remote electronic databases. Properly used, online searching empowered us to introduce patrons to resources previously beyond their reach and to produce packets of data, such as bibliographies, more carefully crafted to their needs than ever before.

Though our appreciation of the utility of online searching was well-placed, we were less cognizant and more tolerant of its attendant problems than our patrons' best interests required. Where we ordinarily bought print data at a fixed cost and retained ownership, for online services we acquiesced in a cost-per-use lease arrangement. We owned nothing and paid each time we accessed the database, even if we had accessed identical information earlier.

Worst of all, the services' price structures inextricably bound our costs to an elastic patron demand for searches. Fearful that we could not afford such an unpredictable and uncontrolled expense, we passed our costs on to our users. This stratagem relieved pressure on our budgets and helped regulate demand. It also caused us to become unwitting proponents of an illogic afflicting modern information delivery, wherein denying access has become our preferred method of providing access. We perceive that we can afford to make a service available only if we ration it by imposing user fees. With one hand we offer patrons remarkable advances in information technology; with the other we restrict their access to the technology and the information by compelling them to pay. Thus is illustrated the paradox of electronic information sources: they can simultaneously broaden and constrict access. This dualism is implicit not in their nature, but in the uses we choose to make of them.

Even at the outset, it was evident that online searching, however phenomenal a development in itself, was but the leading edge of a much more comprehensive new information order. It quickly became clear that this new order promised—some would say threatened—to transform libraries totally. In the early 1990s that transformation is well under way. CD-ROM has already replaced online searching as patrons' favorite gateway to electronic databases; more popular yet are data tapes mounted on online catalogs. Librarians communicate to our users and each other through electronic mail, and we dial into library catalogs worldwide and an array of other remote databases on the Internet. We use electronic list servers to discuss how we expect to acquire and distribute electronic journals.

We have become familiar with, if not yet accustomed to, both change itself and the ever-accelerating pace of change. We see the need to acquire, in the near future, technologies such as hypertext and file transfer protocol to link our users to more powerful local and distant information sources. Further away, but probably not as far as we think, are high-speed fiber optic networks (such as the National Research and

Education Network, NREN). Whether systems mavens or computer illiterates, we all know that much more of the revolution is ahead of us than behind us.

INFORMATION DISTRIBUTION AND COPYRIGHT

As electronic services grow in number and diversity, they confirm our confidence in the information future. They permit us and our users to manipulate masses of data with a speed and rigor previously unattainable. They enable us to vastly increase the number of information sources we can offer patrons. They have already begun to disseminate widely sources once restricted by geography to a relative few. And, not least important, they have amply demonstrated their ability to resolve some of the vexing economic and political problems that characterized online searching.

CD-ROMs in particular have permitted us to purchase as a package data formerly accessible only in separately priced segments. Because most are designed for end-user searching, they lessen the need for labor-intensive mediation by librarians. In short, they make it possible for us to control both our costs and patron demand on staff resources, eliminating the perceived necessity to impose searching fees.

Where online searching conjured up images of powerful databases existing in their entirety in but one locale and under the exclusive aegis of possibly irresponsible corporate owners, the electronic tools in use today impress with their potential to distribute information so universally that for-profit owners fear a loss of control. The affordability of personal computers and the ease of downloading data to portable diskettes liberate information users and threaten information producers. Data sets, both literary and numeric, once previously impractical to photocopy because of their size or format, can now be digitized and recopied (with or without permission) on an almost unlimited basis.

To be sure, there remains a dangerous trend toward concentration of information ownership, and the migration of information from print to digital format is still worrisome in that it offers all too many opportunities for the ill-informed or malicious manipulation of data. Yet the unprecedented capacity of computers to store, transmit, and copy serves as a considerable mitigating influence upon efforts to create and enforce information monopolies. Concern that the technologies of duplication and redistribution surpass, at this point, the technologies of control is probably a prime reason that most commercial publishers are reluctant to venture into electronic publishing.[3] Secure that their property rights are well protected by the relative inelasticity of print, they are understandably wary of fostering a medium that could jeopardize the source of their profitability.

Copyright law, which has served publishers so effectively when applied to print sources, is much less likely to safeguard their interests in the electronic era. If unauthorized photocopying was difficult to police, imagine the daunting, perhaps impossible, task of tracking electronic reproduction.[4] Once a user "captures" the text and images of a copyrighted electronic work, he may so massage and amend the data that identifying the original may be an exercise in futility. Articles in electronic journals are intended for revision by knowledgeable readers and, in their final form (if the term still applies), may be such a collaborative effort that they bear little relationship to their first draft. It remains to be seen whether in such a climate an electronic Kinko's lawsuit could be successful. (Kinko's Graphic Corporation, a major producer of "course packets"—photocopied anthologies for college courses—was successfully sued by eight textbook publishers. The judge ruled that Kinko's could not produce the anthologies without copyright permission from the publishers since they exceeded fair use.)[5]

The radical changes that electronic reproduction and distribution portend may even require us to reexamine traditional concepts of authorship and intellectual property rights.[6] If data is passed from user to user and each user also becomes a contributor, can we continue to define authors in the conventional sense? And if there are no authors, are there authors' (as opposed to publishers') property rights to be violated? Whether copyright law can be reformulated to protect the interests of both producers and user/collaborators of electronic information is very much an open question.

INFORMATION AS PRIVATE PROPERTY

While so many of the features of electronic sources give reason for optimism to those of us who trade in access to information, there are competing tendencies that are ample cause for continued apprehension. Not the least of these is a marked impetus toward treating information principally, if not exclusively, as a proprietary asset. This formidable trend bids to raise our consciousness about information's economic aspects while depreciating its social and political character.

It should not be surprising, given the political temper of the 1980s, that much of the effort to promote information as an economic commodity has come from a federal government grown extraordinarily friendly to business. Rationalizing that much government publication wasted public funds and blocked more efficient free market forces, the Reagan administration undertook a major initiative to "privatize" government-produced data. First came a draconian reduction in government documentation, provided at no cost to the public through depository libraries. Then followed a program to sell or award information gathered at public expense to private companies, who repackaged it and sold it for profit. Privatization proved a most fitting term, for it transformed publicly owned government data into merchandise available only at a price to those who funded its creation. The private sector prospered at the expense of the public's right to know.[7]

Government now attempts to assert a prerogative to restrict the flow of information outside its own precincts. Arguing that awarding research grants conveys rights to regulate the dissemination of research data, federal agencies have sought in court to bar university researchers from publishing or even discussing their government-funded research results without government approval.

While commendably resisting such government efforts to censor intellectual discourse, universities have not been above making their own Faustian compromises in the pursuit of research revenue. In highly prized fields like genetic engineering or cold fusion, institutions often manage their research findings as trade secrets, complete with patent and copyright protection.[8] Safeguarding the economic integrity of potentially lucrative discoveries might be accomplished without limiting the flow of data about the discoveries, but it also invites conflicts of information interest.

Where maximizing income is a paramount institutional goal, the cooperative nature of the research enterprise, which depends upon the unfettered exchange of information, is likely to receive less attention. If knowledge is protected in anticipation of profit, related information may also be deemed too sensitive to share. Implicitly, the proprietary value of information drives decisions about its distribution; the educational and societal benefits derived from enriching a larger pool of research data assume a secondary importance.

In a capitalist system corporate endeavors to merchandise information are to be expected. But when nonprofit entities like government and higher education seek their motivation in the bottom line, they place the public's broad information needs in jeopardy. As technology devises more sophisticated information access tools, actions in the political and economic spheres encourage those who would erect entrepreneurial access barriers.

CONCENTRATION IN THE INFORMATION INDUSTRY

The overcommercialization of information coincides with and complements a financial evolution of global proportions: concentration of ownership in the information industry.[9] Comparatively few hands now control the content and price of mass market (and, increasingly, scholarly) information. Disappearing is the diversity of publishing outlets that nourished a healthy competition in both ideas and cost.

This unsettling phenomenon is largely confined to print publishing at present. The electronic publishing industry, still in its formative state, as yet includes any number of potential major players, among them professional associations, online retrieval services, even telephone companies (who own optical fiber networks).[10] But the industry is unlikely to remain forever immune from the same dynamic of concentration that has shaken the print medium, especially once the attraction of megaprofits supplants qualms over uncontrolled data redistribution in the calculus of current or would-be information conglomerates.

Compounding the worrisome prospect of a reduction in the number of electronic publishers is another equally troubling form of concentration. Unlike print, electronic data accords its producer the means to retain and protect exclusive ownership rights. No longer are publishers confined to packaging data and selling it outright to libraries and other customers to use in perpetuity. They can treat electronic information like rental property, subdividing and leasing it to their customers on terms carefully delimited by contract.

Converting a data set to an electronic format can boost its revenue potential immensely. Where producers ordinarily anticipated one sale transaction per customer for print data sets (monographs, journal volumes, etc.), they may now cheerfully expect multiple sales per customer for each digitized data set. They can segment the set and offer each portion separately; they can lease the set in whole or in part for a fixed period, comfortable in the strong probability of renewal. And by thus wringing every last dollar of income from each product, they can hope to recoup earnings lost through unregulated copying.

LIBRARIES: RENTING VERSUS OWNING

Electronic sources' added value to producers comes, of course, at the expense of customer libraries. In the new economics of digital information, libraries will most likely become renters, not owners, and endure the decreased leverage that this loss of status implies. Our range of control over the materials we acquire will contract. Annual costs for electronic tools might, for example, be pegged to the size of user populations. If we consider enlarging our user base (say, in the case of academic libraries, by including non-faculty/student users), the knowledge that our costs will rise accordingly will be an inhibiting factor. In place of making one payment per title—a payment that incorporates permanent retention rights—we could pay for the same source several times over, only to relinquish everything we have purchased if we terminate our lease.[11]

Lease-in-lieu-of-ownership is a model familiar to us through our experience with online searching, but it has become a central paradigm of library economics as we acquire CD-ROMs and data tapes for public access catalogs. A typical CD-ROM lease fixes an annual price for "current" service, which might include the most recent five years of data. The library lessee who routinely renews this agreement will purchase this year's data once this year, again next year, and consecutively three more years into the future. At the end of the five-year term, the library can customarily obtain six-year-old data, for which it has already paid five times, as an "archival" disc for yet another payment.

Electronic journals, most of which are now supplied with minimal usage restrictions and at little or no cost by small independent publishers, are ripe for the application of lease arrangements.[12] Publishers of a more commercial bent will not likely overlook the lucrative possibilities of introducing user-based pricing and multiple sales of retrospective data to the thriving serials market. The *Online Journal of Current Clinical Trials*, a joint product of OCLC and the American Association for the Advancement of Science, may serve as a prototype for the e-journal of the future. Offered only as a dial-up service, the journal cannot be networked; like print journals, it is available to but one user at a time. If demand exceeds this supply, libraries must place additional subscriptions. Unlike print journals, libraries do not possess the data they purchase (at least, in this case, not current data; fiche backfiles are provided).

DATA INTEGRITY UNDER CONCENTRATED OWNERSHIP

Left unchecked, the dual momentums of concentration in publishing ownership and exclusivity in database ownership could implicate more than the information economy. The integrity of the data itself may not survive every merger and acquisition. The quality and variety of the public's information choices are very much at play in the relentless drive to fashion giant media combines. As the corporate owners of major publishing sources grow fewer in number, opportunities for the expression of diverse opinions diminish in kind. A coterie of multinational publishers, bound by a shared outlook and purpose, will seek to exert a homogenizing intellectual and cultural influence.[13] Unorthodox, radical, and commercially unappealing ideas, especially those challenging the power of the conglomerates, will compete for attention outside the information mainstream. Would trade combinations in electronic publishing be any less predisposed toward the conventional than their print counterparts?

Even if no electronic media oligopoly materializes, the demonstrated resolve of producers large and small to sell only access to, but not control of, their electronic databases is disquieting. When libraries and individuals purchase and maintain complete databases, the data "archives" effectively exist in multiple copies dispersed nationally or internationally. The dispersal itself affords considerable protection against tampering. Digital data archives that reside only in their producer's possession are much less secure. The risk of meddling, whether willful or not, obviously grows in inverse proportion to the number of extant archival sets. Erase or reconfigure the producer's archival sets, and you alter all the subsets leased to libraries and other users.

Careful security may reduce the probability of accidental tampering or vandalism, but there are no safeguards to deter producers themselves from manipulating data deliberately. Concern about such deceit is not only the province of corporate conspiracy buffs; there is enough evidence on the record to warrant at least a healthy skepticism on the part of all censorship opponents. Accounts of businesses suppressing findings of their own research units that impugn product safety are commonplace. Would these companies be any less averse to expurgating comparably displeasing information from their electronic databases? Put another way, would a tobacco concern that acquires a medical database vendor refrain from expunging citations to literature on the hazards of smoking? The empowerment of personal computer users is significantly devalued if the databases they exploit and share are sanitized prior to release.

LIBRARIES AND THE COST OF INFORMATION

It can be (and surely will be) argued that libraries will learn to live with lease arrangements and that fears of data manipulation are overblown. Not so easily dismissed, however, is the most fundamental and still the most formidable obstacle to open and equal electronic access: cost. Hard fiscal experience with sources already on the market is sufficient to brace us for what contemporary argot terms a "challenging" future.

Producers of electronic tools can be expected to devise price structures that make at least occasional access affordable for relatively affluent individuals. Most users, however, will of financial necessity continue to rely on libraries to supply an electronic panoply of CD-ROMs, online databases, e-journals, and so on, to satisfy their comprehensive information needs. They may be disappointed. Libraries, reeling from spiraling serial prices and budget deflation, will be hard pressed to procure expensive electronic resources while maintaining what remains of their investment in print. Cost calculation for electronic items is an exercise emblematic of the extra dimension these materials bring to every level of library decision making. A library's cost for each electronic product is a function not only of what, but also of how, producers choose to charge.

Prices for serially produced CD-ROMs and data tapes cause average print serial prices to pale by comparison, but they do at least exhibit a behavioral consistency cherished by budget managers. Such costs are (or certainly should be) explicit in lease agreements and therefore lend themselves to fund allocation and related planning mechanisms. Conversely, electronic journals, dial-up databases, and other remote access tools may often operate on a more complex cost basis evocative of online searching in their resistance to budgetary order.

Though the economics of e-journal publishing are largely yet to be learned, the elimination of paper would seem to lower production costs.[14] But if, as we strongly suspect, print journal prices bear little direct relation to the expense of production, should we anticipate that e-publishers will pass their savings, if any, on to libraries? Moreover, if publishers fully exploit the revenue potential of charge-per-use pricing or, worse, marry flat subscription fees to charge-per-use, total library access costs for some titles may rival chemistry journal prices.

The opportunities to impose transaction fees for each e-journal use are staggering in their profusion. Paraphrasing one author's apt if depressing metaphor, users may encounter toll booths at every node on the electronic highway.[15] Publishers can, of course, charge for a basic subscription; like the *Online Journal of Current Clinical Trials*, they can require multiple subscriptions for multiple simultaneous users. They can charge for every sign-on, every backfile search, every download, every offprint, every screen dump. Telecommunications charges are another profit center, one which regional phone companies and long distance firms may reserve to themselves. Again the paradox: a technology so rich in its promise of information sharing also awards information producers license to circumscribe access by erecting an array of financial barriers.

Producers can easily raise the same kinds of barriers to regulate—and assess tolls for—the use of other forms of electronic databases. Even NREN, the much-discussed fiber-optic supernetwork conceived as our ultimate gateway to remote data sites, could eventually be commercialized and subjected to fee-based access.[16] Many speculate that the costs of scholarly information (including that produced electronically) could be significantly lessened if both universities and professional organizations were to sever their ties with trade publishers, reclaim their own intellectual product, and self-publish faculty research. This is a hopeful scenario in that nonprofit publishers, according to some studies, tend to price print materials more reasonably than commercial entities. But cynics will question whether the financially stressed academy, even if it musters the wherewithal and the will to become the e-publisher of first resort, will resist the mighty temptation to net top dollar for its output.

Should publishers embrace a cost-per-use model for electronic databases, library expenses will once again be hostage to the elastic and unpredictable patron demand that characterized online searching. In a climate of retrenchment selection decisions about products carrying high fixed costs and/or variable user fees present themselves as a Hobson's choice. Do we forgo acquiring (and providing patron access to) a service we deem prohibitively priced? Or do we defray our costs by passing them on to our users?

If experience is a guide, most libraries will find the latter alternative more compelling. It appeals to both our nobly philosophical and responsibly practical dispositions: philosophical in that it honors a perceived commitment to increase our clientele's information options, practical in that it conserves our already overextended materials funds for other purchases. But it also entails an implied mercenary bargain with producers to use technology as an instrument for impeding open access.

USER FEES AND PUBLIC ACCESS

User fees occupy a pivotal juncture in the electronic information delivery chain not least because they represent perhaps the only point in the process where libraries can intervene to protect the public interest. We may find ourselves powerless to influence global macroeconomic developments like publishing industry combinations or subsidiary monopolistic ploys such as exclusive database ownership (though we might contest leasing arrangements wherever possible). But we can work to preserve equality of access to information in all its forms by repudiating discriminatory practices grounded on ability to pay.

In an era when government vacillates in meeting its obligation to secure the public's information rights, libraries may be the only civic agency positioned to defend the community's stake in equal access. If we accept this essentially democratic trust, it follows that our role is to bridge, rather than widen, economic gaps in the information chain, thereby reasserting the social and political value of information that some would renounce.

Keeping faith with this charge is, of course, at the very heart of our "challenge." Combined with the already oppressive burden of print materials costs, the expense of acquiring and offering free access to electronic data may place some libraries in danger of joining the information poor. Yet our resources have always been insufficient to our needs; we should not expect that electronics will emancipate us from the bleak but enduring financial realities of library service. As we have done so often before, we will have to use our limited means to procure—and provide without charge—a collection of information tools in every format that best addresses our users' requirements. Only thus will we promote the power of electronics to assist us in dispensing information to the broadest possible audience and achieve the highest aims of the electronic revolution.

NOTES

1. Alex Wilson, "The Information Rich and the Information Poor," *ASLIB Proceedings* 39 (January 1987) 1.

2. See my earlier article, "The Politics of Information: Libraries & Online Retrieval Systems," *Library Journal* 111 (1 February 1986): 40–43.

3. Robert Weber, "The Clouded Future of Electronic Publishing," *Publishers Weekly* 237 (29 June 1990): 80; Robert Weber, "Copyright in the Electronic Age," *Publishers Weekly* 238 (22 March 1991): 52; Paul Metz and Paul M. Gherman, "Serials Pricing and the Role of the Electronic Journal," *College & Research Libraries* 52 (July 1991): 321.

4. Francis Dummer Fisher, "The Electronic Lumberyard and Builders' Rights: Technology, Copyrights, Patents, and Academe," *Change* 21 (May/June 1989): 19; Weber, "Clouded Future" 80; Metz and Gherman 323.

5. " 'Textbook Anthologies on Campuses are Curbed by Ruling on Copyrights," *New York Times* 16 April 1991: A14; and Wade Lambert, "Textbook Publishers Win Copyright Case Over Unauthorized Anthologies," *Wall Street Journal* 29 March 1991: B6.

6. Steven W. Gilbert and Peter Lyman, "Intellectual Property in the Information Age: Issues beyond the Copyright Law," *Change* 21 (May/June 1989): 23–26.

7. James F. Govan, "The Creeping Invisible Hand: Entrepreneurial Librarianship," *Library Journal* 113 (January 1988): 36; John Buschman and Michael Carbone, "A Critical Inquiry into Librarianship: Applications of the 'New Sociology of Education,' " *Library Quarterly* 61 (January 1991): 26.

8. Gilbert and Lyman 26.

9. See Ben H. Bagdikian, "The Lords of the Global Village," *The Nation* 248 (12 June 1989): 805–20.

10. Weber, "Clouded Future" 76–78.

11. Ann Okerson, "With Feathers: Effects of Copyright and Ownership on Scholarly Publishing," *College & Research Libraries* 52 (September 1991): 435.

12. Ann Okerson, "The Electronic Journal: What, Whence, and When?" *The Public-Access Computer Systems Review* 2 (1991), section 4.1 (an electronic journal).

13. Bagdikian 807.

14. Metz and Gherman 322.

15. Okerson, "Electronic Journal" section 4.1.

16. Weber, "Clouded Future" 79.

11

Conclusion: Contexts, Analogies, and Entrepreneurial Directions in Librarianship

John Buschman

This volume has been a project to widen the focus of study of information technology in librarianship and to situate those developments in the larger context of critical studies of technology. In so doing, different kinds of questions tend to be raised, different consequences examined. The result has been a survey of scholarly background and the relational issues raised in librarianship. If in the process of this survey certain topics were not explored in enough depth, or others overlooked, the apology must be my own since this is an inevitable consequence of the structure and project of the book. However, it is just such an extension and depth of inquiry that this project is intended to further, and some areas will be suggested in the final paragraphs of this chapter.

EDUCATIONAL FOUNDATIONS: ANALOGOUS DEVELOPMENTS

The endeavor of this book has an intellectual analogy in the field of education that can be profitably explored. Like studies in librarianship, the foundational studies in education—history and sociology—were isolated not so long ago. The history of American education developed "a rather large literature in the area, but too much of it was parochial, anachronistic, and out of touch with main currents of scholarship. [It was] viewed . . . as a device to dignify and inspire a newly self-conscious profession."[1] The sociology of education was "dominated by unrigorous and mediocre 'educationalists' [and] reflected less the application of general sociological principles than the concerns of a subject that considered itself a branch of education."[2] That the foundational studies of education benefited from their connections to broader scholarly themes and inquiry is beyond question. That these connections engendered strong debate and disagreement is also beyond question. The clash of ideas fueled the vitality of both areas.

In broader forms, and focusing on different questions, Wayne Weigand, Michael Harris, and Marcia Nauratil have each stressed such connections. Harris has in fact specifically suggested the critical sociology of education as an interpretive paradigm of particular importance to librarianship.[3] Michael Carbone and I have extended that analysis and further argued the intellectual saliency of the education-librarianship comparison. Briefly put, librarianship and education share historical similarities as institutions and professions in diverse areas such as their founding as free public institutions, the gendered nature of the work and workforce, and the relative status of the professions. Of course libraries also share broadly in the educative mission of schools, communities, and higher education.[4]

In this vein, Amy Gutmann notes the empirical evidence on the role public libraries play in supporting the educational achievements of children during summer, which is especially important for the less advantaged. Like public education, "funding public libraries is a prototypically democratic decision; . . . supplying a good that politics can buy but the market cannot—in the case of libraries, a public culture of learning accessible to all children."[5] Michael Katz and Harris, both historical revisionists, have noted the elite status of nineteenth-century American public education and library reformers, and the similar values placed on immigrant assimilation and the preservation of political order in both reform movements.[6] Finally, like librarianship, the initial changes in historical and sociological scholarship in education were responses to larger social and technological developments. The Ford Foundation initially funded studies of a "new" history of education in "a time of deep public concern over the American schools,"[7] and the invigoration of the sociology of education saw an initial thrust of "technological functionalism . . . emphasizing educational efficiency . . . to produce an adequate flow of scientists and engineers."[8] Those initial scholarly connections and responses went on to spur revisionist historical work and applications of more critical sociological paradigms to educational policy and practice.

The purpose of this analogy is to provide a touchstone to which I will return, and to cite an analogous development in another field of scholarly inquiry. It is my hope that this volume will help spur a similar flourishing of critical inquiry and debate on information technology in librarianship.

BROAD THEME OF THE PROJECT

As I review individual chapters, I see variations on one prominent theme throughout: an emphasis on democratic values permeates each analysis of technology, applications, and libraries. In Part I, Norman Balabanian explored the non-neutrality of technology in an effort to alert us to the need to more democratically control it. Michael J. Carbone has reviewed the critical issues on the underside of educational applications of information technology in order to ensure that the democratic values of schooling are not lost. Sue Jansen has noted the inherently undemocratic values in present structures of media control and discourse. Shoshana Zuboff's work concludes that information technology profoundly affects power relationships in work, and suggests that work must become less hierarchical and more democratic. Steve Slaby notes the events, critiques, and struggles which brought him to challenge the engineering profession to more clearly respond to the technological dangers and to democratic needs.

Part II has seen an extension of those themes in relationship to information technology in librarianship. My own chapter explored the overt and covert issues of censorship engendered by information technology. Carolyn Gray's work explored the importance of information policy in relation to the civic role of libraries in a democracy. Michael Winter examined the democratic and undemocratic effects of information technologies in libraries in the labor process. John Haar does much the same by looking at information technology in libraries in a political and economic context. Finally, this conclusion examines the relationship of this theme to the current entrepreneurial direction of librarianship. All these varied approaches are knit together by a commitment to democratic values and to identifying their absence and presence through a critical analysis of technology (and, in particular, information technology in libraries).

OPPOSITIONS

Democratic values are, it is safe to say, widely supported in American public rhetoric. Yet there are tensions between competing values inherent in American culture. As Samuel Bowles and Herbert Gintis state:

> "Democratic capitalism" suggests a set of harmonious and mutually supportive institutions; each promoting a kind of freedom in distinct realms of social life. Yet . . . capitalism and democracy are not com-

plementary systems. Rather they are sharply contrasting rules regulating both the processes of human development and the historical evolution of whole societies: the one is characterized by the preeminence of economic privilege based on property rights, the other insists on the priority of liberty and democratic accountability based on the exercise of personal rights. [T]here are multiple centers of power in liberal democratic capitalism . . . and this pluralism of powers captures an essential aspect of the conception of a democratic society. . . . Democracy, not the interplay of property rights, should provide the fundamental principle ordering the processes by which we become who we are and by which the rules regulating our lives are continually renewed and transformed.[9]

It is of course not at all difficult to see this tension throughout this volume. For example, one can see it in the examinations of government information privatization and policies, the ownership and control of media and information technology, and the interplay of information technology in work, education, scholarship, and so on.

I contend that the entrepreneurial directions and values in ascendancy in librarianship are changing the role played by our institutions and our profession. Librarianship in its present trajectory is changing sides from one of the democratic "pluralism of powers" to one that primarily supports economic values. Again, I turn to the field of education for a parallel development. As Richard Hofstadter suggests, the American public has long thought of education as having for its purpose the "producing [of] more Sputniks, not for developing more intellect . . . almost suggest[ing] that gifted children were to be regarded as resources in the cold war."[10] But there has been a recent and more fundamental shift toward an economic conception of public education. Henry Giroux has characterized the current debate over the quality of American public education as ushering in a "new" public philosophy which defines schools as places

> to educate students to meet the economic needs of the dominant society [and posits] as an ideal, this model of economic rationality [as] the basis for new relationships between schools and the economic sector. [This approach] suggests that economics is more important to our nation and schools than is our commitment to democratic principles.[11]

As the theme of this volume would suggest, this new public philosophy does not stop at the boundaries of schoolyards. Rather, libraries are another public institution which is similarly subject to the same reordering of priorities. Information technology in libraries, in its form and content, has been the avenue through which corporate and economic values have begun to redefine the values of the profession. Further, this has its clearest expression in the growth of entrepreneurial librarianship.

ENTREPRENEURIAL LIBRARIANSHIP AND INFORMATION TECHNOLOGY

James Govan was among the first to name and critique the entrepreneurial trend in librarianship. With the cumulative changes of government information privatization, the beginnings of library charges for services, access to collections, and copies, and the transformation of information into a valuable commodity, librarians found they were "in the presence of new found 'wealth.' [T]he notion . . . has so beguiled some in the profession [that] subtle but fundamental changes in values and attitudes [have] mov[ed] librarianship more in the direction of the business world."[12]

Govan identified a process well under way. In 1984, for instance, an editor would express frustration at the lack of substantive library scholarship on the marketing of library services: "I am convinced that libraries need to adopt marketing (and other business methodologies) to prosper. [It is] the only hope that library administrators have of winning their fair share of [budgets]."[13] This refrain has become familiar to librarians as they are urged by consultants to charge for services and to make their institutions pay their own way.[14] In discussing librarians as information entrepreneurs, Alice Sizer Warner perhaps states it most baldly: "You've got to like money [and] talking about it. . . . You have to like selling. You have to sell all the time, think about it all the time [and] go where the money is." This applies to more than individual librarians since, as she points out, "non-profit organizations can thrive in the 'enterprise field.' "[15]

Information technology is the most crucial development pushing libraries "to implement entrepreneurially oriented management structures," as Richard De Gennaro notes. The result is a lack of clear demarcation between nonprofit and commercial library organizations, a "blurring of roles" as each performs functions formerly exclusive to the other. While many "were predicting that information technology would put libraries out of business, . . . the evidence is that technology is, in fact, putting libraries into business."[16] This can be seen in the subtle changes in librarianship's expectations for information technology resources: they are expected to produce income, or create a more favorable budgeting and fundraising environment.

The entrepreneurial direction of librarianship has gone far enough that S. Michael Malinconico could state: "There are obviously a growing number of serious competitors prepared to offer a broad variety of library and information services."[17] Clearly, libraries have shifted from a role of public service in which they held the field alone, to some sort of business approach in which they now have "serious competitors." The assumption is that libraries are now just one of many marketers in the information business. Consequently,

> there is no particular reason for all of these resources to be offered through libraries [since they are] not logically, socially, economically, or morally any better or more desirable than other information providers. . . . The current technological trajectory of our profession and our institutions is the primary vehicle behind the shift toward aligning libraries with . . . the [economic] agenda.[18]

Financing libraries on the basis of "more bang for the information buck" holds dangers to the public, to democratic values of service, access, and scholarship, and to public inquiry, as Govan, Haar, Gray, Schuman, Schiller, myself, and others have noted. The ethical compromises inherent in the structures of higher education research funding are a good example. As Ralph Nader asked, "How compatible is academic freedom in a university with trade secrecy and proprietary information?"[19] It does not take much imagination to make the connection and extend these same sorts of problems to entrepreneurial-based budgeting and funding of libraries.

A CONTRASTING VISION

Giroux argues against a vision of education primarily tethered to economic agendas. In offering a contrast, he makes an argument that applies to libraries as well. While the theme of libraries as public institutions supportive of democracy is familiar, Giroux radically extends the concept:

> This means regarding [such public institutions] as democratic sites dedicated to forms of self and social empowerment . . . where [people] learn the knowledge and skills necessary to live in an authentic democracy. Instead of defining [these public institutions] as extensions of the workplace or as front-line institutions in the battle of international markets and foreign competition, [public institutions]

as democratic public spheres are constructed around forms of critical inquiry that dignify meaningful dialogue and human agency, . . . public association and social responsibility. Such a discourse seeks to recapture the idea of critical democracy as a social movement that supports individual freedom and social justice.[20]

This vision stands in direct contrast to the entrepreneurial directions of librarianship and invigorates the articulation of the traditional democratic role of libraries. Such a vision seeks to capture the democratic potentials of information technology. While the approach of this volume has been critical, I do not mean to suggest that such potential does not exist in library technologies. By critically questioning this phenomenon in libraries, we can pierce some of the myths and power in which it is shrouded. By extensively exploring the non-neutrality of information technologies in libraries, and the human decisions behind them, the socially constructed meanings we impart to them are revealed. We face choices in technologies, and we must make those choices free of mystifications.

There is some urgency to this project. I cannot help but notice that those who have pointed to the democratic operations furthered by information technology up to this point have spoken largely of non-corporate societies (China and the former Soviet Union) and the present corporate structure of information.[21] Herbert Schiller sees in our current environment the embattlement of the idea of "social information." It is a battle over whether librarianship remains a profession in the public service, for otherwise "to imagine that [commercial information] services are the sum total of a librarian's contribution is to acquiesce to the emergence of a society in which social aims have been discarded."[22] We are in danger of ceding to the technological metaphor of librarianship, "the very duty to formulate questions."[23] As much as anything, this project is about imagining alternatives through skepticism about the structures of information technology presently in place; retaining the critical distance to raise such questions; and harnessing technologies to the ends of librarianship instead of becoming the end. To borrow one last concept from Giroux, librarians operating in this way become what he calls "transformative intellectuals . . . [who] combine reflection and action in the interest of empower[ment]."[24]

FURTHER STUDY

Many of the questions raised in the chapters deserve further inquiry. Briefly, they might include continuing scrutiny of the political and economic contexts of federal information policy, examination of the corporate control of library information technologies, continued monitoring of the development of information technologies in relation to librarian autonomy and deskilling, and looking at the possibility of information technologies reducing the librarian labor force. Further examinations of the sociology of knowledge in libraries in relationship to information technologies are warranted as are developments in information technology-related censorship, changing patterns and content of student and professorial scholarship related to electronic library resources, and explorations into the fate of print culture in the electronic library environment.

As stated, not all questions have been raised in this venue. For instance, the implications of Lewis Mumford's scholarship bears more inquiry by librarians. His ideas on technological systems as inclusive of human behavior and organization, and the contrast in democratic and authoritarian technics, are highly suggestive of further study of information systems. Both Mumford and Hofstadter have identified particular aspects of "the American mind" which show a particular faith in and fascination with machines and the business ethic. Surely this broad cultural trait has been played out in librarianship as well. The work of the Frankfurt School of Critical Theory, especially in the area of the culture industry, is suggestive of a parallel library inquiry. The broader links of library management training and business management techniques should be explored in their relationship to information technologies. David Noble's work on the history of technology and work is fertile ground for library application. Lastly, the economic assumptions behind the transformations of the information society need to be carefully scrutinized by librarians. It is suggested by many that our economic duty is to convert all available sectors of our society to this vision, but there are holes in this prognosis. Not all economists agree on the forecast that information will take the place of manufacturing. And further, Japan—our chief economic rival— has enjoyed its economic success with a relatively smaller, less developed information industry.[25]

EPILOGUE

My hope is that this work will provide the basis for more critical approaches to information technology in librarianship, and provoke the kind of serious and extended debate over it that we have lacked so far. This has been an effort to look at possibilities, both good and bad. As Karl Jaspers writes:

[I]n order to grasp reality, we must see the possibilities. In the present, a formulation of the possibilities is the area in which I gain certainty concerning what I decide; without possibility, I have no freedom; without a vision of the possibilities, I act blindly; only a knowledge of the possibilities enables me to know what I am actually doing.[26]

NOTES

1. Sol Cohen, "History of Education as a Field of Study: An Essay on the Recent Historiography of American Education," *History, Education, and Public Policy*, ed. Donald R. Warren (Berkeley, CA: McCutchan, 1978) 35, 37.

2. Jerome Karabel and A. H. Halsey, "Educational Research: A Review and an Interpretation," *Power and Ideology in Education*, eds. Jerome Karabel and A. H. Halsey (New York: Oxford University Press, 1977) 2–3.

3. Michael H. Harris, "State, Class, and Cultural Reproduction: Toward a Theory of Library Service in the United States," *Advances in Librarianship* 14 (1986): 236–40; Michael H. Harris, "The Dialectic of Defeat: Antimonies in Research in Library and Information Science," *Library Trends* 34.3 (Winter 1986): 515–31; Marcia J. Nauratil, *The Alienated Librarian* (New York: Greenwood Press, 1989); Wayne A. Wiegand, "The Role of the Library in American History," *Bowker Annual*, 33rd ed., ed. Filomena Simora (New York: R. R. Bowker, 1988) 69–76; and Wayne A. Wiegand, *An Active Instrument for Propaganda: The American Public Library During World War I* (Westport, CT: Greenwood Press, 1989).

4. John Buschman and Michael Carbone, "A Critical Inquiry into Librarianship: Applications of the 'New Sociology of Education,' " *Library Quarterly* 61.1 (January 1991): 15–40.

5. Amy Gutmann, *Democratic Education* (Princeton: Princeton University Press, 1987).

6. Michael B. Katz, "Essay Review of Crisis in the Classroom," *History, Education, and Public Policy*, ed. Donald R. Warren (Berkeley, CA: McCutchan, 1978) 285–95; Michael Harris, "The Purpose of the American Public Library," *Library Journal* 15 September 1973: 2509–14.

7. Cohen 35–37.

8. Karabel and Halsey 8–9.

9. Samuel Bowles and Herbert Gintis, *Democracy and Capitalism: Property, Community, and the Contradictions of Modern Social Thought* (New York: Basic Books, 1986) 3.

10. Richard Hofstadter, *Anti-Intellectualism in American Life* (New York: Vintage, 1962) 5.

11. Henry A. Giroux, "Public Philosophy and the Crisis in Education," *Harvard Educational Review* 54.2 (May 1984): 187–88, 191.

12. James F. Govan, "The Creeping Invisible Hand: Entrepreneurial Librarianship," *Library Journal* January 1988: 36.

13. Gary T. Ford, introduction, *Marketing and the Library*, ed. Gary T. Ford (New York: Haworth Press, 1984) 3.

14. "Make Libraries Pay Their Way, Advises Consultant," *American Libraries* January 1990: 13.

15. Alice Sizer Warner, "Librarians As Money Makers: The Bottom Line," *American Libraries* November 1990: 947–48.

16. Richard De Gennaro, "Technology & Access in an Enterprise Society," *Library Journal* 1 October 1988: 43.

17. S. Michael Malinconico, "Information's Brave New World," *Library Journal* 1 May 1992: 38.

18. John Buschman, "Information Technology, Power Structures, and the Fate of Librarianship," paper presented as part of a panel on "The New Information Technologies: Hidden Agendas, Institutional Power and the Fate of Librarianship," American Library Association Annual Conference, San Francisco, 28 June 1992. See also the arguments presented in John Buschman, "A Critique of the Information Broker: Contexts of Reference Services," *Reference Librarian* 31 (1990): 131–51; and John Buschman, "Asking the Right Questions About Information Technology," *American Libraries* December 1990: 1026–30.

19. Denise K. Magner, "Nader Warns Universities of the Ethical Perils of Increased Links With Big Corporations," *Chronicle of Higher Education* 24 October 1990: A13, A16; see also "The Entrepreneurial University" issue of *Academe* 76 (September-October 1990); David P. Boyd and Jay A. Halfond, "Corporate Ties and Integrity at U.S. Business Schools," *Chronicle of Higher Education* 6 June 1990: A44; and Debra E. Blum, "An Outspoken Critic of Higher Education's Ties to Industry Crusades Against Government-Sponsored Military Research," *Chronicle of Higher Education* 17 July 1991: A11, A16.

20. Henry A. Giroux, *Teachers As Intellectuals: Toward a Critical Pedagogy of Learning* (Granby, MA: Bergin & Garvey, 1988) xxxii.

21. For instance, see Al Kagan, "Liberation Technology," *Progressive Librarian* 5 (Summer 1992): 47–50; and James Flanigan, "The Chip May Prove Mightier Than the Sword," *Los Angeles Times* 14 June 1989, Business sec.: 1, 6.

22. Herbert I. Schiller, "Public Information Goes Corporate," *Library Journal* 1 October 1991: 45.

23. Joseph Weizenbaum, "On the Impact of the Computer on Society," *Libraries in Post-Industrial Society*, ed. Leigh Estabrook (Phoenix: Oryx Press, 1977) 192.

24. Giroux, *Teachers* xxxiv.

25. Glenn Hoetker, "An Overview of the Japanese Information Industry," *Information Today* January 1992: 25.

26. Karl Jaspers, *Three Essays: Leonardo, Descartes, Max Weber* (New York: Harcourt, Brace & World, 1964) 238.

Selected Bibliography

Editor's Note: The works noted in this bibliography are supplemental to those cited in the notes of each chapter author. It is therefore important to use the work of the chapter authors as a basic guide to the critical literature on technology. Only a few items already cited in the notes are repeated here. Those works, in the judgment of the editor, could offer more than the context in which they were cited or discussed would indicate. Also, as implied in the arguments made in this volume, there is more critical work on technology outside of librarianship than in it. Therefore, this bibliography will serve more the function of filling in the foundations of that critique than noting more critical work in librarianship. Most of that work has already been cited in the chapters. Finally, the cumulative works cited in this bibliography and the notes are only a partial guide to the critical work on technology in librarianship and of relevance in other fields. I wish to thank the chapter authors for their contributions to this bibliography.

Arato, Andrew, and Eike Gebhardt, eds. *The Essential Frankfurt School Reader*. New York: Continuum, 1982.

Arterton, F. Christopher. *Teledemocracy: Can Technology Protect Democracy?* Newbury Park, CA: Sage, 1986.

Beniger, James R. "Origins of the Information Society." *Wilson Library Bulletin* (November 1986): 12–19.

Biggs, Mary. "Information Overload and Information Seekers: What We Know About Them, What To Do About Them." *Reference Librarian* 25/26 (1989): 411–29.

Bok, Derek. "Looking Into Education's High-Tech Future." *Harvard Magazine* (May/June 1985): 29–38.

Boorstin, Daniel J. *The Republic of Letters*. Washington, DC: Library of Congress, 1989.

Braverman, Harry. *Labor and Monopoly Capital: The Degradation of Work in the Twentieth Century*. New York: Monthly Review Press, 1974.

Buckland, Michael K. "Information as Thing." *Journal of the American Society for Information Science* 42.5 (1991): 351–60.

Davis, Erik. "Cyberlibraries." *Lingua Franca* 2.3 (February/March 1992): 46–51.

Dennett, Daniel C. "Information, Technology, and the Virtues of Ignorance." *Daedalus* 115.3 (Summer 1986): 135–53.

Dunlop, Charles, and Rob Kling, eds. *Computerization and Controversy: Value Conflicts and Social Choices.* Boston: Academic Press, 1991.

Ellul, Jacques. *The Technological Society.* New York: Vintage, 1964.

Ewen, Stuart. *All Consuming Images: The Politics of Style in Contemporary Culture.* New York: Basic Books, 1988.

Forester, Tom, ed. *Computers in the Human Context.* Cambridge, MA: MIT Press, 1989.

Fromm, Erich. *The Revolution of Hope: Towards a Humanized Technology.* New York: Harper & Row, 1968.

Galnoor, Itzhak, ed. *Government Secrecy in Democracies.* New York: New York University Press, 1977.

Heilbroner, Robert L. "Economic Problems of a 'Post-Industrial' Society." *Dissent* 20.2 (1973): 163–76.

Held, David. *Introduction to Critical Theory: Horkheimer to Habermas.* Berkeley: University of California Press, 1980.

Horn, Zoia, ed. *The Right to Know.* 3 volumes. Oakland, CA: Data Center, 1986, 1988, 1991.

Innis, Harold A. *Empire and Communications.* Toronto: University of Toronto Press, 1972.

Kellner, Douglas. "Critical Theory and the Culture Industries: A Reassessment." *Telos* Issue 62 (Winter 1984–85): 196–205.

Kovel, Joel. "Theses on Technocracy." *Telos* Issue 54 (Winter 1982–83): 155–61.

Kroszner, Randall. "Technology and the Control of Labor." *Critical Review* 1.2 (Spring 1987): 6–16.

Lacey, Paul A. "Views of a Luddite." *College & Research Libraries* 43 (March 1982): 110–18.

Lazere, Donald. *American Media and Mass Culture: Left Perspectives.* Berkeley: University of California Press, 1987.

———. "Literacy and Mass Media: The Political Implications." *New Literary History* 18 (Winter 1987): 237–55.

Lewis, Peter H. "A Fast Way to Discover Patterns in Vast Amounts of Data." *New York Times* 30 August 1992: F8.

Luke, Tim. "Informationalism and Ecology." *Telos* Issue 56 (Summer 1983): 59–73.

"Management of Federal Information Resources; Notice." *Federal Register* 29 April 1992: 18296–306.

Marcuse, Herbert. *One-Dimensional Man.* Boston: Beacon Press, 1964.

Marx, Gary T. "The Case of the Omniscient Organization." *Harvard Business Review* 90 (March/April 1990): 12–30.

———. "Techno-Fallacies of the Information Age." *Citizen Rights and Access to Electronic Information* ed. Dennis J. Reynolds. Chicago: LITA, 1992.

———. "Technology and Privacy." *The World and I* September 1990: 523–41.

Marx, Gary T., and S. Sherizen. "Monitoring on the Job." *Technology Review* 89 (November/December 1986): 62–72.

Marx, Leo. "Does Improved Technology Mean Progress?" *Technology Review* (January 1987): 32–41, 71.

Mitcham, Carl. "What is the Philosophy of Technology?" *International Philosophical Quarterly* 25.1 (March 1985): 73–88.

Mosco, Vincent. *The Pay-Per-View Society: Computers and Communication in the Information Age.* Norwood, NJ: Ablex, 1989.

Mumford, Lewis. "Authoritarian and Democratic Technics." *Technology and Culture* (Winter 1964): 1–9.

———. *Interpretations and Forecasts: 1922–1972.* New York: Harcourt Brace Jovanovich, 1972.

———. *The Lewis Mumford Reader* ed. Donald L. Miller. New York: Pantheon Books, 1986.

———. *The Myth of the Machine: Technics and Human Development.* New York: Harcourt Brace & World, 1967.

———. *Technics and Civilization.* New York: Harcourt Brace Jovanovich, 1962.

Noble, David F. *America By Design: Science, Technology, and the Rise of Corporate Capitalism.* New York: Knopf, 1977.

———. *Forces of Production: A Social History of Industrial Automation.* New York: Knopf, 1984.

———. "Present Tense Technology." 3-part series. *Democracy* 3.2, 3.3, 3.4 (1983).

"OMB Circ. A–130 Revision." *Coalition on Government Information Newsletter* 6.2 (April 1992): 1–2.

Perrow, Charles. "On Not Using Libraries." *Humanists at Work: Disciplinary Perspectives and Personal Reflections.* Chicago: University Library, University of Illinois, Chicago, 1989.

Postman, Neil. *Amusing Ourselves to Death: Public Discourse in the Age of Show Business.* New York: Penguin, 1985.

———. *Technopoly: The Surrender of Culture to Technology.* New York: Knopf, 1992.

Riley, Tom, and Harold C. Relyea, eds. *Freedom of Information Trends in the Information Age.* London: Frank Cass, 1983.

Roach, Colleen. "The Movement for a New World Information and Communication Order: A Second Wave?" *Media, Culture and Society* 12.3 (July 1990): 283–307.

Robins, Kevin, and Frank Webster. *Information Technology: Post-Industrial Society or Capitalist Control?* Norwood, NJ: Ablex, 1986.

Roszak, Theodore. *The Cult of Information: The Folklore of Computers and the True Art of Thinking.* New York: Pantheon, 1986.

Rothschild, Jean. *Turing's Man, Turing's Woman, or Turing's Person: Gender, Language, and Computers.* Wellesley College Center for Research on Women, Working Paper No. 166. ERIC ED 298 946.

Schiller, Herbert I. *Culture, Inc.: The Corporate Takeover of Public Expression.* New York: Oxford University Press, 1989.

Schumacher, E. F. *Small is Beautiful.* New York: Harper & Row, 1973.

Schuman, Patricia. "Social Goals vs. Private Interests: Players in the Information Arena Clash." *Publishers Weekly* (23 November 1983): 56–58.

"Senate 'Electronic' FOIA Hearing Held" and "Justice Department Testimony on S. 1940." *FOIA Update* 13.2 (Spring 1992).

Stearns, P. N. "The Idea of Post-Industrial Society: Some Problems." *Journal of Social History* 17 (Summer 1984): 685–94.

Swan, John C. "Rehumanizing Information: An Alternative Future." *Library Journal* (1 September 1990): 178–82.

Turkle, Sherry. *The Second Self: Computers and the Human Spirit*. New York: Simon and Schuster, 1984.

U.S. Congress. Ad Hoc Committee on Depository Library Access to Federal Automated Databases. *Provision of Federal Government Publications in Electronic Format to Depository Libraries*. Washington, DC: Joint Committee on Printing, 1984.

U.S. Congress. Joint Committee on Printing. *A Directory of U.S. Government Depository Libraries: The Present Law Governing Designated Depository Libraries*. Washington, DC: Government Printing Office, 1985.

U.S. Domestic Council, Committee on the Right to Privacy. National Information Policy. *Report to the President of the United States*. Washington, DC: National Commission on Libraries and Information Science, 1976.

U.S. National Commission on Library and Information Science, Public/Private Sector Task Force. *Public/Private Sector Interaction in Providing Information Services*. Washington, DC: NCLIS, 1982.

U.S. National Telecommunications and Information Administration. *Issues in Information Policy*. Washington, DC: Government Printing Office, 1981.

U.S. Office of Management and Budget. *Improving Government Information Resources Management*. Washington, DC: OMB, 1982.

U.S. Office of Technology Assessment. *Computer-Based National Information System: Technology and Public Policy Issues*. Washington, DC: Government Printing Office, 1981.

Webster, Frank, and Kevin Robins. "Plan and Control: Towards a Cultural History of the Information Society." *Theory and Society* 18.3 (1989): 323–51.

Weizenbaum, Joseph. *Computer Power and Human Reason*. San Francisco: W. H. Freeman, 1976.

Wicklein, John. *Electronic Nightmare: The Home Communications Set and Your Freedom*. Boston: Beacon Press, 1982.

Winner, Langdon. *Autonomous Technology: Technics-Out-Of-Control As a Theme in Political Thought*. Cambridge, MA: MIT Press, 1977.

———. *The Whale and the Reactor: A Search for Limits in an Age of High Technology*. Chicago: University of Chicago Press, 1986.

Woodward, Kathleen, ed. *The Myths of Information: Technology and Post-Industrial Culture*. Madison, WI: Coda Press, 1980.

Zerzan, John, and Alice Carnes, eds. *Questioning Technology: Tool, Toy, or Tyrant?* Philadelphia: New Society Publishers, 1991.

Index

Instrumental reason. *See* Information technology and libraries: scientific rationality and; Information technology in education: instrumental rationality and

Keynes, John Maynard, 20
Kranzberg, Melvin, 24, 29

Language, 70
Libraries: citizens and, 167–70; civic role of, 152–53: democracy and, 213, 216–17;
Library Bill of Rights, 125, 155
Library schools, origins of, 182–83, 194 n.19
Library science research, 6–7
Library services, historical trends, 5–6
Literacy. *See* Print culture
Luddites, 104
Lukacs, Georg, 60

McCormick, Cyrus, 26–27
Marcuse, Herbert, 22, 133
Market censorship, 67–68; and libraries, 128–32
Marx, Karl, 60, 62–63, 178
Mesthene, Emanuel, 29
Moynihan, Daniel P., 29

National Commission on Excellence in Education, 41–42
National Research and Education Network. *See* NREN
Nature, subjugation of, 22–23
Noble, David, 52, 112
NREN (National Research and Education Network), 127, 129, 134, 163–64, 199–200

Objectivity. *See* Technology: neutrality of
Office of Management and Budget (OMB) Circular A–130, 129, 157
Online searching, 198–200; costs of, 199
Orwell, George, 118

Panopticism, 140–143. *See also* Electronic panopticon
Paradigm shifts, 18–19
Peters, John Durham, 137
Pornography, 72
Positivism in library science, 6–7
Postman, Neil, 115–16, 137
Print culture, 136–39, 181–83, 194 n.18. *See also* Scribal culture
Privacy. *See* Information technology and privacy
Privacy Act of 1974, 161–62
Privatization, 64–65. *See also* Information technology and libraries: relationship to privatization
Prodigy, 127
Provenzo, Eugene, 143

Ramo, Simon, 15–16, 24, 28, 29, 32
Regional Bell Operating Companies (RBOCs), 131, 162–63
Rosen, Jay, 138–39
Roszak, Theodore, 5, 49

Schiller, Herbert, 7–8, 217
Schooling and libraries, 212
Science and technology, 70–71
Scientific rationality. *See* Information technology and libraries: scientific rationality and; Information technology in education: instrumental rationality and
Scribal culture, 179–81. *See also* Print culture
Securities and Exchange Commission, 167
Sociology of education and librarianship, 211–12
Software, 119–20

Technological optimism, 15–16
Technological society, premises of, 19–33
Technological systems, 173
Technology: definitions of, 17–18, 39, 105, 174; deskilling and, 85–86 (*see also* Information technology and libraries: librarian deskilling and; In-

Contributors

NORMAN BALABANIAN is an emeritus Professor in Electrical Engineering and Computer Science at Syracuse University. He has authored numerous books, and has been editor of the journal *Technology and Society*.

JOHN BUSCHMAN is Associate Professor-Librarian at Rider College Library. At Rider, he is Coordinator of Collection Development and Acquisitions. His publications and papers on information technology in librarianship are mentioned in this volume.

MICHAEL J. CARBONE is Associate Professor in the Education Department at Muhlenberg College. His past work has focused on issues of technology, teacher empowerment, schools as workplaces, and the liberal arts. He is currently at work on an article concerning technology and school restructuring.

CAROLYN M. GRAY is Associate Director of Brandeis University Libraries. Her previous writing on information technology is mentioned in this volume, and she has been active in the Library and Information Technology Association.

JOHN HAAR is Assistant Director for Collections at Heard Library, Vanderbilt University. His previous publications on information technology in librarianship are mentioned in this volume.

SUE CURRY JANSEN is Associate Professor in the Communications Department at Muhlenberg College. She has published numerous works on technological and feminist issues in communications.

STEVE M. SLABY is emeritus Professor in the Department of Civil Engineering and Operations Research at Princeton University. He is also Director of Technology and Society Seminars at Princeton.

MICHAEL F. WINTER is Behavioral Sciences Librarian at the Library of the University of California, Davis. He has written numerous articles and books on professionalization issues in librarianship. The most recent book was published by Greenwood Press, and is mentioned in this volume.